Derek Walcott and the Creation of a Classical Caribbean

Classical Receptions in Twentieth-Century Writing

Series Editor: Laura Jansen

Each book in this ground-breaking series considers the dialogue with Mediterranean antiquity in a single writer from the 'long' twentieth century. From Virginia Woolf to Judith Butler, Walcott to Soyinka, and Calvino to Foucault, the modalities and texture of this modern encounter with antiquity are explored in the works of authors recognized for their global impact on modern fiction, poetry, art, philosophy and politics.

A distinctive feature of twentieth-century writing is the tendency to break with tradition and embrace the new sensibilities of the time. Yet the period continues to maintain a fluid dialogue with the Graeco-Roman past, drawing on its cultural ideas and claims, even within the most radical thinkers who ostentatiously question and reject that past. Classical Receptions in Twentieth-Century Writing (CRTW) approaches this dialogue from two interrelated perspectives: it asks how modern authors' positions on the ancient classics open new readings of their oeuvres and contexts, and it considers how this process in turn renders innovative insights into the classical world. Interdisciplinarity is at the heart of the series. CRTW addresses some of the most profound shifts in practices of reading, writing, and thinking in recent years within and beyond the arts and humanities, as well as in the poetics of reading antiquity that one finds in twentieth-century writing itself.

Also new in this series

Fellini's Eternal Rome, Alessandro Carrera
Foucault's Seminars on Antiquity: Learning to Speak the Truth, Paul Allen Miller
James Joyce and Classical Modernism, Leah Culligan Flack
J.R.R. Tolkien's Utopianism and the Classics, Hamish Williams
Tony Harrison: Poet of Radical Classicism, Edith Hall
Virginia Woolf's Greek Tragedy, Nancy Worman

Editorial board

Prof. Richard Armstrong (University of Houston)
Prof. Francisco Barrenechea (University of Maryland)
Prof. Shane Butler (Johns Hopkins University)
Prof. Paul A. Carledge (University of Cambridge)
Prof. Moira Fradinger (Yale University)
Prof. Francisco García Jurado (Universidad Complutense de Madrid)
Prof. Barbara Goff (University of Reading)
Prof. Simon Goldhill (University of Cambridge)
Prof. Sean Gurd (The University of Texas at Austin)
Prof. Constanze Güthenke (University of Oxford)
Dr Ella Haselswerdt (University of California, Los Angeles)
Dr Rebecca Kosick (University of Bristol)
Prof. Vassilis Lambropoulos (University of Michigan)
Dr. Pantelis Michelakis (University of Bristol)
Prof. James Porter (University of California, Berkeley)
Prof. Patrice Rankine (University of Chicago)
Prof. Phiroze Vasunia (University College London)

Derek Walcott and the Creation of a Classical Caribbean

Justine McConnell

BLOOMSBURY ACADEMIC
LONDON • NEW YORK • OXFORD • NEW DELHI • SYDNEY

BLOOMSBURY ACADEMIC
Bloomsbury Publishing Plc
50 Bedford Square, London, WC1B 3DP, UK
1385 Broadway, New York, NY 10018, USA
29 Earlsfort Terrace, Dublin 2, Ireland

BLOOMSBURY, BLOOMSBURY ACADEMIC and the Diana logo are trademarks of
Bloomsbury Publishing Plc

First published in Great Britain 2023
Paperback edition published 2025

Copyright © Justine McConnell, 2023

Justine McConnell has asserted her right under the Copyright, Designs and Patents Act, 1988, to be identified as Author of this work.

For legal purposes the Acknowledgements on p. vii constitute an extension of this copyright page.

Cover design: Terry Woodley
Cover image © Derek Walcott at home in Saint Lucia. Photo by Micheline Pelletier/Corbis via Getty Images

All rights reserved. No part of this publication may be reproduced or transmitted in any form or by any means, electronic or mechanical, including photocopying, recording, or any information storage or retrieval system, without prior permission in writing from the publishers.

Bloomsbury Publishing Plc does not have any control over, or responsibility for, any third-party websites referred to or in this book. All internet addresses given in this book were correct at the time of going to press. The author and publisher regret any inconvenience caused if addresses have changed or sites have ceased to exist, but can accept no responsibility for any such changes.

A catalogue record for this book is available from the British Library.

A catalog record for this book is available from the Library of Congress.

ISBN: HB: 978-1-4742-9152-1
PB: 978-1-3503-4314-6
ePDF: 978-1-4742-9154-5
eBook: 978-1-4742-9153-8

Series: Classical Receptions in Twentieth-Century Writing

Typeset by RefineCatch Limited, Bungay, Suffolk

To find out more about our authors and books visit www.bloomsbury.com and sign up for our newsletters.

Contents

Acknowledgements	vii
Introduction: The Homeric Shadow	1
1 Time	37
2 Syncretism	71
3 Re-creation	103
Epilogue	129
Notes	133
Bibliography	167
Index	187

Acknowledgements

Walking across Trafalgar Square, I glance over at the steps of St Martin-in-the-Fields, just in case – this time – I spot an Omeros-figure in conversation. It happens more often than you might think, with a bit of imagination. And so it is that I am grateful to Derek Walcott for creating worlds that have infiltrated my own and I feel lucky to have been able to spend so much time immersed in his writing. I've accrued other debts along the way, too, often ones that were more tangibly built up, and I would like to thank the following people for their support and generosity.

This book began life at the invitation of Laura Jansen, editor of the Classical Receptions in Twentieth-Century Writing series. I am grateful to Laura for her encouragement and vision for the series, and to Georgie Leighton, Lily Mac Mahon and Alice Wright at Bloomsbury for their expertise and guidance along the way, as well as to Roza I. M. El-Eini for her diligent copyediting. Paul Breslin's incisive comments enabled me to improve the book in a myriad of ways, and I am indebted to him for his generosity, wisdom and insights. When I agreed to write this book, I was coming to the end of a Leverhulme Early Career Fellowship at the University of Oxford, based at TORCH (The Oxford Research Centre in the Humanities). I am immensely grateful to the Leverhulme Trust for that fellowship, which enabled the initial work not only on this book but on a number of other projects too. The community I found at TORCH, led by Stephen Tuck and Elleke Boehmer, is one that I will never forget. The TORCH 'Bake-Offs' cemented the friendship of our collection of Early Career Researchers and reminded us just how supportive academia has the potential to be.

I am fortunate to have been part of two other scholarly communities over the course of writing this book. At the Archive of Performances of Greek and Roman Drama (APGRD) at Oxford, I owe particular gratitude to Estel Baudou, Felix Budelmann, Helen Eastman, Constanze Güthenke, Edith Hall, Stephen Harrison, Claire Kenward, David Ricks, Oliver Taplin and, above all,

Fiona Macintosh. Fiona not only read drafts of several chapters but has been an inspiring intellectual interlocutor and an unwavering source of support and encouragement.

At King's College London, I couldn't have hoped for a better community of colleagues in the Comparative Literature department. Through conversations, research seminars and co-teaching, I have learnt such a lot from Matthew Bell, Anna Bernard, Daniela Cerimonia, Jane Darcy, Ziad Elmarsafy, Julia Hartley, Alicia Kent, Tom Langley, Caroline Laurent, Javed Majeed, Sara Marzagora, Sebastian Matzner, Rosa Mucignat, Sinéad Murphy, Zoe Norridge, David Ricks (again!), Michael Silk, Miranda Stanyon and Sebastian Truskolaski. Enormous thanks, too, to Steph Mannion, Monika Shirtliff, Fayeza Rahman and Laura Tull. Beyond Comparative Literature, I am especially grateful to Rosa Andújar, Pavlos Avlamis, Dan Orrells and Emily Pillinger at King's, and to Lucy Jackson and Henry Stead (now) beyond it. Having taught Derek Walcott's work in my 'Myth After Slavery' and 'Caribbean Drama' modules for several years, I am indebted to those students as well as many others for always showing me his work in new lights. Likewise, I owe thanks to the doctoral students I have supervised: Naser Albreeky, Connie Bloomfield-Gadêlha, Rachel Bolle-Debessay, Cai Yi, Lubabah Chowdhury, Rioghnach Sachs, Daniel Whittle and Leslie Wong.

An early conversation with Lorna Hardwick gave me confidence in the shape of the book I wanted to write; Glyn Maxwell and Mac Donald Dixon were generous with their time and insights midway through the research; and later conversations with Imaobong Umoren helped me finalize it. The fact that I had to research Walcott's papers spread across archives in St Lucia, Jamaica, Trinidad and Canada added to the joy of the work, and I am very grateful to the archivists and librarians at the University of the West Indies (UWI) at Mona and St Augustine as well as to Jennifer Toews at the Thomas Fisher Rare Book Library in Toronto. Being able to listen to the terrific recordings of Walcott and others at the Library of the Spoken Word at UWI Mona was a highlight of the research and I am indebted to Sean Mockyen for making that possible and so graciously guiding me round the materials. I am also very grateful to Elizabeth Walcott-Hackshaw, Anna Walcott-Hardy, and the Walcott Estate for granting me permission to include two storyboards from the planned film of *Omeros*.

Finally, my thanks to Hinksey Lido where I do all my best thinking, and to my friends and family for so much else.

Introduction

The Homeric Shadow

> *Why not see Helen*
> *as the sun saw her, with no Homeric shadow*
> Derek Walcott, Omeros (1990: 271)

Derek Walcott's question, quoted as the epigraph to this chapter, is startling. Posed by the narrator more than three-quarters of the way through *Omeros* (1990), the reader of the poem seems to have been encouraged up until this moment to map the tale of St Lucia onto the world of the ancient Greek epics. The poem's very title, *Omeros*, evokes the modern Greek rendition of the ancient poet's name, and as this opening chapter will explore, the resonances, connections and recastings are pervasive. So, why does Walcott stop us in our tracks at this moment and ask us to think again about what it means to seek out the Graeco-Roman allusions in this work of Caribbean literature? That is a question that Walcott raised time and again in his poetry, drama and essays, and it is one that underpins this book; its answers illuminate not only Walcott's corpus of work, but also more widely, artistic responses to Graeco-Roman antiquity that might be broadly designated as 'postcolonial'. The 'Homeric shadow' may, as David Ricks has described of its impact on modern Greek poets, either be 'a helper, a kindly ancestral shade who speaks to them across the ages, or a handicap, a shadow that will loom over their efforts for ever';[1] for a poet from a formerly colonized nation, these two possibilities are freighted with further shadows of modern imperialism.

When Walcott died in 2017, at the age of eighty-seven, he left behind a prodigious oeuvre that spanned seventy-three years, his first poem having been published in *The Voice of St Lucia* in 1944 when he was just fourteen years old.

Brought up in St Lucia's capital city, Castries, his childhood home stood just a five-minute walk from a leafy central square that was named after him following his 1992 Nobel Prize win. That Walcott's name should replace the previous incumbent, Christopher Columbus, is a fitting exemplification of much of Walcott's practice. Awarded the Nobel Prize for Literature in the year that marked the 500th anniversary of Columbus' invasion of the Caribbean, Walcott's work takes on this colonial inheritance but refuses to allow it to predominate. The square that had been named after Columbus not only becomes Derek Walcott Square, but contains a bust of the poet, below which are lines from his poem 'Sainte Lucie':

> Moi c'est gens Ste. Lucie.
> C'est la moi sorti;
> is there that I born.[2]

In these lines are interwoven the languages of the island, and thus the traces of its history, with French, St Lucian Creole and English entwined.[3] In choosing these lines of poetry to stand as the square's epigraph, the public space was transformed from one commemorating colonialism to one which celebrates the syncretism of St Lucia.

Postcolonial Classics

The discipline of 'Classics' embeds its historical assessment of itself in its very name, announcing itself as exceptional. The etymology of this is often traced back to the first census in Rome, thought to have been instigated by the sixth king of early Rome, Servius Tullius (*c.* 578–535 BCE), in which those who possessed the most money and property were termed *classici*.[4] By extension, when Aulus Gellius (*c.* 123–170 CE) wanted to designate the 'top' authors, he adopted Servius Tullius' term in order to distinguish them from lesser writers, and named them *scriptores classici*.[5] For nineteenth-century literary critic Charles Augustin Sainte-Beuve, this intervention points the way towards finding an answer to the question he posed in his 1850 essay, 'Qu'est-ce qu'un classique?' ('What is a Classic?'), a question which was, in turn, asked by T. S. Eliot (1944).[6] For Sainte-Beuve and Eliot, the canonical texts of Graeco-Roman antiquity occupy a substantial space in their vision of which works could be said to be 'a classic'; likewise, Walcott's affinity for the worlds of ancient Greece and Rome affords their literature a prominent place within his own literary vision but does not mark it as different in kind from other works that he deems great.

It is in this sense that the 'classical' of this book's title, 'A Classical Caribbean', should be seen. Contrary to claims that Walcott is in thrall to canonical literature,[7] his 'classical Caribbean' is self-consciously crafted with the intention of creating a space for Caribbean art and asserting its place in the global, transhistorical canon of literature. As Rhonda Cobham-Sander has argued, 'until the twentieth century no cohort of [Caribbean] writers had managed to produce a body of work capable of surviving the amnesiac violence of a world without history'.[8] Walcott, alongside a number of his contemporaries, sets out to change this and, by 1997 at least, is confident enough of their success to scoff at the claim of the Creolists that,[9] 'La littérature antillaise n'existe pas encore. Nous sommes encore dans un état de prélittérature' ('Caribbean literature does not yet exist. We are still in a state of preliterature').[10]

Walcott finds in the contemporary Caribbean 'classical' writers whom he juxtaposes with 'radical' ones, declaring of the former,[11]

> They know that by openly fighting tradition we perpetuate it, that revolutionary literature is a filial impulse, and that maturity is the assimilation of the features of every ancestor.[12]

The 'classical Caribbean' that Walcott endeavours to create is not one indebted to antiquity, but one that has 'paid [its] accounts to Greece and Rome and walks in a world without monuments and ruins'.[13] Created not by Walcott alone, his dialogue with a network of other writers from the Caribbean and beyond, from his own time and from other eras, is significant. Alejo Carpentier's notion of *Mediterráneo caribe* ('the Caribbean Mediterranean'),[14] Édouard Glissant's and Wilson Harris' conceptions of time, and Fernando Ortiz's and Antonio Benítez-Rojo's ideas of syncretism all stand as contemporaneous Caribbean interlocutors, as do V. S. Naipaul and Kamau Brathwaite.[15] At the same time, Walcott takes pleasure in the possibilities of an 'Adamic' role, as we shall see (Chapter 3), and casts himself as a Homer figure whose poetry will correct colonial misapprehensions that the region is 'merely a naturalist's handbook', as his poem 'Roots' describes it, with its call for 'our Homer with truer perception'.[16] This Homer is not one who merely replicates the ancient Greek Homer, but is instead a specifically Caribbean Homeric figure ('our Homer'), exemplifying what Emily Greenwood, drawing from Albert Murray's concept of 'omni-Americans', has termed the 'omni-local' of both ancient and modern works.[17] As this indicates, Walcott's engagement with Graeco-Roman antiquity and other literature of 'the Western canon' is not only about 'writing back' to the metropolitan centre or replicating classical models, even though that is one strand of it. Rather, in pervasive and original ways, he enters into a dialogue with classical literature that goes beyond its bounds to reflect on specifically Caribbean ways of knowing. These epistemological concerns come to the fore as Walcott collapses onto each other conventional ideas of time and space, and distinctions between past Europe and the contemporary Caribbean, setting the two on a par with each other as mutually illuminating and constantly in dialogue.

This vision of simultaneity is central to Walcott's work (see Chapter 1). What is at stake in such simultaneity becomes clear when one turns to the discourses of colonialism and postcolonialism. Overlaying more mercenary motivations of colonial expansion, one often finds a self-serving discourse of aid and development.[18] If the indigenous populations of lands were even acknowledged to exist in colonialist discourses, they were deemed to be 'primitive' and their knowledge was discounted or, alternatively, appropriated and objectified. Modernists such as Paul Gauguin (who features as a central character alongside Vincent van Gogh in Walcott's 2013 play, *O Starry Starry Night*)[19] and T. S. Eliot exemplify the latter approach that was so characteristic of the 'primitivism' that Elazar Barkan and Ronald Bush rightly define as 'an Occidental construction, a set of representations whose "reality" is purely Western'.[20] Indigenous people were often regarded by modernists and imperialists alike as – at best – children.[21] As Anne McClintock succinctly observed, 'in colonial discourse, the movement forward in space is backwards in time';[22] European colonizers crossed the Atlantic and moved from the 'Old World' to the 'New', to a region they conceived of as having only begun when they 'discovered' it. The appellation of newness came to signify not modernity but immaturity for many of those in Europe and the United States, a notion that was further solidified in categorizations such as 'Third World' despite the term's rootedness, on the contrary, in the 'Third Estate' that had played such a key role in the French Revolution, and to which Albert Sauvy alluded in the closing sentence of his article that coined the term.²³

As a result, when European colonial missions included education within their remit, they imposed their own systems on these lands. It is in this act that the roots of the strong links between the discipline of Classics and postcolonial literature can be found. The elitist aspect embodied in the name of 'Classics' meant that knowledge of ancient Greece and Rome came to be seen as a marker of social class for both the colonizers and those they oppressed. Those who worked for the Colonial Ministries and Offices of European powers in governing roles were usually drawn from the wealthy upper classes and despatched around the respective empires to rule over its outposts. They were men (and it was only men employed by colonial ministries as leaders) who had attended schools at which knowledge of Latin and Greek formed a cornerstone of their education, or they needed those languages to pass examinations that would permit them to act as administrators in European colonies around the world and they attended 'crammers' to acquire them.²⁴ As a result, when the European imperial powers colonized other lands, they took with them not only their religion, but also the Graeco-Roman classics, and imposed those on the peoples of the lands they oppressed. Other canonical works were prominent, too, in this wholesale imposition of an educational model but, as Barbara Goff observes, 'classics is preselected as the vehicle of these imperial combinations by its role in Europe as the common coin of the educated metropolitan elite'.²⁵ This enabled imperial powers to use knowledge of Graeco-Roman antiquity as a means by which they claimed superiority over the people they colonized while also building connections between the otherwise potentially disparate European powers. The effect was to consolidate the discourse of colonialism that is so dependent on binaries of self and other, centre and periphery, and thereby emphasize a common cultural heritage between the European colonial powers themselves.

Imposing education systems on the populations they sought to subdue, the European colonial powers held up the discipline of Classics as the subject area to which only the very brightest and best could aspire, and this was no less the case in the Caribbean than elsewhere. Derek Walcott wrote of a 'sound colonial education' ('The Schooner *Flight*'); Lorna Goodison's schooling at the Anglican St Hugh's High School may well have contributed to her engagement with

Graeco-Roman myth in her second poetry collection, *I Am Becoming My Mother* (1986);[26] and Aimé Césaire studied Latin and Greek in Martinique and Paris and returned home to teach both at the Victor Schoelcher school where Frantz Fanon was a student at the time. Each of these writers uses their classical education as both a source of inspiration and a tool of resistance. Césaire, for example, writes his own autobiographical response to the *Odyssey* in his poem, *Cahier d'un retour au pays natal* (1939),[27] in which we are prompted to see that the Cyclops Polyphemus, so vilified in many renditions of Homer's epic, might also be seen as an innocent man, minding his own business. From this perspective, one observes the Cyclops' home being invaded by foreigners who start a fire and steal his cheese – behaviour that starkly contravenes the ancient Greek model of *xenia* (guest-friendship) which the epic is at such pains to endorse – and who are then surprised when he reacts badly. In the Greek, the Cyclops is a huge *man* (an *aner*), rather than the un-human figure he is so often portrayed as.[28] This is a detail emphasized in Césaire's rendering, in which the figure identified by Sylvia Wynter as a Cyclops is vilified simply because of his black skin and his poverty;[29] for Césaire, Polyphemus' single eye could signify, in the modern world, racial alterity.[30]

The ways in which Derek Walcott engages with Graeco-Roman antiquity is, of course, the subject of this book. However, for Walcott, as for many contemporary Caribbean writers, assertions of indebtedness to 'the Western canon' are politically problematic, laced as they are with suggestions of derivative imitation, belatedness and a lack of originality. Walcott countered this with a trifold argument that pervades his work: first, he claims that the temporal axis should be perceived as meaningless, thereby reducing the oppressive power of history. Second, he demonstrates that syncretism lies at the heart of Caribbean life and art, with influences from Africa, Asia and Europe constituting innate parts of Antillean identity alongside its indigenous cultures. And third, he brings centre stage a Caribbean prerogative to re-create and rename the world anew.

Each of these are key concerns of postcolonial theory. Johannes Fabian's idea of the 'denial of coevalness', Dipesh Chakrabarty's work on historicism, and Anne McClintock's on the problems of the term 'post-colonialism', for example, have drawn attention to the way in which difference has been articulated as a temporal gap,[31] instantiated in terms such as 'New World' and 'primitivism'. As well as Homi Bhabha's work on 'hybridity' and Paul Gilroy's on the Black Atlantic,[32] Édouard Glissant's work on 'cross-culturality' and Kamau Brathwaite's on 'creolization'[33] – the latter two both formulated with a specific focus on the Caribbean without their application being limited to the region – have developed new ways to think about cultural intersections and syncretism. Wilson Harris' work, meanwhile, alongside that of Henry Louis Gates, Jr.'s on Signifying, and Elizabeth Alexander's on the reassembly of cultural and historical fragments,[34] have explored the creation of new forms built on what has gone before without concealing the damage wrought throughout history. By adopting these three stances as the structuring principle of my exploration of Walcott's work, the reception of classical antiquity can be explored on his terms, underpinned by these theoretical concerns. The aim is, thereby, to decentre classical antiquity while still focusing on it; to set classical antiquity on a par with the other facets of Walcott's oeuvre. In short, this study implements Walcott's theoretical tenets in its exploration of his work by doing away with the gravitas conferred by historical longevity and chronological distance, by examining the elements with which Graeco-Roman antiquity is syncretized in his work and by focusing on the creative innovations his practice produced.

Henry Louis Gates, Jr.'s theory of Signifying underpins my analysis of Walcott's work, on account of Gates' emphasis upon the 'difference' contained within Signifying's facet of 'repetition with difference' and its rootedness in vernacular traditions occluded by the Western canon, but Signifying's close correspondences with classical reception theory should be apparent too. Gates makes a distinction between 'motivated' and 'unmotivated' Signifying, with the former being akin to parody and the latter to pastiche.[35] Notwithstanding the fact that both Hans Robert Jauss and Wolfgang Iser, two founders of the field of reception theory, conceived of parody primarily as a negating technique,[36] it should be seen as a generative process. 'Motivated Signifying', in terms of classical reception, is seen in works that engage with but radically rethink (in any variety of ways) the ancient texts; 'unmotivated Signifying' corresponds to those in which admiration for Graeco-Roman antiquity remains the driving force of their engagement.

The three central chapters of this book explore elements of classical reception throughout Walcott's oeuvre, considering how they illuminate and interact with ideas of temporality and simultaneity (Chapter 1), syncretism (Chapter 2) and re-naming and re-creating (Chapter 3). These themes recur throughout Walcott's writing, with his approach to them developing over the course of his career; to illuminate that trajectory, each chapter is structured chronologically, revealing the evolution of Walcott's thinking over the decades.

However, before beginning this thematic analysis of his oeuvre, I offer a detailed reading of *Omeros*, which occupies the remainder of this Introduction. *Omeros* is, without doubt, among Walcott's most well-known works; for those with an interest in Graeco-Roman antiquity, this position of pre-eminence is even more secure. Set in the St Lucian fishing village of Gros Islet, on the north-west coast of the island, the poem tells of the lives of Achille, Hector, Helen and Philoctete; of Ma Kilman and the 'No Pain Café'; of the retired expatriate couple, Dennis and Maud Plunkett; and of Seven Seas and the poem's narrator, whose life is closely mapped onto that of Walcott himself. Confirming the centrality of Walcott's trifold theoretical preoccupations with time, syncretism and re-creation, the poem is underpinned by each of these, while its engagement with classical antiquity is thoroughgoing. It constitutes, therefore, an apt starting point for this book.

After the Introduction's reading of *Omeros*, Chapter 1 focuses on Walcott's theory of temporality and simultaneity, as articulated in his 1974 essay, 'The Muse of History', in particular, to demonstrate that this is one of the three major lenses through which he engages with classical myth and literature. By considering works including 'The Almond Trees' (1965), 'Sea Grapes' (1976) and sections from his autobiographical long poem *Another Life* (1973),[37] I show that the engagement of these works with classical antiquity is integrally related to the notion that time must be condensed so that eras are seen as happening simultaneously. As a result, the gap between ancient Greece and Rome and the contemporary Caribbean is confronted and immediately closed. This elision of time is crucial to Walcott's postcolonial vision because it refutes the oft-repeated charge (endorsed by fellow Caribbean Nobel Laureate V. S. Naipaul) that the Caribbean is a place of imitation, not creation. Such charges can be latent in Eurocentric readings of classical reception in Walcott's work, with which he took issue when he denied that *Omeros* was an epic or that the Caribbean could be seen as a 'second-rate Aegean'.[38] Chapter 1 explores the ways in which Walcott's conception of time throughout his oeuvre repudiates

Eurocentric claims of imitation regarding his dialogue with classical antiquity and confronts the historical violence inflicted upon the Caribbean.

Chapter 2 moves to the second major theme within Walcott's philosophy, that of syncretism. Following from the notion of historical simultaneity explored in the previous chapter, Walcott celebrates the multiple roots of the Caribbean (European, African, Asian and Indigenous) as inextricably intertwined in ways that have led to the creation of a 'supersyncretic' Caribbean culture (to adopt Benítez-Rojo's formulation). Walcott has not only repeatedly foregrounded this syncretism in his poetry and drama, but has also often included classical motifs to do so, as will become clear in the chapter's exploration of works such as 'A Far Cry from Africa' (1956), 'The Schooner Flight' (1979), *A Branch of the Blue Nile* (1983) and *The Odyssey: A Stage Version* (1992). To take just one well-known example examined in the chapter, *Ti-Jean and His Brothers*, first staged in Trinidad in 1958, begins with a chorus of small animals (including a frog) reciting 'Greek-croak, Greek-croak' to evoke, simultaneously, the Caribbean exclamation of 'Krik? Krak!' with which oral storytelling begins and Aristophanes' onomatopoeic chorus in the *Frogs*. Walcott's stage version of the *Odyssey* is permeated with notions of Graeco-Roman and Caribbean syncretism, as the blind bard Billy Blue embodies. The dialogues with Graeco-Roman antiquity examined in this chapter not only cast new light on the ancient texts, but also contribute emphatically to the notion of syncretism formulated by Walcott and a number of Caribbean theorists. Even while the chapter examines the ways in which perceptions of canonical literature have been altered by Walcott's syncretic process, it highlights the dynamics of cultural capital and colonial denigration encapsulated in the final line of his poem 'White Magic' (1987): 'Our myths are ignorance, theirs are literature.'[39]

Chapter 3 turns to the third major theme within Walcott's work, that of re-creating and renaming the world around him. A prominent feature of much of Walcott's writing, renaming and re-creating the world anew is a vital aspect of his engagement with classical literature too. Exploring Walcott's conception of the creative potential of mimicry, this chapter examines the Adamic renaming seen in plays such as *Dream on Monkey Mountain* (1967) and *The Isle is Full of Noises* (1982), as well as in his calypso poem, 'The Spoiler's Return' (1981), and 'A Latin Primer' (1988) before considering the plans he had for a film of *Omeros*.

Recalling Walcott's denial of derivative mimicry examined in Chapter 1, this chapter demonstrates that, far from being constrained by 'the classical tradition', Walcott is inspired by it to create something new. The reader is thus propelled forward into Caribbean modernity as well as backwards into Graeco-Roman antiquity, viewing ancient and modern works alike with fresh eyes.

A brief epilogue reflects on how Walcott's ways of knowing shape his engagement with the literature of ancient Greece and Rome, rendering the classical reception in his work inseparable from his artistic and philosophical stance. As a prominent feature of what postcolonial theory, in Salman Rushdie's well-worn phrase, terms 'the empire writes back', classical reception has an important role to play in postcolonial studies. But as Walcott's work exemplifies, it can also 'write forward' to a new modernity; one that includes, but is not overshadowed, by classical antiquity.

Omeros

Famously, Walcott denied that *Omeros* is an epic.[40] The reasons behind this are manifold: the imperialist reverberations of the epic genre;[41] his resistance to a Eurocentric cloak being placed over his Caribbean poem like a shroud;[42] and the connotations of *imitatio* and mimicry that accompany being fitted into such a pre-designated category. Yet, at the very moment of rejecting that generic categorization, he simultaneously accepted it:[43]

> I do not think of it as an epic. Certainly not in the sense of epic design. Where are the battles? There are a few, I suppose. But 'epic' makes people think of great wars and warriors. That isn't the Homer I was thinking of; I was thinking of Homer the poet of the seven seas.[44]

The double qualification of his denial here ('There are a few, I suppose' and 'That isn't the Homer I was thinking of') points to a key facet of Walcott's engagement with classical literature. He 'Signifies upon' the classical canon, to deploy Henry Louis Gates, Jr's theorization of the term; that is, Walcott's reception of Graeco-Roman antiquity is one of 'repetition, with a signal difference'.[45] It is a mode of engagement that is found in jazz too, as Gates identifies, in which 'repetition of a form and then inversion of the same through a process of variation is central'.⁴⁶ Gates' focus is on African American literature, though he specifies in the first edition of *The Signifying Monkey* that his theory can be applied universally to literature because 'all texts Signify upon other texts'.⁴⁷ It is, furthermore, especially apt for the analysis of African diaspora literature more widely because its archetypal figure, the Signifying Monkey, is part of 'an unbroken arc of metaphysical presupposition and a pattern of figuration shared through time and space among certain black cultures in West Africa, South America, the Caribbean, and the United States'.⁴⁸ That is, the trope of 'Signifying' delineated by Gates cuts across the African diaspora, even as it takes altered form in different places and in the hands of different artists, as one would expect of a trope so closely related to a trickster figure. Signifying is an empowered mode of engagement that cannot be elided with the much derided notion of mimicry: Homi Bhabha explains that 'mimicry *repeats* rather than *re-presents*';⁴⁹ Signifying, on the other hand, only comes into being when it enacts a re-presenting that incorporates deliberate alteration. Mimicry, meanwhile, is often seen as 'repetition without sufficient revision',⁵⁰ although this is a perception of mimicry that Walcott powerfully contests in his essay, 'The Caribbean: Culture or Mimicry'.⁵¹ Crucial to Signifying is the centrality of the vernacular.⁵² Not only can vernacular speech be used to communicate to some groups of people while remaining opaque to others (a facet that has been used adroitly at least since the period of the transatlantic slave trade), but developing that feature further allows Black writers 'to ground one's literary practice outside the Western tradition', as Gates' influential monograph made clear.⁵³

But in what ways could Derek Walcott be seen to be rooting his work outside of European literary traditions? He writes in the vernacular from time to time, but scarcely extensively given the size of his corpus of writing; when writing in Creole, he often offers a 'translation' into European English, thereby occluding the possibility of remaining opaque to some audiences; and yet, beyond vocabulary and syntax, there is tone, and Walcott emphasized that tonally, his poetry has always aimed to maintain its Caribbean identity.⁵⁴ Far from separating itself from the European literary tradition, a work like *Omeros* is at pains to engage with many of the most canonical of those works, from Homer and Virgil to Dante and Joyce, yet it is equally absorbed by the history and storytelling traditions of Africa and the Americas. The spoken word is not only key to *Omeros*, it purports to be prized more highly than the written word, as the narrator's awkward admission to Omeros reveals: he admits he has never read the *Odyssey*, 'Not all the way through,' but this is swiftly followed by the confession that, '"I have always heard | your voice in that sea,"' revealing that the initial protestation of ignorance referred only to the act of reading.⁵⁵

The narrator's remark is a clear allusion to the oral roots of the Homeric epics but can also be seen as a more radical manoeuvre: Walcott is displacing Homer from a traditional position at the pinnacle of the literary 'Western canon' and locating the *Odyssey*'s power in its spoken, vernacular instantiation. In doing so, he situates ancient Greek epic outside the Western tradition by affirming that he has heard it in that most geographically uncontainable entity, the sea. In other words, by focusing on oral renditions of the epic heard in the present moment and from the narrator's Caribbean homeland, Walcott dislocates Homeric epic from any specifically 'Western' claims. Rather than engaging with Homer in order to place himself in dialogue with the European canon and situate himself within that milieu, Walcott is – conversely – claiming works from Europe for traditions beyond the West. The balance of power has shifted; to read Walcott only as responding to Graeco-Roman epic, or solely taking inspiration from it, is to misunderstand the more wholehearted manoeuvre that *Omeros* encourages us to make.⁵⁶ Walcott is instead, as Gregson Davis has observed, 'forging a new literary language in the crucible of the local vernacular'.⁵⁷

Yet, even a focus on the vernacular could be seen to align Walcott more closely with European epic, in its allusions both to the Homeric poems' oral roots and to Dante's use of the vernacular in *The Divine Comedy*.⁵⁸ While Dante innovated by his use of the Tuscan vernacular and created an epic poem that stood beyond the confines of the dominating medieval church, Walcott engages with oral traditions and uses St Lucian vernacular speech and rhythms to situate his work beyond the confines of a dominating Western canon. In both cases, the use of the vernacular combined with epic is a far-reaching strategy that does not merely claim a place for itself in the canons of literature, but actually alters the parameters of the epic mode. *Omeros* is composed in a metre that Walcott described as 'rough-textured *terza rima*',⁵⁹ highlighting the riff on Dante's epic form that he conjoins with metrical and melodic cadences derived from Caribbean calypso.⁶⁰ Both *terza rima* and calypso have their roots in oral traditions, with the former believed to have been developed by Dante from the troubadour's *sirventes* song, while calypso was developed on the plantations of Trinidad as a mode of subversive oral communication.[61] When Omeros speaks in a 'Greek calypso',[62] it testifies to creole traditions' incorporation of elements from a range of sources,[63] while also evoking the *Odyssey*'s nymph Calypso.

There is another aspect, too, to Walcott's partial denial that his poem is epic, one that – in Gates' terms – 'Signifies upon' Graeco-Roman literature in a different way. To Signify upon a work is to acknowledge its priorness. To Signify in a motivated way is to do so undaunted by its age or stature; as with parody, the critique is ambivalent, involving an element of respect for the older work even while it is criticized.[64] Just such a manoeuvre is articulated in 'The Muse of History' (1974) when Walcott observes that 'those who break a tradition first hold it in awe'.[65] As Margaret Rose has explained,

> Most parody worthy of the name is ambivalent towards its target. This ambivalence may entail not only a mixture of criticism and sympathy for the parodied text, but also the creative expansion of it into something new.[66]

Certainly, we see this 'creative expansion' in Walcott's work, but Walcott takes one further step: he acknowledges claims of priorness while simultaneously collapsing them, refuting the conception of time as linear even as he engages with earlier literature.[67]

As Gregson Davis has argued, Walcott's 'disavowal' of the epic genre is echoed by the narrator of the poem in a way that recalls the *recusatio* of Hellenistic and Augustan poets such as Callimachus and Virgil.[68] Like the Graeco-Roman *recusatio*, Walcott disclaims the aptness of epic for his purposes while incorporating it into his own work; but unlike the Callimachean precedent in the *Aetia* or the Virgilian one in the *Eclogues*,[69] Walcott incorporates this into a poem that is still recognizably epic. What has been altered in the process, however, is the very notion of epic and the kind of heroism it depicts.[70] As Achille listens to the African griot sing of the horrors of the transatlantic slave trade, the narrator comments: 'But they crossed, they survived. There is the epical splendour.'[71] The imperialistic use of epic is here turned on its head: having survived the horrors of slavery is proclaimed as the true *aristeia*. Walcott Signifies upon epic, repeating and revising it, to shape it into a new form; in the process, he aligns his poem with a new epic tradition being created in the Caribbean, inaugurated by Césaire's *Cahier d'un retour au pays natal* (1939) and continued by Kamau Brathwaite's *The Arrivants: A New World Trilogy* (1973).[72]

Omeros' 'repetitions' of epic conventions may be detected in its length and metre, its celebration of a place and its people, its battles (notwithstanding Walcott's initial denial that these are a feature of the poem), its motifs of an underworld journey and the homecoming it enables, and its relationships between father figures and their sons. Yet, in each case, these are 'revised' so that their role within the poem alters our perception not only of these aspects, but also of what a modern epic can be.

Thus, the *terza rima* is 'rough-textured',[73] evoking Dante but not entirely conforming to the metre of *La Commedia*. Nor does Walcott write in pentameters, so often the metre of heroic verse in English, because this would have given the poem a formality that he felt was true neither to his own creation nor to Homer's:

> I'm not sure it's fair to Homer to do him in pentameter. I don't know Greek but I feel that his is a much more relaxed line; relaxed, but at the same time giving you more space for action than the pentameter – which announces itself as being important, in a sense. And it's very difficult to navigate banality in the pentameter.[74]

What Walcott refers to as 'banality' is not a negative quality except within the narrow conventions of heroic verse; but those conventions are already not fit to encapsulate the environment of the Caribbean. As Kamau Brathwaite memorably remarked, 'The hurricane does not roar in pentameters.'[75] Unable to incorporate 'nation language' into its rhythms,[76] the pentameter in anglophone Caribbean poetry bears the mark of colonialism without syncretizing it with other aspects of the region's culture. Nation language, on the other hand, 'is an English which is not the standard, imported, educated English, but that of the submerged, surrealist experience and sensibility',[77] whose 'forerunner' Brathwaite identifies in Dante's use of the Tuscan vernacular in place of Latin.[78]

The 'banality' that Walcott mentioned is the 'prosaic space [...] the prose element' that he sought for the action of the poem's narrative,[79] which the narrator of *Omeros* also reflects on:

> And I heard a hollow moan exhaled from a vase,
> not for kings floundering in lances of rain; the prose
> of abrupt fishermen cursing over canoes.[80]

Yet the poem shows how thoroughly poetic this 'prose' of fishermen is; even the word 'prose' is a half-rhyme in the lines above, as Oliver Taplin has noted,[81] and Walcott spoke of the poem's hexametrical form as being not only a 'homage to Homer' but achieving 'a kind of prose feel in a verse form'.[82] The reader is reminded, therefore, not to take the narrator's judgement solely at face value, just as the narrator himself will do towards the end of the poem when he criticizes himself and Major Plunkett for the 'Homeric shadow' they have imposed upon St Lucia.[83]

It is in the celebration of this 'prose' and 'banality' that Walcott's Signifying upon epic glorifications of a place and its people comes to the fore. Like Joyce's *Ulysses* (1922), Walcott celebrates the everyday. The trappings of heroism established by ancient epic separate characters from the audience by time and magnitude: even for an eighth-century BCE audience, the heroes of the Homeric epics had lived long ago and were stronger than mortals in the present day.[84] Yet, the Homeric epics are also strikingly full of the quotidian: of preparing meals, washing, falling asleep – in a way that concerned scholars and poets in the seventeenth century to such an extent that ways were found to add gravitas to this aspect of the poems, as we see in Anne Dacier's 1711 preface to her translation of the *Iliad*, in which she argues for a profound religious dimension to the preparation and consumption of food in ancient Greece.[85]

As with his use of metre, so, too, the celebration of the everyday has a connection with Homeric epic, even if Homer's heroes are distinctly part of elite society. Notwithstanding the characterization afforded to Eumaeus and Eurycleia in the *Odyssey*, and Peter Rose's argument that the *Odyssey* expresses 'class ambivalence',[86] the world of the Homeric heroes is a socially elite one not reflected in Walcott's poem. As Walcott insisted, 'All I wanted to do was to celebrate the diurnal, day-to-day heroism of people,'[87] and in so doing he asks of his reader, as Joyce did before him and as Kae Tempest would do after, to recognize what Tempest refers to as 'everyday odysseys'.[88] It is a quotidian heroism that radically Signifies upon epic conventions in a way that Gates would describe as 'motivated', which is to say, it parodies epic while engaging with it.[89] The fishermen of Gros Islet in Walcott's poem, Achille, Hector, Philoctete, are no less heroic than their Greek counterparts, but to recognize their heroism, one must question the qualities required of epic heroism. That these qualities include killing, enslaving, looting and imperialist intentions is laid bare in ironic fashion by an Achille for whom fishing is 'the only slaughter that brought him delight',[90] a Philoctete who, though wounded, is not abandoned by his friends as his ancient counterpart was, and a Hector whose body will be treated with care and respect after his death, even by the man who had become his rival, Achille.

The death of Walcott's Hector alludes to his namesake's killing in the *Iliad*, but with fascinating alterations. It is not only a case, as in Franco Moretti's designation of 'world literature' as incorporating 'foreign *plot*; local *characters*; and then, local *narrative voice*',[91] although this is one dimension of Walcott's syncretizing approach. It is also that Walcott recasts the figure of Hector to such an extent that the reader cannot ignore the particularly modern circumstances that lead to his death. Hector and Achille, in Walcott's poem, are friends who fall out over their rivalry for Helen. Yet, as with the myths surrounding the Homeric Helen, retold by Euripides and Stesichorus, of a shadowy phantom in Troy and the woman herself in Egypt, so, too, in *Omeros* the two men fight over 'an old bailing tin crusted with rust', which is only a shadow that stands in for the woman herself.[92]

Hector's death comes not at the hands of Achille in Walcott's poem, but in a road accident: while driving the minibus-taxi by which he makes his living after his boat is destroyed in a storm, Hector swerves to avoid a piglet in his path and crashes.[93] The piglet reminds Hector of Plunkett, who has a pig farm and previously had reflected, 'If History saw them as pigs, History was Circe';[94] as he swerves, Hector refuses that imposed imperial mindset and avoids the piglet at the cost of his own life. His minibus, 'the Comet', so often referred to as a chariot in the poem, evokes the Homeric chariot behind which the Greek Achilles dragged the corpse of the Trojan Hector around the walls of Troy. As with the *Iliad*'s retelling, *Omeros*, too, offers a reconciliation after Hector's death, but in contrast to the tragic death that awaits the Homeric Hector's son, Walcott's approach is one of repetition and revision once more. Unlike in the *Iliad*, in *Omeros* the child who may be Hector's son has a hopeful future ahead, as Taplin has observed, noting the way in which the contrast is emphasized by

Achille's reflections on Helen's pregnancy, in which the 'mound' alludes to the conch-shells heaped up on Hector's grave:[95]

> The sail of her bellying stomach seemed to him
> to bear not only the curved child sailing in her
> but Hector's mound.[96]

The imagery of these lines exemplify Walcott's conception of simultaneous time, with the present of Helen's 'bellying stomach' combining both the future of the 'curved child' she will bear and the past of Hector's life.

'the echoes were prediction and memory'[97]

While genealogical models such as those of George G. M. James (1954), Cheikh Anta Diop (1974), Martin Bernal (1987) and Samir Amin (1989) have all highlighted the previously neglected interactions between Greece, Africa and the ancient Near East that led to many of the innovations that were for a long time attributed to ancient Greece alone,[98] Walcott's primary connection between Africa and Graeco-Roman antiquity is found in a less traceable proposal. Set forth most adroitly in his essay, 'The Muse of History', it is a conception of time that sidelines the linearity that underpins many dominant ideas of 'history' and asserts simultaneity in its place. This philosophy, held by writers from the Americas who engage with, but also break free from, the traditions disseminated and imposed by colonialism, is, for Walcott, 'revolutionary, for what they repeat to the New World is its simultaneity with the Old'.[99]

Rejecting, as Walcott declares, 'the idea of history as time for its original concept as myth',[100] opens the way for an understanding of temporality that is not purely linear. Condensed into a non-sequential moment, time is located on the same axis as space, with eras happening simultaneously. Yet, paradoxically, the 'New World' has already experienced the horrors of colonialism despite this simultaneity; it is the very events of history that caused what Édouard Glissant terms 'nonhistory',[101] as Walcott later encapsulates in 'The Muse of History' when he writes, 'In time the slave surrendered to amnesia. That amnesia is the true history of the New World.'[102] This kind of approach to history is shared with a number of Caribbean writers, Glissant and Harris most notably,[103] the latter of whom engaged with Graeco-Roman myth among many others and whose novel *The Mask of the Beggar* (2003) is in intricate dialogue with the *Odyssey*.[104] It is a philosophy that confronts the proclaimed temporal gap between Graeco-Roman antiquity and the Americas and immediately closes that gap by the assertion of simultaneity. As Emily Greenwood has elucidated, in the work of Walcott and Harris, this is enacted by the use of myth: 'myth is used as a stratagem to counter the historical inequality between Old World and New World'.[105]

Walcott's troubling of temporal linearity displaces classical Greece from its time-honoured pedestal but does so without lowering its value. Instead, the removal of temporal hierarchies makes way for the removal of hierarchies of cultural capital that struggle to assign value to more modern works because they have not yet had the opportunity to stand the test of time. Walcott's conception of simultaneity is not only an intricately argued philosophical position, but also a logical conclusion: if ancient Greece has so much in common with the modern Caribbean, then the gap of three millennia need be granted no more power than it is when modern and ancient Greece are compared.

Alongside the philosophical conception of time as non-linear stands geological history: if, rejecting the ideology that underpins colonialism, people should embrace a notion of simultaneous time, the validity of such an approach is endorsed by the chronological parity of the Greek and Caribbean archipelagos, which gives the lie to the nomenclature 'New World'. As Walcott explained,

> The shape, the geographic reality of the Caribbean, is the cultural reality of the Caribbean, and the cultural reality of Greece is the geographic reality of the Aegean, the archipelago. The Caribbean islands existed at the same time; they didn't decide to imitate the Aegean, they were there at the same time.[106]

If the islands are coeval with each other, to see them as anything other than on a par with each other is to adopt the colonial gaze that asserted a chronological belatedness on the part of the Caribbean.[107] By extension, *Omeros* and the Homeric epics can be seen as contemporaries (just as Walcott asserted of Joyce and Homer),[108] which is not to deny that the former engages with the latter, but rather to acknowledge what Walcott refers to as 'belief in a second Adam, the recreation of the entire order'.[109] This is not, as he is at pains to make clear, a naïve re-creation. It is, instead, a re-creation that contains the experience of the past yet begins anew: 'the apples of its second Eden have the tartness of experience'.[110]

While the poem as a whole embodies this philosophy of simultaneity, certain episodes within *Omeros* illuminate what is at stake with particular poignancy. Among these, Achille's hallucinatory journey to Africa, the figure of Philoctete and his wound, Helen's stroll along the beach,[111] the narrator's meeting with Omeros in London and Plunkett's imagined genealogy of father and son, are the most striking. Significant, too, is the way that the concept of time as non-sequential overlaps with Walcott's exploration of the process of syncretism, which will be considered later in this chapter.

Fishing far out at sea one day and suffering from sunstroke, Achille dreams that he is voyaging to Africa, his boat towed by the sea-swift whose 'speed outdarted Memory'[112] and who serves as a unifying figure of the narrative, crossing back and forth across the poem, stitching it together.[113] As Lorna Hardwick observes, the journey Achille makes is a kind of *katabasis*, a descent to an underworld, but one which refutes any misconceived idea that this deployment of a motif traditionally associated with epic implies that Walcott's riff on it is derivative.[114] Key to this refutation are the differences between Walcott's and other literary *katabaseis* and the ways in which global history forms part of *Omeros*' *nekuian* episodes; there is another key intertext within this episode too, that of Kamau Brathwaite's *The Arrivants: A New World Trilogy* (1973), in which the poet 'returns' to Africa and encounters his ancestors.[115] Walcott's Achille journeys 'back to Africa' where he meets his ancestors, learns their myths and history from the griot, and witnesses a raid that enslaves many in the community. In his efforts to fight off the enslavers, he is felled by his now proverbial Achilles' heel:

> Then a cord
> of thorned vine looped his tendon, encircling the heel
> with its own piercing chain. He fell hard.[116]

At this moment, Achille fulfils the classical expectations of his name by being brought down by his heel, while simultaneously disappointing those expectations by being unable to defeat the slave-raiders. At the same time, as

John Van Sickle has noted, the vulnerability of Achille's heel is naturalized by the setting in the mangroves, while the 'piercing chain' of the vine evokes the history of enslavement that Achille was striving to avert as he fell.[117]

The dreamlike quality of this episode is a result of Achille's sunstroke-induced slumber,[118] while also resonating with the otherworldliness of some of its epic predecessors. Among these are Enkidu's dreamed visit to the underworld in the epic of *Gilgamesh* (Tablet 7), as well as the conversations with the dead in the *Odyssey* (book 11), the *Aeneid* (book 6) and *The Divine Comedy* (especially *Inferno*). The episode in *Omeros* is shot through with the sense that time is no longer functioning in the way we might expect. Walcott has explained that 'the journey he [Achille] makes is supposed to take place in an instant, during a moment of sunstroke which is magnified in time'.[119] This magnification of time, which is made clear in Achille moving from his own contemporary moment, reversing the route of the Middle Passage,[120] and passing through global colonial history in an instant,[121] exemplifies the simultaneity of time by which the legacy of slavery and colonialism remains present in the contemporary moment.

The tourism of St Lucia is posited as an extension of this history from the poem's opening lines, with the cameras of the wealthy travellers from elsewhere trying to steal away the souls of the local people:[122]

> 'This is how, one sunrise, we cut down them canoes.'
> Philoctete smiles for the tourists, who try taking
> His soul with their cameras.[123]

Achille, Philoctete and all the characters of *Omeros* live in a present moment so interwoven with its past that to separate them is a false manoeuvre; and this, the poem suggests, is not particular to St Lucia. Hence the centrality of the simultaneity of time to Walcott's vision. It is this simultaneity, too, that encourages us to recognize that a writer like Walcott can both respond to earlier literature (as we see in his engagement in this episode with Homer, Virgil and Dante) and be their contemporary: alongside the linear trajectory of time exists 'art as a simultaneity'.[124]

Achille's *katabasis* explores another central theme that simultaneously reflects upon Walcott's own role as composer of this poem. This is the act of naming and deriving meaning from names, and more broadly, the meaning that accrues to the world around us by the language used to describe it. In Walcott's writing, language and naming is often proposed as a route by which a person may be released from historical paralysis, enabling them to reclaim an original freedom, as Paul Breslin has observed.[125]

When Achille meets his ancestor Afolabe during the hallucinatory dream sequence, the older man declares:

> A name means something. The qualities desired in a son,
> and even a girl-child; so even the shadows who called
> you expected one virtue, since every name is a blessing,
>
> since I am remembering the hope I had for you as a child.
> Unless the sound means nothing. Then you would be nothing.
> Did they think you were nothing in that other kingdom?[126]

For Afolabe, one's name is a signifier of identity. His suggestion that a name with no meaning indicates a disregard for that person's humanity poignantly evokes the process of renaming enslaved people that was often integral to the practice of slavery. As Orlando Patterson observed, 'the changing of a name is almost universally a symbolic act of stripping a person of his former identity'.[127] Robbed of their names, those who were enslaved were deprived of a part of their identity. Most frequently, new names were imposed by the enslavers who drew from literary sources, very often Graeco-Roman literature, in an effort to assert their power, highlight their own education and declare the centrality of what they saw as European culture.[128] The imposing of new names, alongside the breaking up of family units and the refusal to formally recognize relationships of kinship, were tactics designed to ensure the 'natal alienation' and 'social death' (to use Orlando Patterson's terms) of those who were enslaved.[129]

At the 8th West Indian Literature Conference in 1988, where Walcott first read aloud in public an extract from *Omeros*, which he was still in the process of composing, he remarked upon this aspect of slavery:

> All through the Caribbean and also, y'know, in southern America, slaves were given heroic names like Pompey and Achilles and so on. The unfortunate thing is that what was meant to be patronising was actually justified.[130]

Despite the efforts of the enslavers to strip those they enslaved of their identities, Walcott sees the names as being more apt than was intended, at least in terms of the character traits they evoked. Thus, the names Pompey and Achilles evoke heroism in a way that befits those who endured the horrors of enslavement, but the precise details of the historical or mythical Graeco-Roman figures are rendered unimportant. This manoeuvre, which rejects the primacy of European antiquity, is echoed in Achille's initial response to Afolabe:

> I do not know what the name means. It means something,
> maybe. What's the difference? In the world I come from
> we accept the sounds we were given. Men, trees, water.[131]

This may be a defensive reflex on Achille's part ('What's the difference?'), but it is also a celebration of sound that foreshadows the narrator's later declaration to Omeros that, '"I have always heard | your voice in that sea"'.[132]

Nonetheless, Achille's response also brings to mind again Walcott's idea that, 'In time the slave surrendered to amnesia. That amnesia is the true history of the New World,'[133] and he accepts the truth of Afolabe's words, understanding that, to Afolabe, he is merely an insubstantial ghost. Having crossed back through time, Achille is a ghost to his ancestors ('Are you the smoke from a fire that never burned?')[134] because, existing only in the future as he will, he has not yet lived,[135] while also signifying the social death that was enacted upon his ancestors by their enslavers. This leads to an inversion of the Homeric situation: while Odysseus and Achille both journey to a deathly underworld and learn from the figures they encounter there, in Walcott's poem it is Achille, not the inhabitants of that world, who are ghostly, and it is he who will be questioned rather than doing the questioning.[136] His experiences in this underworld enable Achille to throw off the ghostliness that Afolabe perceives in him: by connecting with his ancestral past, he emerges from the 'social death' previously imposed by the enslavement of his ancestors. This opens the way for Achille to embrace a future kinship by bringing up Helen's child, whether the child is biologically his or Hector's, reclaiming the right to establish kinship ties that were denied by enslavers.[137]

While this episode's exploration of the importance of names and naming reflects on the Caribbean's history of slavery, reading it alongside the *Odyssey* and Virgil's *Aeneid*, evoked as they are by Achille's *katabasis*, illuminates both the ancient and modern poems. The *Odyssey*'s short excursus relating how

Odysseus came by his name (*Odyssey* 19.396–412) makes clear that, in the Homeric world too, a name had meaning and could link its bearer with their past and their ancestry.[138] But it is in the Homeric episode of the Cyclops Polyphemus that the issue of names takes centre stage: to survive, Odysseus abandons his name and adopts the pseudonym, 'Nobody'. As Max Horkheimer and Theodor Adorno wrote, at that moment Odysseus 'saves his life by making himself disappear'.[139] The loss of one's name, then, can be a necessary survival technique. While those who were enslaved had no choice in the loss of their names, unlike Odysseus for whom this decision heralds one of his greatest moments of renown, Walcott's dialogue with Homer in this episode pushes the reader to recognize the *kleos* that should (counterintuitively perhaps, given the etymology of the word)[140] accrue to those who lost their names. Those who were enslaved are thereby aligned with the hero Odysseus.[141]

Afolabe's fear that a name without a meaning designates its holder as nothing is countered by the value that the *Odyssey* accords its hero's name of nothingness. At the same time, it resonates with an established trope that has figured the Caribbean as a blank space. The roots of the latter idea follow the logic of the colonial assertion of *terra nullius* even when that claim was acknowledged to be palpably false. James Anthony Froude, for example, wrote in *The English in the West Indies: Or, The Bow of Ulysses* (1888):

> There are no people there in the true sense of the word, with a character and a purpose of their own.[142]

Walcott quotes this in the epigraph to his poem, 'Air', first published in *The Gulf* (1969),[143] and the Trinidadian writer V. S. Naipaul had used it as an epigraph to *The Middle Passage* (1962), in which he would give perhaps the most famous articulation of this notion of 'nothingness' in the Caribbean when he declared that 'nothing was created in the West Indies'.[144]

Walcott, however, following a precedent set by Aimé Césaire in *Cahier d'un retour au pays natal* (1939),[145] turns dismissals such as Naipaul's on their head: for Walcott as for Césaire, 'nothingness' can be a positive. By highlighting the oppressive uses to which technology has so often been put, particularly during the colonial era, Césaire celebrates what has been cast by European societies as a lack of inventiveness on the part of people of African descent.[146] Both Césaire and Walcott turn from the denigration of 'nothingness' to a celebration of it that is rooted in the recognition of value that remains unobserved by those who equate technological advances with unquestionably positive 'progress'. Just as Césaire celebrates négritude, the natural world around him and a close connection to it, so, too, Walcott proclaimed, 'We must look *inside*. West Indies exists but we must find it.'[147] This is not to say that Walcott endorsed Césaire's conception of négritude (he did so only grudgingly, as his essay 'Necessity of Négritude' declares even within its title), but on this point of the value of that which some have deemed 'nothing', they were in agreement.

Achille's conversation with Afolabe reflects all three of these aspects: the erasure enacted by colonialism and the Middle Passage; the celebration of what modern European ideologies have deemed to be insignificant and worthless; and the endorsement of the Homeric recognition of the value of 'nothingness' contained in Odysseus' period as 'Nobody'.[148] However, escaping Polyphemus, the Homeric Odysseus cannot resist calling out his true name because, in Horkheimer and Adorno's reading, he fears that having proclaimed himself 'Nobody', he risks becoming nobody again.[149] Walcott's Achille, on the other hand, less caught up in this bourgeois concern,[150] recognizes that there is value in a name that evokes erasure. Achille understands that his name is a palimpsest of his past, including the historical erasure of his African roots; Odysseus, on the other hand, fears the void of his adopted pseudonym and rejects its palimpsest even though it contains his most distinctive trait, his *mētis* (cunning) within it.[151] Achille, accepting his Caribbean history, keeps the name imposed by slavery and syncretizes this past with ancient African traditions, as his participation in the Boxing Day celebrations and his wish to give Helen's baby an African name with a meaning make clear.[152]

'All that Greek manure under the green bananas'

The syncretism at the heart of Walcott's work is neatly encapsulated in *Omeros*' memorable image of the 'Greek manure under the green bananas',[153] as is Walcott's ambivalence towards that European inheritance, which is both fertile in its nourishment of Caribbean art and repulsive in its association with imperialism.[154] Yet, it is the syncretism of European forms with African, Asian and Indigenous ones that combine to create a new, specifically Caribbean whole that Walcott both celebrates and contributes to, and which, as Barbara Goff and Michael Simpson have explored, is most thoroughly modelled in *Omeros*.[155] As the renowned cultural theorist Stuart Hall remarked, '*Omeros* is, without question, a great poem of the creolizing imaginary.'[156]

Despite the dislocation from their ancestral home, despite the acknowledgement that the loss of one's homeland is the greatest pain of all ('the one pain | that is inconsolable, the loss of one's shore'),[157] Walcott denies that the African continent is the true home of people from the Caribbean.[158] While in Africa, Achille believes that it must be his home because his ancestral roots are there ('the sadness sank into him slowly that he was home').[159] Yet, gazing at his reflection in the river, he sees that it

> seemed homesick
> for the history ahead, as if its proper place
> lay in unsettlement.[160]

This is the beginning of Achille's celebration of his Caribbean identity, in all its complexity and with all the pain of the region's history of enforced diaspora. While on the Congo River, he dreams of Philoctete back in St Lucia, and of walking along the seabed past 'the huge cemeteries || of bone and the huge crossbows of the rusted anchors',[161] this time journeying in the direction of the Middle Passage, back to St Lucia. The poem in this respect offers a celebration of the Caribbean as a homeland, encompassing its multitude of cultural influences and elements alongside the atrocities of the colonial past and the trade in enslaved people, as well as its own indigenous creations, reflecting what Antonio Benítez-Rojo termed the 'supersyncretism' of the Caribbean.[162] The syncretism of all of these strands, so characteristic as it is of the Caribbean, indicate that Achille's hallucinatory voyage to Africa is a *katabasis*, rather than a *nostos* ('homecoming'), because it is only one step, albeit a crucial and enabling one, on his journey home. Such a reading of the episode is also denoted by the Virgilian resonances of Achille's underworld meeting with his male ancestors and the presence of 'Sybils',[163] indicating that his homeland – like Aeneas' – is to be found in a new place after being forcibly removed from his original home. This chimes with Walcott's stance espoused throughout his oeuvre, that Caribbean identity is not to be found in Africa alone. Instead, by embracing the present alongside the past, it is formed by a process of syncretism:

> For us, whose tribal memories have died, and who have begun again in a New World, Negritude offers an assertion of pride, but not of our complete identity, since that is mixed and shared by other races.[164]

In this way, the Homeric *Odyssey*'s central theme of *nostos* is refigured in *Omeros* in a way that speaks to the postcolonial present of the Caribbean. There is no single place to which each character may return; instead, the poem echoes Stuart Hall's conception of cultural identity as being 'always constructed through memory, narrative, fantasy, and myth',[165] as we see in Achille's *katabasis* and in *Omeros* as a whole.

Given that undertaking a *katabasis* is a step on the way for an epic hero to achieve their quest, the multiple *katabaseis* within *Omeros* remind us that, if this is an epic poem, it is of a new kind. Here there are multiple heroes, each questing in different, often seemingly small ways, befitting the poem's celebration of 'the diurnal, day-to-day heroism of people', as we have seen.[166] Major Plunkett, for example, who has retired to St Lucia with his wife Maud, is also given a kind of heroic journey, for all that he is at times a preposterous figure, though well aware of his own occasional pomposity,[167] and depicted with affection by Walcott. The narrator, too, undertakes a katabatic journey.[168]

For both these characters, the *katabasis* is restorative. Plunkett, sceptical yet desperate with grief, seeks Ma Kilman's help to communicate with his now-dead wife and finds, to his surprise, that this connects him not only with Maud once more, but with the people of St Lucia:[169]

> And her [Ma Kilman's] shut eyes watered while his own were open.
>
> That moment bound him for good to another race.[170]

The narrator, meanwhile, is led by Omeros through an underworld that is both distinctly Dante-esque and particularly St Lucian, being located as it is in the volcanic town of Soufrière, on the west coast of the island in the shadows of the Pitons, and featuring a syncretic pantheon 'of Hephaestus or Ogun'.[171] The *katabasis* will free the narrator of the strictures of the Western canon, equipping him – like Achille before him – to incorporate this element of his heritage into his life and work without it dominating.[172] Achille and the narrator, therefore, not only share the role of protagonist in *Omeros* but, in seeking a sense of identity and of home,[173] they both undergo a *katabatic* journey led by the sea-swift.[174]

Achille's *katabasis*, which rejects the linearity of time and imagines the contemporary man conversing with his ancestors, leads to his embrace of the syncretic nature of the Caribbean. Similarly syncretic, in Walcott's rendition of it, is the motif of the wound that runs throughout the poem. Early on in *Omeros*, the narrator declares 'affliction is one theme | of this work',[175] and so, just as a descent to an underworld is experienced by several characters, so, too, several figures of the poem are wounded physically or metaphorically, and often both.

That Walcott adopted a motif so closely associated with postcolonial literature may come as a surprise after his earlier vehement rejections of what Jahan Ramazani has termed a 'poetics of affliction'.[176] In his autobiographical poem, *Another Life* (1973), Walcott castigated Caribbean poets for their reverence of 'the festering roses made from their fathers' manacles',[177] and the following year, he criticized poetry that 'limits [its] memory to the suffering of the victim'.[178] Yet, the imagery regarded with scorn in *Another Life* is reprised in *Omeros*:

He believed the swelling came from the chained ankles
of his grandfathers. Or else why was there no cure?[179]

This may be unsurprising, given the time that had elapsed between the two, yet it stands as a salutary reminder that Walcott's work was always evolving and what may be true of his earlier work does not always hold of the later pieces. Even the rejection of Afrocentrism seen in Achille's imagined journey to Africa, does not conform to what might be seen as a postcolonial, African diasporic perspective, as Ramazani has discussed.[180]

Philoctete's wound that 'came from the chained ankles of his grandfathers' personifies the violence inflicted upon the Caribbean by slavery and colonialism. So too, exemplifying Césaire's observation that 'colonization works to *decivilize* the colonizer, to *brutalize* him in the true sense of the word',[181] Plunkett – as the poem's colonial figure – is also wounded. In keeping with Walcott's vision of a world in which the division between the colonizer and colonized is not wholly insuperable, the wound serves as a unifying motif (afflicting, whether physically or emotionally, the narrator, Catherine Weldon and Hector, as well as Philoctete and Plunkett) even while it evokes a well-established postcolonial trope.[182] This sharing of a wound across any divisions of 'race' and nationality is an aspect of Walcott's cross-culturalism that is seen not only in his rejection of Afrocentrism, but also in the episodes of the poem that focus on indigenous peoples of both the Caribbean and North America, highlighting the parallels between their experiences of colonial barbarism without conflating them.[183] In literary terms, the cross-cultural connections of the wound motif can also be seen to represent the way in which Walcott is simultaneously in dialogue with literature of the African diaspora and the European canon, a conjunction that is embodied by the St Lucian Philoctete's wound being born both of Greek myth and colonial history.

Likewise, Omeros in his various instantiations as Seven Seas, the African griot, the Sioux 'shaman'[184] and the ancient Greek Homer, is a syncretized figure whose presence incorporates not only geographic and cultural creolization, but a temporal one of the kind we see in Walcott's proposition of the simultaneity of time. Just as a new conjunction of elements jostling side by side is revealed by time being flattened onto the same plane as space in Walcott's notion of simultaneity, so, too, the syncretism embodied by Omeros brings together seemingly disparate elements. Personified in the shape-shifting figure of Omeros is the multiplicity of narrative traditions at play in the poem, which recall Claude Lévi-Strauss' notion that myth consists of all its versions simultaneously, as Gregson Davis has perceived.[185] The indeterminacy is deliberate here: throughout his oeuvre, Walcott has reflected on the entwined multiple aspects of Caribbean culture; consequently, it would be a mistake to attempt to identify the bardic figure of *Omeros* with any single tradition.

Walcott's conception of Homer as 'the poet of the seven seas'[186] indicates an identity unbounded by regional demarcations. No longer a primarily ancient Greek bard, he has become a global poet in the sense of one who is rooted in multiple locations simultaneously. The term 'seven seas' first appears around 2300 BCE, in the eighth of the 'Sumerian Temple Hymns' of Mesopotamian poet, Enheduanna.[187] This echo of Mesopotamian literature links Omeros to origins that predate those of the ancient Greek Homer, refuting the primacy of the Homeric text and setting forth a syncretized poetic figure in its place. The idiomatic sense of 'the seven seas' as the world's oceans gives the character his nickname, as well as naming him after a brand of vitamin pills with deliberate bathos:

> Old St. Omere.
> He claimed he'd sailed round the world. 'Monsieur Seven Seas'
>
> they christened him, from a cod-liver-oil label
> with its wriggling swordfish. But his words were not clear.
> They were Greek to her. Or old African babble.[188]

For Ma Kilman, Omeros' words are, colloquially, 'Greek to her': equally incomprehensible wherever they are from, she draws no differentiation between Europe and Africa. The commonality between Europe and Africa is further emphasized by the figure of the griot to whom Achille listens during his hallucinatory *katabasis*, whose presence and song quash any claims that epic poetry does not exist in the continent of Africa.[189] His role, as we see in Homer's bards, too, is one both of entertainment and of the preservation of history. His subject matter, meanwhile, is strikingly cosmogonic resonating with the tales retold in, for example, the Sumerian hymns, Hesiod's *Theogony*, and Akan mythology,[190] and reinforcing the connections Walcott makes between ancient Europe, the Near East and Africa.

As well as the syncretized figure of Omeros and the creolization evident in Achille and Philoctete's Francophone renditions of ancient Greek names, which make the traces of slavery and colonialism ever-present, the cure for Philoctete's wound also exemplifies syncretism. On her way back from Catholic Mass, Ma Kilman finds the healing herb, whose seed was brought over from Africa by a swift; praying to Haitian and Yoruba gods alike, she is both a 'sibyl' and an 'obeah-woman', thereby uniting the Caribbean, the African, the Graeco-Roman and the Judaeo-Christian to find a cure.[191] When Philoctete emerges cured, it is as an Adamic figure in the Garden of Eden, and the rebirth of both island and fisherman is accomplished:

> So she threw Adam a towel.
> And the yard was Eden. And its light the first day's.[192]

As with Achille's experience following his katabatic journey, for Philoctete, too, the recovery of the past allows for a syncretic healing process that paves the way to a new future that Walcott deems 'Adamic'.[193]

It is this syncretism that is celebrated in the poem's Boxing Day rites. When Achille joins Philoctete at the Boxing Day carnival,[194] it is with a renewed understanding of the celebration's African roots. Achille had seen the same costumes and dances in his dream-voyage to Africa,[195] while Philoctete, though cured now, is suffused once again with the suffering of the Middle Passage:

> All the pain
>
> re-entered Philoctete, of the hacked yams, the hold
> closing over their heads, the bolt-closing iron,
> over eyes that never saw the light of this world.[196]

The Boxing Day celebrations syncretize the island's African ancestral past with its St Lucian contemporary present, nodding to the Christianity brought by European colonizers in its timing the day after Christmas.

'So she threw Adam a towel'[197]

The Boxing Day rites also exemplify the third major theme that is explored throughout Walcott's oeuvre: that of re-creating and re-naming. As with the syncretic cure for Philoctete's wound that leaves him emerging as an Adamic figure to whom Ma Kilman throws a towel,[198] this rebirth is often the result of syncretization. The poem, I have argued, changes our understanding of what epic is by altering elements and combining them afresh in new ways like a mosaic, as Walcott and John Figueroa term it;[199] in similar fashion, the celebrations on Boxing Day take a new, specifically St Lucian form. Rather than focusing on the process of syncretism at this moment, attention shifts to the syncretic result. Just as a mosaic or artistic collage is initially seen as a whole, before closer examination causes it to jump back and forth in our appraisal between its various elements and the sum of those parts, so Walcott encourages us simultaneously to see in *Omeros* its unified whole and the way he has stitched together many different elements. He deploys a metaphor of sewing on several occasions in the poem; when applied to the artist's process, the echo of the etymology of the ancient Greek rhapsode (ὁ ῥαψῳδός – 'one who stitches songs together') is unmistakeable. Thus, the narrator reflects on 'This wound I have stitched into Plunkett's character,'[200] eliding the wound and its healing suture, as Ramazani has noted.[201] It is a metaphor to which the narrator returns at the poem's close:

> I followed a sea-swift to both sides of this text;
> her hyphen stitched its seam, like the interlocking
> basins of a globe in which one half fits the next
>
> into an equator, both shores neatly clicking
> into a globe.[202]

The narrator and the sea-swift bind the world together ('both shores neatly clicking into a globe') in a unifying action that begins to heal the rifts human history has inflicted on the world, re-creating a unity that the 'interlocking basins of a globe' always held.

The notion of stitching together an artwork, whether visual or literary, resonates with the creation of collages and Walcott once remarked that Romare Bearden's 'Odysseus Series' of collages from 1977 may have influenced his writing of *Omeros*.[203] Writing of Bearden's work (among which is also a series of artworks from the 1940s based on the *Iliad*), Elizabeth Alexander identifies 'fragmentation and reassemblage' as a feature of African American culture as a result of the Middle Passage, which is evoked and embodied by Bearden's collages.[204] This points to part of its appeal for Walcott too, with the fragmentary nature of the collage recalling the enforced fragmentation (geographic, familial, psychological) of diaspora.

Even the very title of Walcott's poem embodies this process of re-naming and creating anew from the fragments of the past. 'What is needed is not new names for old things, or old names for old things, but the faith of using the old names anew,'[205] proclaimed Walcott in 'What the Twilight Says', and as Robert Hamner has observed, 'Walcott sees mimicry as part of the process of beginning anew.'[206] The etymology Walcott offers for the poem's title combines the modern Greek, the ancient, the contemporary St Lucian English, the colonial French, the Antillean creole and even the Latin roots:

> 'O-meros,' she laughed. 'That's what we call him in Greek,'
> stroking the small bust with its boxer's broken nose,

> and I thought of Seven Seas [...]
>
> > I said, 'Omeros,'
>
> and *O* was the conch-shell's invocation, *mer* was
> both mother and sea in our Antillean patois,
> *os*, a grey bone, and the white surf as it crashes
>
> and spreads its sibilant collar on a lace shore.[207]

The multiple strands that contribute to Caribbean culture are incorporated into a new whole that takes the word firmly from exclusively European roots to the language and natural environment of the Caribbean. As Laurence Breiner has argued, Walcott does not set up an opposition between Caribbean and European languages, rather his is a 'creolizing impulse',[208] which allows him to bring together languages and narrative traditions in syncretic ways.

Walcott's linguistic and literary syncretism is part of his move towards the creation of new forms. Antillean creole is used sparingly throughout *Omeros*, and when it is, Walcott tends to 'translate' it within the text itself,[209] as we see in the early argument between Achille and Hector:

> '*Touchez-i, encore: N'ai fendre choux-ous-ou, salope!*'
> 'Touch it again, and I'll split your arse, you bitch!'
> '*Moi j'a dire – 'ous pas prêter un rien. 'Ous ni shallope,*
>
> *'ous ni seine, 'ous croire 'ous ni choeur campêche?*'
> 'I told you, borrow nothing of mine. You have a canoe,
> and a net. Who you think you are? Logwood Heart?'
>
> ' *'Ous croire 'ous c'est roi Gros Îlet? Voleur bomme!*'
> 'You think you're king of Gros Îlet, you tin-stealer?'
> Then in English: 'I go show you who is king! Come!'
>
> Hector came out from the shade. And Achille, the
> moment he saw him carrying the cutlass, *un homme
> fou*, a madman eaten with envy, replaced the tin
>
> he had borrowed from Hector's canoe neatly back in the prow.[210]

Translations such as these indicate an intended audience beyond St Lucia, exposing Walcott to criticisms such as Kamau Brathwaite's claim that he is 'speaking away from' the St Lucian people.[211] Yet, Rhonda Cobham-Sander is surely right to draw attention to Walcott's engagement with Brathwaite's work, seen in *Omeros* in Achille's dream-journey back to Africa and in Walcott's use of St Lucian Creole language and rhythms,[212] making her reading of the quarrel between Hector and Achille as a reflection of the fraught relationship between Walcott and Brathwaite especially appealing. Such observations also remind us, yet again, that classical epic is not the only intertext at work in Walcott's poem.

If Walcott's translations of the passages of Creole in his poem accommodate an international audience, it is also true that he plays games with audiences who have insufficient knowledgeable of those languages. Philoctete's bilingual pun of '*blessé*' and 'blest' is one such example that lays bare on the page the capacious multilayers of creole languages.[213] Walcott's decision to write a poem which invites categorization as an epic, and to include St Lucian Creole within it, could be seen to demand an acknowledgement of Antillean creole as a language rather than a dialect, in line with Alexander Beecroft's suggestion that 'a language is a dialect with a literature'.[214]

Although Walcott's metre is varied throughout, or 'rough-textured' in his terminology, Lance Callahan has noted that not only are some of the poem's most crucial lines rendered in strict metre, but also that this is a direct inversion of the tradition within much European verse of diverging from the metre for the most significant lines.[215] Focusing on the first three lines of the quotation above, Callahan suggests that the translation that falls between the first two lines of Creole is metrically a blend of the two lines it separates, with Hector's first line following the rhythm used most pervasively throughout the poem. The implication is that St Lucian speech rhythms, rather than European metrical patterns, structure the poem and that there is no radical contrast between classical metre and St Lucian speech patterns.[216]

Walcott's use of language is part of the broader strategy that he explicated, albeit elusively, in 'The Muse of History'. Despite the inseparability of the English language and canonical texts of Europe from the history of imperialism, they can be deployed anew. For Walcott, as we have seen, 'revolutionary literature is a filial impulse, and [...] maturity is the assimilation of the features of every ancestor'.[217] As a result, Walcott regards his approach as one that – far from being in thrall to a European literary tradition and imperialist language – instead moves beyond the limitations of an oppressive canonicity. To pursue a wholesale break with that tradition would be, for him, a less liberated move: 'by openly fighting tradition we perpetuate it'.[218]

Herein we see the philosophy that leads to Walcott's simultaneous use and subversion of epic conventions and classical characters in *Omeros*. 'The Muse of History' suggests that an Adamic poetics is liberated from an obsession with the colonial past without denying or concealing its existence;[219] for Walcott, it is part of a 'cunning assimilation' developed by peoples in the Caribbean, which brought renewal rather than 'surrender'.[220] Walcott, then, can engage with the epics of Homer, Virgil and Dante without his work being overshadowed by them. To return to Gates' theory, Walcott Signifies upon the European canon, but it is the 'signal difference' that has at least as much potency as the 'repetition'; this is the literary aspect of that 'cunning assimilation' through which 'the language used is, like the religion, that of the conqueror of the God. But the slave had wrested God from his captor.'[221] Walcott's New World Adam possesses the Edenic Adam's power to 'name' all that surrounds him, yet in a seeming contradiction with the biblical figure's status as the first man, he has ancestors. Likewise, Walcott mobilizes both these facets, the newness and the lineage, within his poetry.

A final striking instance of Walcott's re-creation of past forms comes at the close of *Omeros*, when he riffs on the traditional trope of the invocation of the Muse, 'repeating with signal difference' the opening of the *Iliad*:[222]

> I sang of quiet Achille, Afolabe's son,
> who never ascended in an elevator,
> who had no passport, since the horizon needs none
>
> never begged nor borrowed, was nobody's waiter,
> whose end, when it comes, will be a death by water
> (which is not for this book, which will remain unknown
>
> and unread by him). I sang the only slaughter
> that brought him delight, and that from necessity –
> of fish, sang the channels of his back in the sun.[223]

Walcott echoes yet simultaneously, in Joseph Farrell's terms, 'systematically inverts' the opening lines of the *Iliad* in order to close his epic poem.²²⁴ This is a double-edged nod to the ancient source, characteristic of Walcott's engagement with earlier literary traditions and of 'motivated Signifying' more broadly: far from being a humble acknowledgement of his Homeric intertext, Walcott's transformation of the opening invocation of the Muse creates a closing emphasis on his own role as artist by replacing the Muse with himself; the anger of the Greek Achilles is reshaped in Walcott's hands into the quietness of Achille; and the slaughter of fish ('from necessity' only) is implicitly praised over the human carnage of the Trojan War.

The 'repetition with difference' highlights the close points of similarity all the more poignantly. Just as the poem has refused to allow a reader to map the St Lucian Achille only onto the ancient Greek Achilles, so, too, the moments in which Achille has become an Odysseus-like figure in the poem are recalled here. In these closing pages, Achille's prophesied death is directly mapped onto that of Odysseus: both will die after the close of the poems in which they have featured so centrally, but the modern Achille, unlike the ancient Odysseus, has no interest in the *kleos* that these poems will bring and he has replaced Achilles' anger with his own calm. In fact, Walcott's Achille lives a life that is not dissimilar to that which Homer's Achilles in the underworld longs for:

βουλοίμην κ' ἐπάρουρος ἐὼν θητευέμεν ἄλλῳ,
ἀνδρὶ παρ' ἀκλήρῳ, ᾧ μὴ βίοτος πολὺς εἴη,
ἢ πᾶσιν νεκύεσσι καταφθιμένοισιν ἀνάσσειν.²²⁵

    I would prefer to be a workman,
hired by a poor man on a peasant farm,
than rule as king of all the dead.²²⁶

Recalling the times in *Omeros* when Achille is forced to find work on Plunkett's small pig farm cements the comparison.²²⁷ Likewise, Teiresias predicts that Odysseus will die ἐξ ἁλὸς (*Odyssey* 11.134) in the Homeric epic;²²⁸ Walcott's poem preserves the ambiguity by predicting that Achille will die 'by water'. In both poems, the ambiguity regarding the preposition, whether it is one of agency or location, persists.

This closing engagement with the opening of the *Iliad* underlines the overarching re-creation, of epic and other narrative traditions, that Walcott enacts in *Omeros*. While Froude suggested in his *The English in the West Indies: Or, The Bow of Ulysses* that the British Navy and its exploits in the Caribbean were worthy of an epic poem,[229] Walcott answers this claim by penning an epic poem not of the imperialists, but of the everyday heroism of the people of St Lucia. The poem is not so much an adaptation of Graeco-Roman forms and myths as it is a creation of epic for the modern era, as the characters, form, language and plot, all confirm. Signifying upon multiple traditions and texts within *Omeros*, Walcott created a radically new poem that proffers itself as a novel kind of epic for the contemporary Caribbean.

1

Time

These writers reject the idea of history as time for its original concept as myth, the partial recall of the race. For them history is fiction, subject to a fitful muse, memory. Their philosophy, based on a contempt for historic time, is revolutionary, for what they repeat to the New World is its simultaneity with the Old.

Derek Walcott, 'The Muse of History' (1998: 37)

At the core of Derek Walcott's conception of time is the idea of history as myth.[1] This wholehearted reconceptualization of history disarms the discourse of the colonizers and destabilizes the power dynamics that produce 'history'. If history and myth are indistinguishable, the narratives of the powerful (recorded as 'history') and the dispossessed (often perceived as 'myth' by dominant powers) are accorded equal credibility and status, with assertions of fact over fiction becoming redundant. Far from being mutually exclusive, myth and history are entwined, as the work of many prominent Caribbean writers has explored.[2]

This chapter focuses on Walcott's multifaceted notions of time, examining how he articulates these ideas in his essays and embodies them in his poetry and drama. Beginning with an analysis of the sometimes elusive conceptualizations of time contained within his non-fiction, and considering the ways in which his ideas compare with two other prominent Caribbean thinkers, Édouard Glissant and Wilson Harris, I proceed to explore how these ideas take shape within Walcott's plays and poetry over the course of his career, starting with his first history play, *Henri Christophe: A Chronicle in Seven Scenes*, written when he was just nineteen years old.[3] Attention to temporality in Walcott's work not only illuminates a persistent thread in his thinking but demonstrates the ways in which notions of time are intricately connected to the postcolonial condition in the Caribbean, to understandings of originality and mimicry, and to Walcott's engagement with Graeco-Roman antiquity.

Walcott's words that are cited as the epigraph to this chapter echo in poetic timbre those of the anthropologist Jack Goody and literary scholar Ian Watt, who, in their 1963 essay 'The Consequences of Literacy', wrote of the culture of the Tiv people of Nigeria, 'Myth and history merge into one: the elements in the cultural heritage which cease to have a contemporary relevance tend to be soon forgotten or transformed.'[4] While, for Walcott, such merging of myth and history is laudable, for Goody and Watt – who came to their conclusion after observing during fieldwork that it was the written word that made the past unchangeable – find it problematic.[5] Given the implication of anthropology with oppressive conceptions of time, encapsulated in Johannes Fabian's notion of 'allochronism' that will be discussed shortly,[6] this divergence is unsurprising.

Walcott's most sustained conceptualization of time and history is found in two of his essays, both originally published in 1974.[7] 'The Caribbean: Culture or Mimicry?' and 'The Muse of History' have striking if unsurprising correspondences with each other; both articulate Walcott's notion of time in ways that shed light on his work and on the Americas more broadly, and both respond to contemporaneous political events, global and regional, most notably the independence movements of the Antilles and Trinidad and Tobago's Black Power Revolution of 1970.

Walcott's conception of time, in which the 'New World' is simultaneous with the 'Old', is fundamental to understanding his engagement with Graeco-Roman antiquity and the refutation of charges that his work is derivative. The latter is a criticism often levelled at artists from the Caribbean, as I will discuss below, as well as being a well-rehearsed, post-Romantic snipe at any writer who seeks to adapt the work of previous writers. However, even in the most classically inflected of Walcott's works, canonical texts do not provide the sole key to unlocking the new works' meanings and resonances nor to recognizing their significance. They have a role to play, of course, and Walcott's persistent dialogue with canonical works indicates how generative he found them, but the classical scholar who reads only the Graeco-Roman in Walcott's writing overlooks much else that is there (as Chapter 2 on syncretism will explore) and risks enacting a neocolonial appropriation of his work.[8] Walcott's conception of time, then, allows his writing to serve as a model for how research on classical reception can avoid the pitfalls of appropriation and dominance that have plagued the discipline of Classics at certain moments in its history.[9]

Walcott's philosophical understanding of time, explored in a number of his essays, poems and plays, resonates with that expounded by two of his Caribbean contemporaries, the Martiniquan writer Édouard Glissant and Guyanese writer, Wilson Harris. Writing separately but frequently in artistic dialogue with each other, these three thinkers advocate an epistemology not underpinned by European understandings of chronology; their conceptions of time are, instead, rooted in the experience of the Caribbean region. As Glissant argued, 'Parce que le temps antillais fut stabilisé dans le néant d'une non-histoire imposée, l'écrivain doit contribuer à rétablir sa chronologie tourmentée' ('Because the Caribbean notion of time was fixed in the void of an imposed nonhistory, the writer must contribute to re-constituting its tormented chronology').[10] For Harris, as for Walcott, a primary way of 're-constituting' chronology is to conceive of time in terms of simultaneity, as he explores in 'Quetzalcoatl and the Smoking Mirror' (1994):

> To arrive in a tradition that appears to have died is complex renewal and revisionary momentum *sprung from originality and the activation of primordial resources within a living language*. We arrive backwards even as we voyage forwards. This is the phenomenon of simultaneity in the imagination of times past and future, a future that renews time in its imaginary response to gestating resources in *the womb of the present and the past*. It is unlike the linear biases that prevail in conventional fiction.[11]

The 'linear biases' Harris identifies in fiction replicate those of European historiography but are inadequate for the Caribbean. Even the assertion of a 'standard time' (embodied in Greenwich Mean Time) is a facet of coloniality, which Black temporality opposes, as Tao Leigh Goffe has argued.[12]

However, that European epistemologies are not universal is something dominant European powers have been unwilling to concede. As Michel-Rolph Trouillot argued in *Silencing the Past: Power and the Production of History* (1995), the understanding of history developed in Europe rests on a denial that other ways of knowing have validity; a denial that would have been more accurately represented as an acknowledgement of European historians' inability to understand other forms of knowledge. As Trouillot observes:

> The classification of all non-Westerners as fundamentally non-historical is tied also to the assumption that history requires a linear and cumulative sense of time that allows the observer to isolate the past as a distinct entity. [...] The pernicious belief that epistemic validity matters only to Western-educated populations, either because others lack the proper sense of time or the proper sense of evidence, is belied by the use of *evidentials* in a number of non-European languages.[13]

The 'evidentials' to which Trouillot refers are grammaticalized constructions that enable languages to express certain epistemologies, and which, as he observes, are more intricate in some languages than others.[14] Furthermore, as Paget Henry has explored, the 'imploded worldviews' that Caribbean philosophy has been compelled to confront as a result of the physical and epistemic violence inflicted upon the region has led to a specifically Caribbean reconceptualization of the fragmentation, union and transformation of the Antilles.[15]

Despite an insistence on the objectivity, and therefore universality, of 'clock time',[16] there is a significant area in which those in a position of dominance have undermined it, thereby accidentally highlighting its constructedness and the power dynamics contained within it. This is laid bare by Johannes Fabian in *Time and the Other*, first published in 1983, in which he argues that a 'denial of coevalness' underpins the discipline of anthropology's written discourse, fabricating a temporal separation between the anthropologist and the people they study.[17] The 'othering' that Edward Said explores in *Orientalism* (1978) is revealed in temporal form in Fabian's work, which shows it to be an integral feature of anthropological discourse; both have been fundamental to much colonial discourse.[18] While at pains to note that his book was completed in 1978 but not published until five years later,[19] Fabian observes 'similarities in intent, method, and occasionally in formulations' between his study and Said's, which he attributes to the era in which they were working, the influence of Michel Foucault on their thinking, and certain convergences between their intellectual biographies and experiences.[20] Fabian's work, no less than Said's, sheds light on artistic work often designated 'postcolonial', a term which itself runs the risk of both temporalizing and 'othering' simultaneously.

The relevance of this to Walcott's work becomes clear when one considers Kathleen Gough's succinct remark, made in an influential article in 1968, that 'Anthropology is a child of Western imperialism'.[21] The 'schizogenic use of

Time' that Fabian identifies in anthropological studies, whereby one conception of time is at play when anthropologists conduct their fieldwork and quite another when they write,[22] is a version of the slippage that is foundational to imperial ideology. That is, in order to justify the invasion and settlement in another's land, which requires the dismissal of the law of physics that asserts that a single space cannot be occupied by two bodies simultaneously, 'one assigns to the conquered populations a *different* Time.'[23]

Allochronism

Fabian adopts the term 'allochronism' to indicate that the fabricated temporal distance he identifies in anthropological studies is deliberate and systematic, rather than accidental. The 'denial of coevalness' is not an anachronism but rather the 'allochronism' of the discipline's discourse.[24] This term could have been just as aptly adopted by Walcott, resonating as it does – albeit in altered form – with his conception of time. It is allochronism that Walcott, Glissant and Harris urge us to recognize in the Caribbean, though their conceptions of it extend beyond the confines of Fabian's anthropological focus. For these three writers, to understand the Caribbean, one must rid oneself of the strictures of what Arjun Appadurai termed 'Eurochronology',[25] and understand that there is another time that 'the West' has failed to perceive. As Antonio Benítez-Rojo has remarked, in terms that are especially resonant with Walcott's work in its evocation of the sea,

> The culture of the Caribbean, at least in its most distinctive aspect, is not terrestrial but aquatic, a sinuous culture where time unfolds irregularly and resists being captured by the cycles of clock and calendar.[26]

What Walcott, Glissant and Harris argue, in their different ways, is that there are different ways of knowing and that in the Caribbean, Antillean ways of knowing are an important key to apprehending the region, both in terms of time and more widely. Such an argument – made prominently in several of Walcott's and Harris' essays,[27] as well as in Glissant's *Le Discours antillais* (1981) – rejects colonially imposed epistemologies and articulates the specifically Caribbean epistemologies already in existence but overlooked by dominant powers in thrall to 'Western' ways of knowing.

Before turning to the specifics of Walcott's conception of time, as articulated in 'The Muse of History' and 'The Caribbean: Culture or Mimicry?', it is worth considering the work of his Martiniquan interlocutor Édouard Glissant. As Emily Greenwood cautioned in her foundational work on classical reception in the Caribbean, *Afro-Greeks: Dialogues Between Anglophone Caribbean Literature and Classics in the Twentieth Century* (2010), 'the study of the reception of Classics in the anglophone Caribbean needs to focus not just on the dialogue with the literatures of Greece and Rome, but also on the dialogue between Caribbean authors themselves'.[28] Naturally, in a book dedicated to the exploration of a single artist such as this one, the overwhelming focus is on Walcott's work, but his connections, influences and dialogues with other Caribbean writers will be seen to be important too.

Like Walcott, Glissant was both a creative and a theoretical writer, but while Walcott prioritized his creative output, Glissant (notwithstanding his significant creative oeuvre) prioritized his theoretical works. Where, in Walcott's essays, one finds fleeting hints, tantalizing ambiguities and provocations that question and unsettle conventional assumptions, Glissant's writing offers a more sustained theoretical approach. Nonetheless, there are striking similarities in their conclusions, and their dialogues with each other, both literal and metaphorical, highlight the importance of considering their collected thoughts on Caribbean epistemologies in tandem, particularly those related to time and history.

If, for those primarily or solely familiar with 'clock time', the idea of a non-linear way of measuring time initially seems misguided, it is worth bearing in mind that the dominance of certain forms of knowledge is closely related to the power of the proponents of those ideas. Even when mistakes have been discovered, traces of those errors have, at times, taken hold and been incorporated into our cultural knowledge in all their wrongheadedness. The example of Christopher Columbus' voyage to the Caribbean is a case in point, and one which Glissant dramatized in his epic poem *Les Indes* (*The Indies*), published in 1955. Setting sail for the region then named by Europeans as the East Indies, Glissant's Columbus is unfazed by his navigational error when he makes landfall in the Caribbean:

> Et si les Indes ne sont pas de ce côté où tu te couches, que m'importe!
> Inde je te dirai. Inde de l'Ouest: afin que je regagne mon rêve.[29]

> And if the Indies are not where you are, I do not care.
> Indies you will be. West Indies, so that my dream will be.³⁰

What Glissant's Columbus asserts not only resonates with the imperial practice of imposing names as if no prior ones existed (whether of lands or of people), which itself is to assume a *tabula rasa* that was embodied in the claim of *terra nullius*, it also recognizes that knowledge is created rather than absolute.³¹ Such a recognition opens the way to new epistemologies that rethink the world around us. Michael Dash has argued persuasively that *Les Indes* 'proposes nothing less than a new way of viewing New World history'; its vision of history is not demarcated by events 'but organised in terms that are more imaginative, cyclical and less narrowly chronological'.³² Similarly, in Walcott's work an imaginative understanding of time and history seeks to unsettle the predominance of history as a series of events recorded and preserved by the victors, which in the Caribbean has for so long been dominated by European perspectives. As Glissant observed,

> L'une des conséquences les plus terrifiantes de la colonisation sera bien cette conception univoque de l'Histoire, et donc du pouvoir, que l'Occident a imposée aux peuples.³³

> One of the most disturbing consequences of colonization could well be this notion of a single History, and therefore of power, which has been imposed on others by the West.³⁴

The conceptions of time and history developed by both Walcott and Glissant contest this oppressive power by articulating new ways of understanding time that embrace ambiguity, plurality and indeterminacy; in this sense, their theorizations of time should be seen as part of a revolutionary anti-colonial resistance.

And yet, Walcott's stance – like his notion of time – is also plural: he both resists and embraces the colonial legacy of the Caribbean. These new visions of history are not about rejecting those established in Europe, but about holding in mind several different understandings simultaneously. For Walcott, Glissant and Harris, to seek singularity would be to fail to do justice to the complexity of the world and of the Caribbean region in particular.³⁵ Thus, Glissant urges his fellow Martiniquans to confront history rather than, in Freudian terms, to repress it, as Celia Britton has argued; only by doing so does he see hope for the people of Martinique to move forward as a collective not still in thrall to France.[36] Walcott, too, does not shy away from confronting the region's past. His exploration of the history of imperialism and enslavement has been discussed in the Introduction in terms of Achille's reverse Middle Passage in *Omeros*, but Walcott's extensive engagement with Graeco-Roman antiquity throughout his oeuvre should also be seen in this light. To be in dialogue with European canonical works has the potential to stage a confrontation with colonial history that overtly situates both interlocutors in the same time and space. It is just such a dialogue that is brilliantly staged in *Omeros* in the conversation between the narrator and Omeros on the steps of St Martin-in-the-Fields.[37]

This positioning of the ancient and the contemporary in a shared moment is a refutation of the belatedness that historicism has ascribed to formerly colonized lands.[38] But it is not only postcolonial literature that has been preoccupied with this concern; there is, as Charles Pollard notes in his exploration of Derek Walcott's and Kamau Brathwaite's engagement with the work of T. S. Eliot, 'a shared modernist and postcolonial anxiety about being belated'.[39] Contrary to the idea, rooted in the elitism of high modernism, that postcolonial and modernist literature have little in common, Pollard has shown how important modernism was for Walcott and Brathwaite. Walcott and Brathwaite both Signify upon Eliot's work, engaging with it but making crucial changes,[40] which is not to say – as Greenwood stresses – that it was more influential than the many other resources from which Caribbean writers have drawn.[41] Walcott's assertions of simultaneity can thus be understood in terms of postcoloniality and modernism, but these are just two of the numerous theoretical strategies with which he engages.

The Haitian Trilogy

It was in Walcott's first published play that an overt concern with history took centre stage.[42] *Henri Christophe: A Chronicle in Seven Scenes*, written and first performed in 1949 shortly after Walcott finished school, is a traditional history play that wears its indebtedness to Elizabethan drama on its sleeve.[43] Unlike

Alejo Carpentier's *El reino de este mundo* (*The Kingdom of This World*), published that same year and also depicting the Haitian Revolution and the first and last king of Haiti, Henri Christophe, Walcott's play has none of the fantastical features of Carpentier's novel that were signalled by the Cuban work's famous preface in which Carpentier first introduced the term *lo real maravilloso* ('the marvellous real').[44] Yet, as Paul Breslin has discussed, one might see in the emplotment of *Henri Christophe* a pattern familiar from *El reino de este mundo*, with both eliding some of the most traditionally significant events of the period they depict.[45]

Despite the early date of *Henri Christophe*, one glimpses the seeds of ideas about history that Walcott developed in his later work. The violent disjunctures of the region's history, most significantly imposed by the Middle Passage but also enacted by momentous changes inflicted by colonial powers,[46] are alluded to in the play's disjointed structure that might be seen to be signalled in its subtitle 'A Chronicle in Seven Scenes'. The omission of Toussaint L'Ouverture from the play, rendering him an absent presence, resonates with the 'amnesia' that Walcott will later identify as being caused by the traumatic history of the Caribbean. As he explains in 'The Caribbean: Culture or Mimicry', written twenty-four years later,

> In the Caribbean history is irrelevant, not because it is not being created, or because it was sordid; but because it has never mattered, what has mattered is the loss of history, the amnesia of the races, what has become necessary is imagination, imagination as necessity, as invention.[47]

Coupled with the Caribbean's trauma-induced amnesia is the wider world's 'silencing' (to use Trouillot's term) of that history, and of the Haitian Revolution in particular.

That the Haitian Revolution has been relegated to a marginal place in global histories despite being 'the only successful slave revolt in history' as C. L. R. James emphasized,[48] and despite being – or rather, because it was – in Susan Buck-Morss' words, 'the crucible, the trial by fire for the ideals of the French Enlightenment',[49] exemplifies the subjectivity of history that Walcott encapsulated in his idea that the 'original concept' of history was as myth.[50] As Trouillot argued, the Haitian Revolution has been 'silenced' by two strategies that he terms 'formulas of erasure' and 'formulas of banalization', which have worked in tandem to relegate the revolution from 'Western' historiography.[51] Walcott anticipates one of Trouillot's core arguments, namely that the Haitian Revolution was literally 'unthinkable' for those in Europe because it breached their understanding and categorizations of the world.[52] Walcott upends Naipaul's remark about nothing ever being created in the Caribbean with his contention that 'Nothing will always be created in the West Indies, for quite a long time, because what will come out of there is like nothing one has ever seen before'.[53] The failure, in other words, will be on the part of those who fail to see, let alone understand, the events and art of the Caribbean.

Walcott, however, provides some guidance to such people in his deployment of European analogies that help locate his readers and audience. This is not the only reason for Walcott's engagement with myth and literature from around the globe, of course, but it is a reminder that – like the theorization underpinning classical reception theory – the illumination goes both ways: if Walcott's dialogue with Graeco-Roman antiquity signals his debt to European traditions, it must also be recognized that he uses it to help audiences unfamiliar with the Caribbean locate themselves within the worlds and epistemologies he develops.

It is in *The Haitian Trilogy* (2002a) that Walcott's most thoroughgoing engagement with the Haitian Revolution is found. The trilogy comprises plays that were written and first performed over a span of thirty-five years: *Henri Christophe* (1949), *Drums and Colours* (1958) and *The Haitian Earth* (1984). As Edward Baugh has argued, the sequence of plays registers a development of Walcott's ideas concerning heroism in the Caribbean which, with increasing confidence, Walcott grounds in the people rather than in their leaders, in what he termed in *Another Life* (1973) 'heraldic men' rather than 'heroes'.[54] The focus on 'great men' that dominates *Henri Christophe*, with its centring of Jean-Jacques Dessalines and Henri Christophe, gradually gives way in the later plays to a broader focus. While *Drums and Colours* still pivots around 'four heroes' as the Prologue labels them,[55] their depiction is more rounded and the play's framing by a Carnival band facilitates 'the appropriation of the grand historical narrative by the grassroots tradition', as Baugh observed.[56] By the time of *The Haitian Earth*, the people take centre stage and it is their perspective on the Haitian Revolution, and its impact on them, that is the play's focus.

However, at the age of nineteen when Walcott wrote *Henri Christophe*, he was still – in his own words – 'a bewildered boy' who 'saw history as hierarchy and to him these heroes, despite their meteoric passages, were damned to the old darkness because they had challenged an ordered universe'.[57] This assessment, articulated in Walcott's 1970 essay 'What the Twilight Says', is coupled with his recollection that, at that stage, he felt of Haiti's history that, 'The parallels were there in my own island, but not the heroes.'[58] C. L. R. James' *The Black Jacobins* (1938) had given renewed prominence to the history of the Haitian Revolution and, alongside Césaire's *Cahier* (1939), had cast Toussaint L'Ouverture firmly as a hero, with James' work following what David Scott has identified as a 'Romantic inclination to privilege the historic role of the heroic personality.'[59] Walcott also exhibits this Romantic trait in his earliest play on the Revolution, but it conspicuously begins with those on Haiti awaiting news of Toussaint's fate. Moments later, news of his death reaches them.[60] The play opens, then, with the death of the revolution's most lauded hero having already taken place off-stage, marking it as a drama not so much about the success of the Haitian Revolution as about the terrible events and tragic trajectory that followed it,[61] with the 'heroic personalities' being those of Dessalines and Christophe. Dramatic form, which centres the present moment both by the embodiment of characters by actors and by the enactment of the narrative in the moment, further foregrounds the question of what the Haitian Revolution might mean for audiences and communities today.[62]

A Messenger relays to characters and audience alike news of Toussaint's death, in a passage that owes much to the messenger speeches of Greek tragedy and closes with his declaration that Haiti is now 'rudderless'.[63] This same Messenger will reappear later in the play, rushing on stage out of breath (again, a trope familiar from Greek tragedy), and telling of the massacre of Haiti's white population in vivid, violent terms:[64]

> Two hours we raged the city, raping, rioting,
> Turning with slaughter the chapels into brothels.
> I skewered a white martyr under an altar,
> We flung one girl in an uncertain arc
> Into the bloody bosom of the pier, and over us
> This King [Dessalines] rode, looking as though he chewed his corpses.[65]

The visceral violence of this narrative and its delivery by a Messenger bring to mind the messenger speech in Euripides' *Bacchae* in which the peaceful

Maenads – under attack – become violent, ripping apart cattle with their bare hands and flinging the dismembered limbs around:[66]

>αἳ δὲ νεμομέναις χλόην
>μόσχοις ἐπῆλθον χειρὸς ἀσιδήρου μέτα.
>καὶ τὴν μὲν ἂν προσεῖδες εὔθηλον πόριν
>μυκωμένην ἔχουσαν ἐν χεροῖν δίχα,
>ἄλλαι δὲ δαμάλας διεφόρουν σπαράγμασιν.
>εἶδες δ᾽ ἂν ἢ πλεύρ᾽ ἢ δίχηλον ἔμβασιν
>ῥιπτόμεν᾽ ἄνω τε καὶ κάτω. κρεμαστὰ δὲ
>ἔσταζ᾽ ὑπ᾽ ἐλάταις ἀναπεφυρμέν᾽ αἵματι.[67]

> But with their bare hands,
> Not with weapons of iron, then they began
> To attack the grazing herds. You would have seen
> One woman by herself with just her hands
> Pulling in two a big young heifer that
> Had swelling udders and was bellowing,
> And meanwhile others were dismembering
> The full-grown cattle, flaying them to shreds.
> You would have seen the ribs and hooves hurled up,
> Thrown down, flying through the air, and pieces
> Hanging from the trees, still dripping blood.[68]

Where Euripides' description of the dismemberment of the cattle bellowing in fear and pain casts them in an anthropomorphic light, in *Henri Christophe* this indication is fully realized as human beings are the victims of the violence.

Philip Kaisary notes that, in contrast to James' account of this episode, Walcott gives no contextual information that would make Dessalines' orders more understandable.[69] Yet, if Walcott did have the *Bacchae* in mind at this moment – and certainly by 1957, his play, *Ione*, contains a scene of *sparagmos* ('ripping apart of limbs') that evokes Euripides' tragedy,[70] and earlier in *Henri Christophe* Dessalines has spoken of 'bacchanals'[71] – then the seeds of this reading are embedded in that reference because the Bacchants only turn violent when under attack. As James argues, Dessalines' orders were issued in response to the threat of a trade embargo by the British and should be seen in light of French massacres of Haitian people, such as that ordered by Charles Leclerc at Le Cap in 1802 in which more than 1,000 men were slaughtered. The historical massacre narrated here by the messenger is therefore an instance of 'the calculated savagery of imperialism'.[72]

Alongside the Messenger speech's overt nod to Greek tragic form is *Henri Christophe*'s Jacobean framework, with character-types drawn from the canon of English Renaissance drama and the play's epilogues from Shakespeare's *Hamlet* and *Richard III*.[73] In a play on words with James' heroic 'black Jacobins', Walcott reflected that,

> They [the black Jacobins of Haiti] were Jacobean too because they flared from a mind drenched in Elizabethan literature out of the same darkness as Webster's Flamineo, from a flickering world of mutilation and heresy.[74]

As this indicates, Walcott's view of the Haitian Revolution was significantly less positive than that of C. L. R. James, a perspective he illustrates by the depiction of the lives of Haiti's first two rulers, Jean-Jacques Dessalines and Henri Christophe, as following a trajectory of 'the corruption of slaves into tyrants'.[75] In the latter two plays of the trilogy, Walcott shifts his heroic focus from these giants of history to the ordinary people, as we have heard, a move that is signalled not only by his detailed depiction of these fictionalized figures, but also by the inclusion of a Greek-style chorus (albeit played by a single actor in each case). This movement from a focus on rulers to a primary concern with the people ('heraldic men')[76] runs alongside Walcott's increasing confidence in syncretizing European canonical traditions with Caribbean ones: his chorus resonates with Greek drama but also with Carnival traditions, as the embodiment by a single actor akin to the leader of a Carnival band, indicates.

One of these new kinds of hero in each play is named Pompey, though this is not a recurrence of the same figure but rather two characters of the same name. As in *Omeros*, such a name is a legacy of the island's history of enslavement, but it is significant that Walcott chose for two of his heroes the name of a Roman general. While in *Drums and Colours*, Pompey is a member of the Carnival band that frame and introduce the pageant to follow, in *The Haitian Earth* he is a man who had previously been enslaved on the same plantation as Toussaint. There is, in fact, yet another 'Pompey' in *The Haitian Earth*: the first name of the historical Baron de Vastey, secretary to Henri Christophe and a prolific anti-colonial writer and historian, was Pompey, as Walcott flags towards the end of the play.[77]

Yet, the reason for this choice of name for Walcott's fictional hero remains somewhat opaque: Chris Bongie has suggested that the doubling of the two Pompeys in *The Haitian Earth*, a feature drawn attention to only once and fleetingly in the play, is a trace of the 'ambivalent identification' with Vastey that Walcott exhibited in the earlier *Henri Christophe*.[78] The evocation of the Roman Pompey may be a nod to his role in the suppression of the slave revolt led by Spartacus in 71 BCE, given that the nickname often applied to Toussaint L'Ouverture is 'the Black Spartacus'. But that analogy would fall apart on closer inspection, as Walcott surely knew, because it seems to cast the Haitian Pompey as a power-hungry ruler, which is entirely out of keeping with his two fictional depictions in the plays. One is tempted to recall Walcott's admonition from *Omeros* that we should see Helen 'with no Homeric shadow' and allow the name both to evoke the Roman Republic and simultaneously signify the very disconnectedness that names imposed upon enslaved people inflicted on the individuals themselves.

This latter reading is in keeping with a criticism often made of Walcott's trilogy: that in focusing on Dessalines and Christophe as tragic characters, he separates them from their historical context in problematic ways.[79] But as Paul Breslin has observed, *Henri Christophe* could be seen as marking the start of Walcott's 'quarrel with history'.[80] As we have seen, Walcott himself lamented his youthful attitude that 'saw history as hierarchy' and felt there could be nothing other than a bitter end for those who challenged the power structures it had established.[81] Yet, Walcott is already beginning to play around with time in this play. When it opens, Dessalines is setting himself up to be ruler of Haiti, but Haiti did not yet exist when news of Toussaint's death (in April 1803) reached the island: it is only on 1 January 1804 that Dessalines would declare its independence and the island would assume the name of 'Haiti' in recognition of its indigenous Taíno name, Ayiti. The trilogy posits a cyclical view of history in which violence and tyranny continue to be a catalyst for each other no matter who is wielding the power. As the priest Brelle warns in *Henri Christophe*,

> The extreme of tyranny happens when
> The gaoled turned on their gaolers.[82]

In Walcott's rendering, this cycle is not disrupted even by as significant a change in the ruling order as the Haitian Revolution.[83]

This may seem troubling when Walcott's subject is historical events, but it is in keeping with his disruption of linear, hierarchical time, and conforms to the cyclical view of time expressed in a poem such as the later 'Sea Grapes' (1976).[84] Such a disruption to temporal structures signifies the ways in which, to draw on Trouillot once more, the Haitian Revolution was 'unthinkable' for so many even as it happened because it did not fit into categorizations prescribed by dominant powers. Beyond anachronism, Walcott also disrupts clock and calendrical time in the trilogy. It is an approach that, ten years later, Édouard Glissant would develop even more extensively in his own play about the Haitian Revolution, *Monsieur Toussaint* (written in 1959, first published in 1961),[85] in which time and space is refigured according to Glissant's concept of *Relation*,[86] creating a Caribbean-inflected allochronism that shifts the dynamics of power described by Fabian.

'A Map of the Antilles'

Drums and Colours, the middle work in Walcott's Haitian trilogy, was commissioned to be performed at the opening of the first Federal Parliament of the West Indies in April 1958.[87] As Walcott remarked in his 1960 'Author's Note' prefacing the publication of the play, its trajectory is one of 'discovery, conquest, exploitation, rebellion, and constitutional advancement', rendering it an optimistic drama despite Walcott's own scepticism about the impact that changes in ruling powers have when the overarching frame is still one of coloniality.[88] But the West Indies Federation was short-lived, lasting only from 1958 to 1962, and Walcott's disappointment in the failure of the project can already be glimpsed in 'A Map of the Antilles', first published in *London Magazine* in August 1960 and included in the collection *In a Green Night* (1962).

The poem begins with the misperceptions others hold of the region, including the opening observation that, 'On maps to Federalists the Antilles may seem | a single chain.'[89] The tensions already apparent in the West Indies Federation put the lie to such a view, but the poet despairs of his ability to correct such delusions:

Nothing which I assert can prove them fools
Since men invent those truths which they discover.[90]

What follows is an imaginative approach to cartography, offering an alternative epistemology centred around the magnetic south and by extension the Global South, rather than the north:

> My compass keeps avoiding all the facts
> To find that South is its magnetic mover.[91]

The poem implies that such an understanding of space need be no less true than that of the 'scholars' in the opening lines, who suggested they had found the Hesperides in the Caribbean.[92] 'A Map of the Antilles' unsettles the objectivity of established cartography in favour of imaginative map-making in a way that matches the contestation of European temporal frameworks that Walcott will go on to develop.

At the same time, Walcott echoes the scholars' identification of the Hesperides with the Caribbean when he makes his own connection with the voyage of Odysseus. Deploying his notion of simultaneity that locates time on the same axis as space,[93] the poem turns to the myth of Odysseus as it contemplates the contemporary political situation of the West Indies Federation. The federation was intended to create unity among the Caribbean islands still ruled by Britain's waning colonial regime, but Walcott understood the divisions between the islands to be no less distinct than those which Odysseus encounters on his journey, nor are the gaps between them any easier to navigate than the seas across which Odysseus sails:

> And so an emerald sea, wild as this one
> Seemed to Odysseus a destructive ocean,
> Even as he lingered in Circean seas.[94]

The poem suggests that an assimilationist mindset that allows the West Indies Federation to be viewed through an Odyssean gaze ultimately leads to the Federation's disintegration, just as a federation founded on the colonial holdings of the British Empire was too Eurocentric to have a long-term future. There is, Walcott suggests, a flaw in the new political structure while the region remains in the perilous context of Circe's grip, which can be read as the colonial oppression to which the region continued to be subjected, foreshadowing *Omeros*' claim that 'History was Circe',[95] even while Walcott seems to identify the Caribbean region (rather than just one island) as home.

'The Almond Trees'

Five years later, the imposition of an identity onto the Caribbean remains in Walcott's mind, prompting a relatively early formulation of his alternative epistemology that reclaims the idea of 'nothingness'. 'The Almond Trees' (1965)[96] opens with a wry allusion to Froude's and Naipaul's claims that there is 'nothing' in the Caribbean:[97]

> There's nothing here
> this early.[98]

With the poem advancing through a day, 'early' refers both to the morning and to the history of the Caribbean as understood by Eurocentric criteria. But in mapping the two loosely onto each other, the poem reveals the limitations of this anthropocentric obsession with the monumental. The poem's eponymous trees protest against such a conception of history: there they stand, aged and enduring, contesting the idea that there is 'no visible history' there.[99]

> The fierce acetylene air
> has singed
> their writhing trunks with rust,[100]

yet still they thrive. Unlike the ruins of Pompeii evoked just a few lines earlier by the mention of women on the beach, sunbathing in 'Pompeian bikinis',[101] the poem's trees and its people 'endured their furnace'. Not only that, but the welding property of acetylene unites the trees and the people, as the poem forges a connection between the two that Signifies upon the myth of Daphne and Apollo in Ovid's *Metamorphoses*, paralleling it, but also repeating it with a 'signal difference'.[102]

The alteration lies in multiplicity where the ancient text suggests singularity, simultaneity in place of consecutive events, and strikingly, an inversion of roles. For the sunbathing women of Walcott's poem are

> brown daphnes, laurels, they'll all have
> like their originals, their sacred grove,
> this frieze
> of twisted, coppery, sea-almond trees.[103]

Where Ovid's Daphne, fleeing Apollo, transforms into a laurel tree, in Walcott it is the trees that seem to transform into women. The sea-almonds lining the shore are, by noon, joined by 'the forked limbs of girls toasting their flesh' – a phrase that brings to mind the 'forked limbs' of a tree trunk as it divides into two. But they also evoke King Lear's famous proclamation that 'unaccommodated man is no more but such a poor, bare, forked animal as thou art'.[104] What is significant here is that Lear's phrase not only comes immediately after the tormented old man struggles to distinguish between his own situation and that of the disguised Edgar, assuming that both must have been betrayed (as he sees it) by their children. It is also that the phrase recalls Shakespeare's crucial reconceptualization of 'nothing' as a positive trait. When Cordelia refuses her father's invitation to flatter him, she responds that she can say 'Nothing, my lord' (*King Lear* I.i.87).[105] It is this positive conception of 'nothing', misunderstood by Lear, that reverberates throughout the tragedy. Likewise, in 'The Almond Trees' and throughout much of Walcott's work,[106] we find a positive (and if one sees the poet aligned with Cordelia, a true) understanding of 'nothingness' in contrast to Naipaul's Lear-esque blinkered vision. At the same time, Lear's observation is made as he attempts to rip off his clothes and mirror the scarcely clad Edgar, who is exposed to the tempestuous elements on the heath in a way that is reflected in the women on the beach exposed to the no-less-brutal heat of the midday sun. Once again, Walcott refutes clear demarcations between people, envisioning instead a syncretization that is fundamental to much of his work, as Chapter 2 will explore.

Like the sunbathing women as 'daphnes', the heat that the trees have endured becomes metaphorical, too, evoking the horrifying experiences of enslavement and the Middle Passage that lie at the heart of the poem, and uniting the trees with the people:

Welded in one flame,
huddling naked, stripped of their name,
for Greek or Roman tags, they were lashed
raw by wind.[107]

The 'huddling naked' trees recall the horrors of confinement of human beings in the hold of the slave ship; Apollo's attempted rape of Daphne now foreshadows the sexual assaults committed by enslavers; and the re-naming of enslaved people and the brutal physical treatment they endured is enacted and reinscribed on the almond trees. As Edward Baugh notes, the sea-almond grows wild in the Caribbean but is not indigenous to the region; and when brought there, was re-named by European botanists as *Terminalia catappa* before being informally re-named again by a variety of titles riffing on the title of 'almond', all of which 'designate it an imitator, mimicking the "real", prized, commercially grown almond of the temperate North'.[108]

The reference to the myth of Daphne and Apollo opens Walcott to the charge of imitation, but the manner in which he Signifies upon Ovid is generative. Having 'the faith of using the old names anew' ('What the Twilight Says'),[109] Walcott refigures Daphne's desperate flight from Apollo, in which she takes root in the soil and is transformed into a laurel tree,[110] into that of enslaved people escaping the dominant imperial powers, taking root in a new place, and transforming themselves from enslaved African people into free Caribbean people. The myth of Daphne and Apollo appears in the first book of Ovid's *Metamorphoses*, soon after the epic's cosmological opening, which highlights its potential as an origin myth. This makes it an apt point from which Walcott will refute the poem's opening suggestion that 'there's nothing here', and argue instead that, as John Thieme has observed of the poem, 'the traumas of the Middle Passage and slavery have been transformed into a history of endurance and cultural pride'.[111] With Walcott's conception of time as one of simultaneity that, all the same, does not ignore linear, hierarchical time, the 'welding' of trees and people means that they are both simultaneously united (as in the imagery of the slave ship) and that the trees are ancestors of the people.

This notion is one that Walcott discussed in an essay that same year, 'The Figure of Crusoe',[112] explaining the inspiration for the poem that he found when he 'saw the figures of ancient almond trees in a grove past Rampalangas on the north coast [of Trinidad], as a grove of dead, transplanted, uprooted ancestors',[113] and it is one that the final verse of 'The Almond Trees' affirms, albeit with a more positive, living sense:[114]

> One sunburnt body now acknowledges
> that past and its own metamorphosis
> as, moving from the sun, she kneels to spread
> her wrap within the bent arms of this grove
> that grieves in silence, like parental love.[115]

Walcott's engagement with Ovid's tale is thus refigured not only in a Caribbean setting, but to offer a different trajectory: the language of these trees, he tells us, is not like 'some running hamadryad's cries', but rather, an 'enduring sound' of grief. While in Ovid, the people were the ancestors of the trees, Walcott's trees are ancestors of the people, reminding us that monuments built by people and histories rooted in human 'achievements' are not the only way to tell a tale.

'Air'

The reclaiming of a notion of 'nothingness', seen in 'The Almond Trees', is returned to in 'Air' (1969),[116] which opens with a quotation from Froude in an echo of Naipaul's epigraph to *The Middle Passage* that quotes a longer passage that includes those same lines.[117] Walcott 'mocks the colonialists' denial of history and achievement in the Caribbean', as Isidore Okpewho has noted,[118] while also pointedly taking issue with Naipaul's then-recent endorsement of the colonial view. The poem's title reflects the fact that the attribution of 'nothingness' is made only by those who fail to see, just as only a lack of understanding would allow someone to declare the 'air' a void. Humankind's refusal to pay sufficient attention to nature (the rain forest is 'unheard', its 'shell-like noise [...] roars like silence') is coupled with a human tendency to attribute blame to it rather than accept responsibility themselves: the forest is said to have 'devoured | two minor yellow races and | half of a black',[119] the adjective 'minor' signalling the colonialist perspective.[120] The poem ends with the sardonic retort, 'There is too much nothing here,' reclaiming 'nothing' as a potent and vibrant force recognized by Caribbean ways of knowing.

This reclamation of 'nothingness' has correspondences with a striking passage from Césaire's *Cahier d'un retour au pays natal*:

> Eia pour ceux qui n'ont jamais rien inventé
> pour ceux qui n'ont jamais rien exploré
> pour ceux qui n'ont jamais rien dompté
> mais ils s'abandonnent, saisis, à l'essence de toute chose
> ignorants des surfaces mais saisis par le mouvement

de toute chose
insoucieux de dompter, mais jouant le jeu du monde

Hurray for those who have never invented anything
for those who have never explored anything
for those who have never vanquished anything
but they surrender, possessed, to the essence of every thing
ignorant of surfaces but possessed by the movement
of every thing
unconcerned to vanquish, but playing the game of the world.[121]

Here, in a manoeuvre akin to the coining of the word *négritude*, Césaire takes criticisms that have been levelled against people from Africa and of the African diaspora and affirms them as positives. At the same time, similar to Walcott's conception of time, this passage is also about another way of knowing; as Abiola Irele notes (of the previous stanza in *Cahier*), 'beyond its polemical intent, the passage is also a poetic statement of an alternative path to knowledge'.[122]

Another Life

While 'The Almond Trees' and 'Air' take to task declarations that there is 'nothing' in the Caribbean, highlighting the narrowness of a mindset that makes such proclamations, in Walcott's most extended piece of poetry before *Omeros*, he develops his notion of contemporary St Lucia's simultaneity with the ancient Graeco-Roman world. The first book of *Another Life* (1973),[123] his autobiographical epic poem, exemplifies this especially evocatively. Walcott composes an A–Z (minus a few letters) of Castries, depicting the people of the town in what Baugh has observed is a kind of Joycean 'comic odyssey',[124] a connection Walcott highlights with the punning line a little later in the same book, 'when he ulyseed, she bloomed again'.[125] This classically infused meditation is prompted by the young Walcott reading two collections of Greek myths written for children, Nathaniel Hawthorne's *Tanglewood Tales* (1853) and Charles Kingsley's *The Heroes: Or, Greek Fairy Tales* (1855), and a schoolteacher's sharp interruption, 'Boy! Who was Ajax?'[126] The answer begins the depiction of Walcott's hometown, eschewing the Joycean mapping of Dublin found in *Ulysses* in favour of an alphabetical one that Baugh and Colbert Nepaulsingh suggest is intended to 'make it appear thorough, complete, easy to remember; it is the bedrock of his art, as the English alphabet is the bedrock of his writing'.[127]

Castries' Ajax, conjured in response to the teacher's barking question, is a cart-horse who, on one day of the year only, becomes a thoroughbred race horse, sensing on the race-track 'the scent of battle' in place of the usual smell of discarded food scraps that surrounds him.[128] Helen is 'the town's one clear-complexioned whore', Cassandra an old woman to whom no one listens, 'her drone unheeded', Midas a successful businessman, 'pillar of business and the Church'.[129] Castries itself is 'Troy town', destroyed by a fire that ravaged the city in 1948, reminiscent of the Greeks setting light to the Trojan city.[130] Some of these St Lucian characters are the Graeco-Roman figures, some are merely akin to them, so that the alphabetical episode slips in and out of temporal planes in a way that is fitting for the construction of mythology, which is seldom constrained by clock time. Bringing the alphabet to a close, Walcott reflects on how he has shaped the world around him into something mythological:

These dead, these derelicts,
that alphabet of the emaciated,
they were the stars of my mythology.[131]

Although Walcott's career had already spanned two decades by this stage, *Another Life* is, nonetheless, a relatively early creative instantiation of Walcott's conception of time that recurs throughout his myth-infused writings. It is developed most extensively in *Omeros* and *The Odyssey: A Stage Version*,[132] with Lorna Hardwick remarking of the latter, that Walcott's 'dramatic strategy involved disruptions of historically and culturally constituted narrative',[133] pointing to the way that his approach to time resonates with his approach to art more widely.

'The Medusa of the New World'

Although 'The Muse of History' was published one year after *Another Life*, it was written three years earlier, hard on the heels of the Black Power Revolution in Trinidad.[134] Walcott claims in the essay that history is 'the Medusa of the New World'.[135] The essay is a meditation on time, identity and art, which should be read alongside his more traditionally creative works that contemplate many of the same issues. The essay articulates Walcott's philosophy in a way that serves as a counter both to the criticism directed at him for being overly enamoured with 'the Western canon', and to the praise heaped upon him by those who delight in spotting his canonical allusions. As he remarks, perhaps too pointedly for the scholar engaged in studying classical reception, 'it is only academics and frightened poets who talk of Beckett's debt to Joyce'.[136]

Key to the essay is Walcott's reformulation of the perception of time: no longer should the linear trajectory of time proposed by European thinkers predominate. This is both a contestation of colonially imposed ideas, as we have seen,[137] and key to Caribbean ontology more widely, as Glissant noted in his essay 'The Quarrel with History':

> Quereller l'Histoire, c'est peut-être, pour Derek Walcott, affirmer l'urgence de cette mise en question des catégories de la pensée analytique.[138]

> The quarrel with History is perhaps for Derek Walcott the affirmation of the urgency of a revaluation of the conventions of analytical thought.[139]

Glissant's essay takes its inspiration from a talk by Edward Baugh on Walcott,[140] and includes Glissant's striking formulation, '"Là où se joignent les histoires des peuples, hier réputés sans histoire, finit l'Histoire." (Avec un grand H.)'[141] ('"History (with a capital H) ends where the histories of those peoples once reputed to be without history come together"').[142] Resonating with Walcott's notion, quoted as the epigraph to this chapter, that the New World and the Old World are simultaneous, both writers reject History with a capital H 'for its original concept as myth'.[143] As Glissant articulates it, 'L'Histoire est un fantasme fortement opératoire de l'Occident, contemporain précisément du temps où il était seul à "faire" l'histoire du monde'[144] ('History is a highly functional fantasy of the West, originating at precisely the time when it alone "made" the history of the World').[145]

This model of history, the 'fantasy of the West', is underwritten by notions of superiority and inferiority which map directly onto age and newness: to be new and to ponder ideas found in other works is to be derivative; newness stands not for innovation if it can be connected with ideas that have gone before, but for imitation. Ezra Pound's radical formulation of Modernism, 'Make it New', was radical for the very reason that it was so unusual: for what Pound proposed was not that artists dismiss what had gone before in order to create something utterly new, but rather that they build on those past works, engaging with them but also creating something so fresh that the 'it' (the past, often the canonical works of the past) became new.[146] Poets, Walcott claims (implicitly concurring with Pound's maxim), can only be original once they have 'absorbed' all the work that has gone before them.[147] As Walcott argues of Carnival in his essay 'The Caribbean: Culture or Mimicry?', 'From the viewpoint of history, these forms originated in imitation if you want, and ended in invention'.[148] This is a position that succinctly articulates his approach to Graeco-Roman antiquity too, including his acknowledgement in that same essay that his engagement with Classics is not disconnected from the colonial oppression that likewise gave rise to Carnival in the Caribbean.[149] Walcott echoes the Modernist dictum as he reflects on the unrepeatability of Carnival: 'an entire population of craftsmen and spectators compel themselves to this regeneration of perpetually making it new'.[150] Walcott contests any notion of originality that does not spring from repetition, claiming that 'everything is mere repetition'.[151]

To compare Walcott with Pound can be jarring: notwithstanding their engagement with epic, embodied in *Omeros* and the *Cantos*, respectively, and the influence of Pound on Walcott's early work, especially *Epitaph for the Young: XII Cantos* (1949),[152] their ideologies were very different. Line Henriksen has suggested that Walcott's 'anxiety' regarding his writing of epic is generated not only by the literary weight of Dante, Milton and the Graeco-Roman epics, but also by the knowledge that to write an epic poem in the twentieth century is to write in the shadow of Pound's fascism and the critical failure of the *Cantos*.[153] There is also an underlying introspection and decadence to high modernism that is at odds with Walcott's more politically engaged approach, even while he did not shy away from autobiographical self-reflection. Moreover, an understanding of modernism rooted only in its European instantiations occludes recognition of its Caribbean form that Glissant articulated in his essay 'The Novel of the Americas':

> L'irruption dans la modernité, l'irruption hors tradition, hors la «continuité» littéraire, me parait être une marque spécifique de l'écrivain américain quand il veut signaler la réalité de son entour.[154]

> The irruption into modernity, the violent departure from tradition, from literary 'continuity', seems to me a specific feature of the American writer when he wishes to give meaning to the reality of his environment.[155]

As Dash notes, Glissant proposes a modernism rooted in the Americas and 'profoundly connected with resistance and a suspicion of any transcendent systems of centralization or totalization'.[156] Just as Walcott's conception of time is in dialogue with Glissant's, so, too, his engagement with modernism must be seen through the lens of its Caribbean instantiation rather than merely as a European movement.

Bearing that in mind, there remain ways in which the dialogue between Walcott's work and that of European modernists is illuminating. Among the works of high modernism is a proliferation of art that engages with classical antiquity (as can be found in so many literary eras, especially in Europe), but which marks its engagement by difference as well.[157] Joyce's *Ulysses*, for example, self-consciously marks its difference from Homer's *Odyssey* in its form, its geographic and temporal scope, and in the nature of its protagonist's heroism, while also adapting the Homeric settings and themes, and (sometimes) providing the Homeric episode, all of which compel the reader to make a comparison with Homer.[158] The combination casts the worlds of both Odysseus and Leopold Bloom in a new light, and goes beyond this, too, as T. S. Eliot famously noted: 'In using the myth, in manipulating a continuous parallel between contemporaneity and antiquity, Mr Joyce is pursuing a method which others must pursue after him.'[159] Walcott can be seen to extend the 'mythical method'[160] in new directions by not only setting up a 'parallel' between past and present, but seeing them as co-existent as well, just as Joyce likewise did.[161] But to read Walcott's work as solely or even primarily deploying the 'mythical method', even in a poem so overtly engaged in this approach as *Omeros*, would be a mistake. What Walcott avoids is the decadence that lies at the nub of Ekwueme Michael Thelwell's criticism of high modernism, which he sees as having reached a point at which 'the creation of new and vital formulations and interpretations of cultural reality becomes secondary to the parody and cannibalization of earlier works'.[162] While Thelwell overstates the case, his argument illuminates the ways in which Walcott's work shares in elements of modernism while also sidestepping its pitfalls by its exploration of contemporary 'cultural reality'.

As Paula Burnett has noted, there are significant correspondences between Eliot's essay and Walcott's 'The Muse of History',[163] but even more thoroughgoing is the dialogue between Walcott's essay and Eliot's slightly earlier piece, 'Tradition and the Individual Talent' (1919), in which both writers recognize linear time but assert simultaneity as a more pertinent way of understanding a tradition.[164] Eliot encapsulates this in his conception of tradition:

> What happens when a new work of art is created is something that happens simultaneously to all the works of art which preceded it. The existing monuments form an ideal order among themselves, which is modified by the introduction of the new (the really new) work of art among them.[165]

This idea of tradition, freed from the constraints of calendrical time, is very appealing to Walcott and his engagement with it leads to what Pollard terms his 'ironic New World classicism'.[166] The respective contexts from which Eliot and Walcott were writing were, for different reasons, rife with fragmentation, and this conceptualization of tradition offers a way to create a whole out of fragments.

However, for Walcott, there is another element at play too, and it is one that has exacerbated the tendency to see literature from the Caribbean not only as belated, but as derivative as well. Despite its wrongheadedness, this attitude is almost inevitable if one adopts a Eurocentric idea of movement forward in time equating with 'progress', as Walcott has explained:[167]

> If you think of art merely in terms of chronology, you are going to be patronizing to certain cultures. But if you think of art as a simultaneity that is inevitable in terms of certain people, then Joyce is a contemporary of Homer (which Joyce knew).[168]

It is not only as a contemporary writer, then, that Walcott fears this slight on his originality; it is also as a Caribbean one. The 'New World' – a misnomer that embodies the colonial arrogance of European imperialists – and the Caribbean, in particular, has a long history of being perceived as a place in which nothing is created, as we have seen. It is a perception that Walcott aptly deemed a 'curse' when he referred to Naipaul's infamous claim that 'nothing was created in the

West Indies'.[169] Walcott's 'The Muse of History' can in part be seen as a response to this essay too, for the opening clause of Naipaul's proclamation is, 'History is built around achievement and creation'; 'history' retorts Walcott, is more complex than that. It can, Medusa-like, petrify the potential of the Caribbean, but it can also liberate.

To pursue Walcott's Medusa-metaphor further, time itself may be an innocent victim akin to Ovid's Medusa assaulted by Neptune (*Metamorphoses* 4.791–804). Neptune's rape of Medusa, and Minerva's subsequent punishment of her, transforms the beautiful Gorgon into a monster whose gaze turns all to stone. Similarly, imperialism (metonymically represented by Neptune and Minerva as gods of sea and war, respectively, in Walcott's analogy) turned time into petrifying History, as Fabian's work in *Time and the Other* confirms. History, then, is the transformed and previously innocent Time that, Medusa-like, fixes formerly colonized worlds in a state of stasis, at least in the eyes of those who adopt the colonially inflected gaze.[170]

Those writers who are most constrained by the region's colonial past, most petrified by History's Medusa-like gaze are, Walcott argues in 'The Muse of History', those he terms 'radical':

> In the New World servitude to the muse of history has produced a literature of recrimination and despair, a literature of revenge written by the descendants of slaves or a literature of remorse written by the descendants of masters.[171]

Lamenting this approach, he argues that the finest writers of the New World (among whom, he numbers Walt Whitman and Pablo Neruda) 'reject this sense of history'.[172] In its place is a mode that is aware of, but unencumbered by, the past. In this new mode, the hierarchy of linear time is flattened, leading to the simultaneity that makes questions of indebtedness or charges of imitation illogical. He singles out Graeco-Roman antiquity as one of those potentially encumbering histories, but sees it stripped of its negative power, leaving only the generative aspects behind: 'he [the vision of man held by the great writers of the New World] has paid his accounts to Greece and Rome and walks in a world without monuments and ruins'.[173]

It is this ability to inhabit ancient Greece and Rome imaginatively without setting it apart, on either a pedestal or in the distant past, that is central to understanding Walcott's engagement with it. He places Graeco-Roman antiquity on the same temporal plane as himself, so that neither the decay of its ruins nor the intervening period's oppressive use of its monuments intrudes. The effect is to replace linear time with simultaneity; or as Walcott suggests, 'So the death of a gaucho does not merely repeat, but is, the death of Caesar.'[174]

It is not only the hierarchical structure of linear time that is removed by this vision of simultaneity, but also the social hierarchies that might designate Caesar as being of more importance than a gaucho. Walcott will again put the lie to this in *Omeros* when he chooses village fishermen as the heroes of his poem, just as he did with the trajectory of his Haitian trilogy and its movement from a focus on 'great men' to 'heraldic' figures. Combined with the mention of Jorge Luis Borges just two sentences earlier in the essay, Walcott's words bring to mind José Hernández's epic poem *El Gaucho Martín Fierro* (first published in two parts in 1872 and 1879), which was the subject of Borges' 1953 volume *El 'Martín Fierro'*, co-authored with Margarita Guerrero. Hernández's poem, as Borges himself notes,[175] is often compared with the *Odyssey* and one might illuminatingly see Hernández as another poet with whom Walcott is in contemporaneous dialogue as he writes *Omeros*.

Walcott's contention here, that events do not repeat other ones so much as *are* other ones, might be seen as the flipside to Fabian's argument about anthropology's allochronism: instead of occupying the same temporal space but placing 'the other' in a different one, Walcott situates what we might traditionally think of as past and present on the same temporal plane as each other. This refutes the 'othering' that is deployed by those who regard later writers as indebted to earlier ones rather than in dialogue with them, although such 'othering' is not always stated explicitly but instead reverberates through charges of imitation and mimicry.[176] For Walcott, this new reckoning of time is to be celebrated:

> Fact evaporates into myth. This is not the jaded cynicism which sees nothing new under the sun, it is an elation which sees everything as renewed.[177]

With everything 'renewed', the hierarchy of time is removed and replaced with equality.

'Sea Grapes'

Walcott's conception of time, as one of both simultaneity and a non-linearity produced by the 'amnesia' imposed by colonial violence, is enunciated in poetic form in the title poem of his 1976 collection, *Sea Grapes*. The poem was originally entitled 'Sour Grapes',[178] a term that remains embedded in the version published in the collection, but the idiom derived from Aesop's fables has ceded its place of priority to the fruit indigenous to the Caribbean (formally known by the Latin name, *coccoloba uvifera*).[179] The palimpsest of these changes echoes the trajectory of the poem itself, which moves from seeking answers in a model from ancient Greece (whether that be in the reflection 'could be Odysseus' or in Aesop's 'sour grapes') to the realization that 'The classics can console. But not enough.' This palimpsest of alternative renderings is also what the poem itself debates: is the boat on the water a Caribbean schooner or Odysseus' ship? Or is it instead, like Walcott's model of simultaneity, both at once? 'Sea Grapes' puts into action the understanding of time that Walcott outlined and advocated in 'The Muse of History'.

The poem opens with a boat making its way home. Gazing out to sea, the narrator reflects that it could just as easily be a boat in the Aegean as the Caribbean, sailing by in antiquity or in the present:

a schooner beating up the Caribbean

for home, could be Odysseus,
home-bound on the Aegean.[180]

There is no question of resolving this temporal uncertainty; rather, the poem asks that the uncertainty be embraced: times and spaces usually perceived as different are mapped onto each other, whether in a simultaneous moment or a cyclical one. The cartography of 'the New World' that was sketched out by imperial forces is destabilized by the fact that the Caribbean could just as easily be the Aegean; likewise, the designations of priorness and belatedness contained in the terms Old and New Worlds are dismantled: the boat at sea could be in either place or time.

The rest of the poem continues to embody this concept of time that Walcott sketched in 'The Muse of History', doing so both at the narrative level and, as

Emily Greenwood has highlighted, at the level of language: 'Walcott's concept of time infuses and informs his use of language,'[181] seen particularly in his use of temporal adverbs and other markers of time.[182] The poem is one of divisions but it is Walcott's conceptualization of time that points the way to overcoming these ruptures, much as it also offers a way beyond the Manichean divisions imposed by European epistemologies. An 'ancient war between obsession and responsibility' is at the heart of the poem. It is there in the simultaneously centripetal and centrifugal drive towards and away from home, and in the pull of the wife and child ('that father and husband's | longing') that conflicts with 'the adulterer hearing Nausicaa's name | in every gull's outcry'. So, too, there are divisions in the distinction between the sea-voyager and the land-wanderer, between Odysseus' ship and the Caribbean schooner, between the 'consolation' of classical literature and its insufficient power to console. But crucially, these divisions are united by the simultaneity of time: that 'ancient war' 'will never finish and has been the same': the spectre of linear time is here, but its hierarchies have been removed in favour of a cyclical vision of time. As Greenwood notes of that line, the verb tenses 'raise the aspect of time as if only to negate it: this situation is eternal and unchanging.'[183]

The Homeric allusions of the poem not only illustrate Walcott's theorization of time, but also interleave 'Sea Grapes' with several of the preoccupations that regularly recur throughout his oeuvre. In particular, the themes of homecoming, romantic betrayal and Signifying upon canonical literature which, in this poem as in many other Walcott works, are explored in part through a lens suffused by the *Iliad* and *Odyssey*.[184] For Edward Baugh, Walcott's work 'has constructed for him an Odyssean persona, hooked on wandering but always yearning for home,'[185] as we saw in the figure of the poet-narrator of *Omeros*. In this vein, the line 'This brings nobody peace' resonates intriguingly through 'Sea Grapes'. On the one hand, the most direct reading of the line is surely valid: that this battle between obsession and responsibility is vexatious for everyone and 'brings nobody peace'. On the other hand, given the Odyssean motifs of the poem, which are further consolidated in the penultimate verse's Cyclopean reference to the 'blind giant's boulder' thrown into the sea, it is impossible not to hear Odysseus' most famous pseudonym in the mention of 'nobody'.

By this reading, the one person who gains a sense of peace is Odysseus, but only the Odysseus as he is for that short moment in the Cyclops' cave when, as

Horkheimer and Adorno articulate it, 'He declares allegiance to himself by disowning himself as Nobody.'[186] Unable, according to Horkheimer and Adorno, to bear the loss of subjectivity that is embodied in the name 'Nobody', Odysseus scurries back to the security of a non-dialectical position by reclaiming his name as he taunts the Cyclops to disastrous effect while making his escape (*Odyssey* 9.473–540).[187] In so doing, Odysseus reclaims his identity and returns to his position as a 'prototype of the bourgeois individual',[188] a figure of the Enlightenment which values singularity over plurality.[189] Moreover, it is not only this prioritization of singularity that is at odds with Walcott's conception of time and which would explain why 'Nobody' can find peace in the multiple temporal domains of the poem, it is also that the Enlightenment thinking that Odysseus is so quick to return to has always had the oppression of others at its heart.[190] The moment at which Odysseus allows himself to be 'Nobody', then, is the one in which he is furthest from the position of a protocolonial figure and so least invested in the colonial power dynamics that regard the Caribbean as belated. When he reverts to the position of Enlightenment thinking, he reclaims his identity as would-be oppressor, and it is in that role that Polyphemus hurls the rock after him, which Walcott imagines bringing the Homeric epic to Caribbean shores:

> and the blind giant's boulder heaved the trough
> from whose ground-swell the great hexameters come
> to the conclusions of exhausted surf.[191]

Walcott thereby models the attack on indigenous people by agents of imperialism in terms of Odysseus' invasion of Polyphemus' home, in a way that has commonalities with Aimé Césaire's vision in *Cahier d'un retour au pays natal* and,[192] much further back, with Lucian's in *Dialogues of the Sea-Gods* (2nd century CE).[193] In so doing, though, he highlights that this is a two-way process: colonialism caused the Greek epic to reach other shores, but the Cyclops has a creative role to play in its continued existence and diffusion, since it is his rock that gives the momentum for the hexameters to reach the Caribbean. The result is a contestation of the model of imposed tradition; instead, Walcott sees the epic's survival in the Caribbean as being as much dependent on the formerly oppressed as it is on the colonial forces.

If Walcott were to see the Homeric Cyclops episode in a similar way to Horkheimer and Adorno, either by having read *Dialectic of Enlightenment* (1944) or by his own engagement with the *Odyssey*, the line 'this brings nobody peace' takes on new meaning. For the multiplicity that the poem explores, namely the contestation of two opposing forces (seen in 'the ancient war | between obsession and responsibility'), is one that Odysseus-as-Nobody can handle. The possibilities of multiple conceptions of time, including the linear hierarchy of European chronology and the simultaneity of Caribbean time, may well bring that 'Nobody' peace and advocate for similarly plural understandings of the world around us.

'Map of the New World'

Five years later, Walcott's 'Map of the New World', published in his 1981 collection, *The Fortunate Traveller*,[194] picks up this theme of simultaneity, again in the context of Homeric epic and the Trojan War, as we saw also in 'A Map of the Antilles'.[195] The poem's Caribbean is a space of simultaneity in which the *Odyssey* is about to be written, as the closing verse of the first section of the poem, entitled 'Archipelagoes', depicts:

> The drizzle tightens like the strings of a harp.
> A man with clouded eyes picks up the rain
> and plucks the first line of the *Odyssey*.[196]

It is possible that the poet is about to re-perform Homer's epic, but the preceding stanza, in which the Trojan War is over but Helen is alive if aged and Troy is still a 'white ashpit', suggests that these events are not so far in the past and that the song that is about to begin will be a composition of the *Odyssey* itself, akin – as Thieme has suggested – to Pierre Menard's verbatim writing of *Don Quixote* in Borges' short story, 'Pierre Menard, Autor del *Quijote*' ('Pierre Menard, Author of the *Quixote*').[197] This can be seen as a kind of precursor to Walcott's own composition of *Omeros*, further endorsed by the allusion to the myth of Tristan and Yseult in the next section of 'Map of the New World', prefiguring Walcott's engagement with a range of myths in *Omeros*, although the originality and syncretism of *Omeros* make it a new work rather than a retelling of any epic that has gone before.

'The Sea is History'

The temporal ambiguity of 'Map of the New World' is another instance of Walcott's insistence on the importance of plural perceptions of time, which must be understood as being directly related to the colonial violence inflicted upon the region. As Simon Gikandi has argued in *Writing in Limbo* (1992), 'Caribbean writers simultaneously represent colonial history as a nightmare and affirm the power of historicity in the slave community.'[198] It is this combination that helps explain why history and its more objective counterpart, historicity, have been such central concerns for Caribbean writers. The Joycean notion of history as a nightmare from which we struggle to awake, which Gikandi evokes here,[199] was quoted by Walcott in his 1989 talk, 'The Sea is History':[200] 'History, Stephen said, is a nightmare from which I am trying to awake.'[201] Or rather, Walcott fractionally misquotes it, removing Stephen (perhaps merely for syntactical convenience) and more significantly, substituting a definite article where Joyce has an indefinite one: 'History is *the* nightmare from which I'm trying to awake.'[202] The effect is to proclaim history the predominant nightmare of those in the Caribbean.

Walcott goes on to explain the importance of freeing oneself from the constraints of history:

> For the artist to deliver himself from the bondage of time, which is called 'history' is the only way he himself can burst through. And the bondage of time involves language. It involves the idea of language being the tool that dominates the colonial.[203]

As the language of bondage makes clear, Walcott's exhortation is not to ignore history but to strip it of its paralysing power. His poem 'The Sea is History' (*The Star-Apple Kingdom*),[204] written ten years earlier and which he performed in the middle of the later talk of the same name, suggests how this might be done. It begins:

> Where are your monuments, your battles, martyrs?
> Where is your tribal memory? Sirs,
> in that gray vault. The sea. The sea
> has locked them up. The sea is History.[205]

The vastness and power of the sea give 'an idea of time that makes history absurd'.[206] Claiming the sea as history scorns this vision of historical progress in which monuments and ruins stand as commemorations of human achievement. The sea contains history, having witnessed and 'locked up' the horrors of the transatlantic slave trade (paralleled in the poem with biblical narratives in deliberately incommensurable ways), but it refuses the commemoration of any human events.[207] In place of history's linearity is the unceasing cyclical rhythm of the sea, with which Walcott brought the final lines of *Omeros* to a close: 'When he [Achille] left the beach the sea was still going on'.[208]

For Walcott, what is at stake in his reconceptualization of time and his advocacy of simultaneity in place of linearity is accentuated by History (with a capital H, to borrow from Glissant again)[209] for the simple reason that so little space and value has been afforded the Caribbean in hegemonic historiographies. As Shabine, the protagonist of 'The Schooner *Flight*' recalls, 'I met History once, but he ain't recognize me.'[210] An answer, then, is found elsewhere: in the simultaneity that Walcott promulgates and also in the syncretism that is the subject of the next chapter. For it is not only Walcott's conception of time that asks for multiple moments to be merged; the syncretism that his work enacts and celebrates mirrors this conception as well.

2

Syncretism

If the geological form of an archipelago evokes both fragmentation and connection, the colonial history of the Caribbean looked set to ensure that it was the rupture and dispersal of the former that was forever associated with the region. But rather than focusing on fragmentation, it is the processes of connection that artists, and in turn scholars, of the Caribbean have shown to be a defining characteristic. From Fernando Ortiz's concept of 'transculturation' to Antonio Benítez-Rojo's 'repeating island' to Kole Omotoso's 'kaleidoscope', syncretism is a fundamental aspect of the Caribbean.[1]

A term that had come to acquire pejorative overtones, especially in the context of comparative studies of religion where it was developed, 'syncretism' has been reclaimed by Caribbean theorists, as Benítez-Rojo's 1989 conceptualization of the region as a place of 'supersyncretism' proclaims.[2] So much so, that the anthropologist James Clifford declared, 'We are all Caribbeans now in our urban archipelagos.'[3] At the heart of a pejorative understanding of syncretism is both a disdain for 'mixture' and a mistaken belief that any tradition or culture is 'pure'.[4] These two ideas have long been understood as fallacies, the propagation of which has often been political. As Édouard Glissant explained, not only have all peoples been part of the 'cross-cultural process', but the idea of syncretism (or creolization, as Michael Dash translates *métissage*) has been reconceptualized:

> Affirmer que les peuples sont métissés, que le métissage est valeur, c'est déconstruire ainsi une catégorie «métis» qui serait intermédiaire en tant que telle entre deux extrêmes «purs». [...] Le métissage comme proposition suppose la négation du métissage comme catégorie, en consacrant un métissage de fait que l'imaginaire humain a toujours voulu (dans la tradition occidentale) nier ou déguiser.[5]

> To assert peoples are creolized, that creolization has value, is to deconstruct in this way the category of 'creolized' that is considered as halfway between two 'pure' extremes. [...] Creolization as an idea means the negation of creolization as a category, by giving priority to the notion of natural creolization, which the human imagination has always wished to deny or disguise (in Western tradition).[6]

It is this concept of syncretism, a kind of continuous 'cross-cultural poetics' (to use Glissant's term) that is so crucial to Derek Walcott. This is a syncretism that can incorporate the Graeco-Roman without making obeisance to it – however much the 'Western tradition' may flinch at what it fears is a loss of status. Syncretism can be, as Christopher Balme has argued, 'a response to what is perceived as a peculiarly Western tendency to homogenize, to exclude, to strive for a state of "purity", whether it be racial or stylistic'.[7] Its capacity to stage an active resistance towards Eurocentrism is also evident in Abdul JanMohamed's observation in the mid-1980s that 'the domain of literary and cultural syncretism belongs not to colonialist and neocolonialist writers but increasingly to Third World artists'.[8]

Coining the term 'transculturation' in his 1940 work, *Contrapunteo Cubano del tabaco y el azúcar* (*Cuban Counterpoint: Tobacco and Sugar*),[9] Ortiz explained its superiority to the word 'acculturation' by noting that while the latter expresses the acquiring of a new culture, 'transculturation' also encompasses the loss of elements of a previous culture and the creation of new cultural forms born out of that transition.[10] For Benítez-Rojo, claiming the archipelagos of ancient Greece and the modern Caribbean as 'meta-archipelagos' with neither limits nor centres, and drawing from Chaos theory, the Caribbean must be understood as 'a chaos within which there is an island that proliferates endlessly, each copy a different one, founding and refounding ethnological materials'.[11] While, for Omotoso, prefiguring the imagery of the Creolists Jean Bernabé, Patrick Chamoiseau and Raphaël Confiant, the Caribbean 'is like a kaleidoscope where new colours and new colour combinations keep turning up'.[12] In each of these, the ways and extent to which the Caribbean synthesizes the divergent aspects of its cultures and its history, bringing together the Indigenous, the African, the Asian and the European elements to form new wholes,[13] is identified as being key to the region. As Michael Dash remarked of the particularity of the Caribbean,

> Including the Caribbean in any [literary] survey means ultimately more than simply expanding the literary canon to include new minorities or the heretofore marginalized. It means dismantling those notions of nation, ground, authenticity, and history on which more conventional surveys have been based and exploring concepts of cultural diversity, syncretism, and instability that characterize the island cultures of the Caribbean.[14]

It is this ever-evolving syncretism,[15] and the ways in which it features in Derek Walcott's work, that is the subject of this chapter. His syncretizing approach, as well as the syncretism of the Caribbean region itself, are integral to his writing and to the ways in which he engages with the Graeco-Roman world and with canonical literature more widely.

Walcott offered an evocative image of Ortizian transculturation in his Nobel Prize acceptance speech, 'The Antilles: Fragments of Epic Memory' (1992):

> I am only one-eighth the writer I might have been had I contained all the fragmented languages of Trinidad.
> Break a vase, and the love that reassembles the fragments is stronger than that love which took its symmetry for granted when it was whole. The glue that fits the pieces is the sealing of its original shape. It is such a love that reassembles our African and Asiatic fragments, the cracked heirlooms whose restoration shows its white scars. This gathering of broken pieces is the care and pain of the Antilles, and if the pieces are disparate, ill-fitting, they contain more pain than their original sculpture, those icons and sacred vessels taken for granted in their ancestral places. Antillean art is this restoration of our shattered histories, our shards of vocabulary, our archipelago becoming a synonym for pieces broken off from the original continent.
> And this is the exact process of the making of poetry, or what should be called not its 'making' but its remaking.[16]

The imagery of the broken vase, rebuilt in ways that incorporate its history, serves as a metaphor for the Caribbean region. Fragmented at both the geological level, as islands broken off from the original whole, and human level, as the strategies of imperialism ripped people from their homelands and scattered them throughout the Americas, the unity of the region and the identity of its peoples is stronger and more valued than that which went before; as Kamau Brathwaite memorably pronounced, 'the unity is submarine'.[17] In this, Walcott's words resonate closely with those of Benítez-Rojo, who argues that 'Caribbean discourse carries [...] a myth or desire for social, cultural, and psychic integration to compensate for the fragmentation and provisionality of the collective Being.'[18]

Yet, despite the fixity that Walcott's image of the mended vase may evoke, his vision is of an ongoing, open-ended syncretism in line with Glissant's idea that 'creolization is the unceasing process of transformation' (*'la Relation n'est sans cesse qui relais'*).[19] The recurrent sea imagery of Walcott's work, the Adamic re-naming that is the subject of Chapter 3, and the combining and re-combining of a figure like *Omeros*' Seven Seas-Omeros-Homer-griot character confirms this, while the poignant refusal of closure in *Omeros*' final line encapsulates it: 'When he left the beach the sea was still going on.'[20]

Epitaph for the Young

Given that syncretism is an ever-evolving process, both at the individual and collective levels, it is no surprise that Walcott's very earliest works exhibit an incomplete syncretism that is not wholly successful. Having self-published his first collection of poetry, *25 Poems* in 1948 at the age of eighteen,[21] *Epitaph for the Young: XII Cantos* was published the following year.[22] In *Epitaph for the Young*, an 'attachment to the colonizer's tradition coexists with the no less sincere desire to pioneer a new and native art', as Patricia Ismond observed:[23] Walcott strives to foster creativity from the combination of a diverse range of elements in this collection, but the syncretic fusion of his later works has not yet been achieved. Nonetheless, Walcott would go on to draw links between *Epitaph* and both *Another Life* and *Omeros*, regarding the early poem as a significant precursor to the later ones,[24] and one might see in this proposed genealogy an acknowledgement of the earlier work's effort to attain that which the later poems achieve.

Epitaph for the Young offers an insight into Walcott's development as a writer, but it also contains much that is of interest in its own right as well: for example, as George Lamming recognized when he riffed on the phrase for his

1953 novel, *In the Castle of My Skin*, Walcott's line, 'You in the castle of your skin, I the swineherd,' has a magnificence that belied Walcott's teenage years.[25] In its fleeting evocation of the *Odyssey*'s loyal, enslaved swineherd, Eumaeus,[26] the line also captures the long history of enslavement that contributes to the divisive racial prejudice separating the speaker from the addressee while highlighting the constructedness of 'race' by alluding to an ancient system of slavery that was not based on skin colour, yet likewise deprived people of their freedom, their family and their roots.

Homer, along with Dante, Baudelaire, Eliot and Pound, is a persistent presence in *Epitaph for the Young*. The poem as a whole is cast as a sea voyage, with the narrator a still-young questing hero, more Telemachus than Odysseus, as his search for literary and personal father figures suggests. Walcott is, at this stage, very much an 'apprentice'; as he commented in an interview with Edward Hirsch in 1977:

> You just ravage and cannibalize anything as a young poet; you have a very voracious appetite for literature. The whole course of imitations and adaptations is simply a method of apprenticeship.[27]

The eighth canto of *Epitaph for the Young* exemplifies the incomplete syncretism of the collection,[28] while engaging with texts and themes that will remain important to Walcott throughout his career. It opens with a quotation from the *Odyssey*, of Telemachus seeking news of the still-wandering Odysseus; the smouldering ruins of Troy form a parallel to the condition of Walcott's hometown, which had so recently been devastated by the fire that destroyed much of Castries in 1948, rendering it a 'city of burnt desires, and ashen fires' in the young Walcott's eyes.[29] Alongside the Homeric referents, the influence of T. S. Eliot looms distractingly large in this section of the poem: not only in the direct allusions of 'A Little Giddying', but tracing back that 'chain of reception' (to use Jauss' and Martindale's term), Walcott engages with one of the very same encounters from Dante's *Inferno* that Eliot conjures. Thus, in his evocation of Dante's meeting with his mentor Brunetto Latini, filtered through Eliot's rendition yet Signifying upon it by restoring the direct address 'Ser Brunetto' that Eliot eventually chose to omit, Walcott places himself in this lineage of poets as an inheritor, but also a son seeking his father as the Odyssean allusions confirm.[30] When Eliot's famous speech to the Virgil Society, 'What is a Classic?'

is directly referenced in the poem,[31] the poetic persona's quest is confirmed as both personal and artistic. Keith Alleyne was not wrong when he remarked of *Epitaph* that, 'With Walcott, Eliot is not merely an influence, but a complete formula',[32] but only because Walcott has not yet achieved the kind of syncretic fusion that his later works will attain. As Stewart Brown notes, 'after *Epitaph* Eliot is essentially absorbed, has become one of the masters in the mature poet's archive of imagination'.[33] While the ever-evolving process of syncretism continued, Walcott's early works illuminate the period before syncretism, where the different elements jostle with each other but do not yet fully cohere to create a new whole.

'A Far Cry from Africa'

The difficulties of achieving the kind of fusion that creates an effective syncretism is considered on a personal (rather than artistic) level in Walcott's early poem 'A Far Cry from Africa', written around 1953,[34] and later included in the collection *In a Green Night* (1962). The impact of the region's colonial history on the individual is seen in different ways in the scars of the vase, the wounds of *Omeros* ('affliction is one theme | of this work') and, as we shall see, the characters of Walcott's 1983 play *A Branch of the Blue Nile*.[35] In 'A Far Cry from Africa', Walcott articulated the dilemma of a divided identity in such powerful terms that the poem became one of his most well-known works.

The poem opens with a scene of the Mau Mau uprising that was taking place in Kenya when Walcott composed the poem. Immediately, the tussle of opposing forces bubbles to the surface, not only in the scenes of violent conflict depicted but in the narrator's own perspective. The country is described as a 'paradise', the violence is 'a wind [...] ruffling the tawny pelt' of the continent, the Kikuyu people are compared with flies;[36] it is, as Breslin notes, a 'ventriloquism of colonialist attitudes', that satirizes such perspectives yet also recoils at the violence of the conflict and the slaughter of innocent children carried out by the Kenyan fighters.[37] Nonetheless, as the poem goes on, its stance and its sympathies shift along with its poetic style, embodying the poet's ambivalence.[38]

The poem turns, in its final verse, to self-reflection, as the narrator asks,

I who am poisoned with the blood of both,
Where shall I turn, divided to the vein?
I who have cursed
The drunken officer of British rule, how choose
Between this Africa and the English tongue I love?
Betray them both, or give back what they give?[39]

Being 'poisoned with the blood of both', the speaker feels implicated in the atrocities carried out by both sides in the conflict, and he 'betrays them both' by the very form of the poem, written in the English language and deploying iambic pentameter, yet expressing ambivalent concern for the resistance movement in Kenya. Contained within this anguish of divided identity is a corrective to those who claim that to write in imperial languages or engage with works of the European literary canon is to be in thrall to the colonizer.[40]

This is a reproach that has repeatedly been levelled at Walcott, whether in Kamau Brathwaite's assessment that he 'speaks away from' the people of the Caribbean,[41] or Errol Hill's sense that he is 'buttered up by the culture of Athens',[42] or Dionne Brand's disparagement that 'He has appealed from the beginning to foreign critics and foreign needs' and 'plays to the belief that colonization brought civilization, brought culture'.[43] The force of these criticisms is borne out by some of Walcott's writing: for example, in a later essay, 'Meanings' (1970), he writes that,

> It's the greatest bequest the Empire made. Those who sneer at what they call an awe of tradition forget how old the West Indian experience is. I think that precisely because of their limitations our early education must have ranked with the finest in the world. The grounding was rigid – Latin, Greek, and the essential masterpieces, but there was this elation of discovery. Shakespeare, Marlowe, Horace, Vergil – these writers weren't jaded but immediate experiences. The atmosphere was competitive, creative.
> It was cruel, but it created our literature.[44]

The description of colonial education systems as 'the finest in the world' and the stalwarts of the Western canon as 'the essential masterpieces' rankles, as could the idea that those 'created our literature'. Crucially, though, it is not the imposition of European works themselves but rather the 'competitive' context that provides the conditions for Caribbean creativity.[45] That competition, in which the European classics are felt as 'immediate experiences' just as the culture of the islands are, jostles different aspects of the Caribbean together, which, in rubbing against each other, mutually transform the other, and in the process, produce the potential to create new syncretic wholes.

However, in a poem as early as 'A Far Cry from Africa', Walcott has not yet found a way to enact the syncretism that many of his later works achieve and celebrate. The portrayal of the violence of the Kenyan freedom fighters combined with the poem's metre that adheres so closely to the iambic pentameter of much canonical English literature might seem to indicate Walcott's greater connection with the colonial aspects of his identity at this stage in his career, until it clashes with the poem's more anti-colonial perspective.[46] The division and plurality signalled in the poem's title (indicating both that the poet has heard a cry from all the way across the Atlantic and that he, or his poetry, is very different from what he perceives 'Africa' to be) thus persists throughout the poem, without finding a way to achieve a syncretic wholeness. Instead, the African and British aspects of his heritage are 'poison' and the questions at the poem's end remain unanswered.

'Ruins of a Great House'

Another early poem, 'Ruins of a Great House',[47] continues this theme of division. Published three years after 'A Far Cry from Africa' was written and positioned immediately following it in the 1962 collection, *In a Green Night*, 'Ruins of a Great House' (1956) asks the reader to focus for a time on fragmentation rather than synthesis, to move from contemplation of the effect of empire on the individual to its impact on a collective, and to see the way in which a quiet resistance is staged, here personified in the creeping war of attrition undertaken by nature. The poem's 'Great House' has a triple resonance: as an old colonial home, fallen into disrepair; as the British Empire disintegrating but still doing damage: 'The rot remains with us, the men are gone';[48] and as a cultural monument such as 'the Western Canon', imposed as if it were an unchangeable monolith. The poem concludes on a more elegiac note that seeks connection rather than the apportioning of blame, reflecting on Britain's own former status as a colonized land.

It is an ending that was foreshadowed by the poem's opening lines, for if in the penultimate verse we hear, 'That Albion too, was once | A colony like ours',[49] the poem began by alluding to Horace: 'Stones only, the *disjecta membra* of this Great House.'[50] Horace's '*disiecti membra poetae*' ('limbs of a dismembered poet') may be a literary metaphor,[51] but Glenn Most has persuasively argued that, a few decades later, the motif of fragmentation gains prominence in Neronian literature in response to the sense of disconnectedness that the vastness of the Roman Empire was engendering in its people,[52] a vastness that included Britain. Walcott's allusion to Horace gains a new sense once Roman Britain is evoked, as the *disjecta membra* are imagined also to exist in Britain as persistent traces of the Roman imperial project.

These connections that Walcott builds between colonial powers, who were still claiming most of the Caribbean as their own in 1956 when the poem was written, and the people of the Caribbean, seldom made him popular.[53] They do, however, indicate another aspect of the appeal of Graeco-Roman literature for him. Combined with his refutation of the importance of linear time that we saw in Chapter 1, and the fleeting alignment of himself with the Roman Horace in the citation of his words, Walcott identifies Britain both as a formerly colonized land and a current imperial power, troubling the notion of binary oppositions and tallying with Walcott's sense that his own heritage is one of conflicting aspects, as he explored in 'A Far Cry from Africa'.[54] Further endorsing the sense that Manichean oppositions are oversimplified is the poet's aghast recognition that enslavers and imperialists, 'men like Hawkins, Walter Raleigh, Drake' were both 'ancestral murderers and poets';[55] that, as Ismond notes, 'the literature and crimes of the empire were produced from one and the same source'.[56] This complexity that Walcott identifies in colonial powers is another aspect that leads him to resist direct oppositions of colonizer and colonized, even at this early stage of his writing when St Lucia was still fully under British control.

Ione

If 'A Far Cry from Africa' ended with a series of unanswered questions about how aspects of one's identity can be resolved, and 'Ruins of a Great House' contemplates fragmentation while identifying points of connection even with the proponents of brutal atrocities of imperialism and slavery, one year later Walcott's play *Ione* attempts a creative syncretism of artistic influences.[57] In its sustained engagement with Graeco-Roman literature alongside its Caribbean setting and context, the play can be seen as a very early prefiguration of some of the ideas motivating *Omeros*, but unlike the later work, *Ione*'s syncretism is less successful, with the plethora of classical referents threatening to overwhelm the play's coherence.[58] Nonetheless *Ione* remains an important work in allowing us to understand the ways in which Walcott developed his own contribution to the making of a classical Caribbean. The roots of his later approaches can be glimpsed in the play, while the ways in which these fail to compel an audience in *Ione* throw into sharp relief the more effective strategies of his later work.

Ione is overflowing with ideas and embedded narrative references. Among the relatively overt intertextual allusions are ones to Homer's *Iliad*, Aeschylus' *Agamemnon* and *Seven Against Thebes*, Euripides' *Bacchae* and *Medea*. The result, as Jamaican theatre director and critic, Norman Rae, observed of the play's premiere in 1957, is a work that feels more like an academic exercise than an artistic work:

> Walcott has woven a story to match the Greeks, as full of blood and thunder as *Agamemnon*, of women's matters as *Electra*. But the exercise remains an academic one. He presents the people and he presents the plot and hardly ever do the twain meet. The manipulation of the people for plot purposes is even more overt than in the Greek plays and because of the brevity of character exposition they do not make themselves very well known.[59]

What Rae pinpoints here in the gap between Walcott's characters and the play's plot is an aspect of the fragmentation that runs counter to the syncretism that so many of his later works achieve. In *Ione*, the fault lines of Walcott's intertextual engagement threaten to rip apart the play into non-cohesive segments, whereas in a work such as *Ti-Jean and His Brothers* (first performed the following year), Walcott syncretizes the ancient Greek with the Caribbean folktale.

That Walcott was striving for unity, even if *Ione* does not attain it, is indicated by a note at the start of the play that evokes the neoclassical Aristotelian unities: 'The action of the play takes place between two hill tribes in the island of St

Lucia, West Indies, and lasts for one day'. Unity of time thus asserted, the play also observes, for the most part, unity of place; but unity of action is jeopardized by the paralleling of two plots that are connected through character though not by event.

Nonetheless, it is worth keeping Walcott's impassioned response to Rae's review in mind. In a letter to the editor of Jamaica's *Daily Gleaner*, Walcott protests Rae's characterization:

> Sir: – If your reviewer Norman Rae imagines that he is writing for an audience which cares for the intricate lecture on what is great classical drama, he is five thousand [*sic*] years too late.
>
> It is not I who am trying to make an audience think and react like Grecians, it is Mr Rae who is doing this, and I cannot think of anything more academic [...] I also cannot imagine the Greek audience checking on their Aristotle before they entered the theatre.[60]

The backdrop to the play is a tussle over ownership of the land, with the opposing sides led by half-brothers, Victorin and Alexandre. Into this simmering conflict comes Achille who, like his later incarnation in *Omeros*, is in a relationship with Helene. Helene, daughter of Victorin, has an affair with Alexandre's son Diogene, which prompts the escalation of conflict, just as Helen's relationship does in both Homer and *Omeros*. Full of rage in Walcott's play not for the Iliadic slight on his honour, but as a reaction to the infidelity of his wife, Achille flies into a frenzy and cuts to pieces not only his wife's lover but also his own child, driven by the fear that the child is not really his own. Meanwhile, Helene's widowed sister, Ione, is pregnant by an American anthropologist and awaiting a letter from him that she hopes will invite her to join him in the United States; but when the letter arrives, it contains $50 and the suggestion that she have an abortion. Ione goes off-stage and just 11 lines later we learn that she is dead.

Such a plot summary indicates its resonances with Greek myth, and with Greek tragedy in particular. Combined with the names Helene and Achille (as well as others associated with Greek antiquity) and the fact that the killing takes place off-stage, the two brothers at war over the land brings to mind *Seven against Thebes*; the murder of the partner's lover and his own child evokes *Medea*, albeit with the gender roles inverted, while the dismemberment of the bodies recalls the *Bacchae*, especially in the killing of a child by their parent. The play also features a blind prophet, Theresine, whose name evokes Teiresias but whose qualities – in particular, the fact that she is doomed to prophesy without being believed – is more reminiscent of Cassandra, while the Iliadic intertext of Achille's and Helene's names is further highlighted when the former drags the body of Diogene through the dust. Yet, despite the preponderance of Greek myth, Walcott's incipient syncretization can be seen. Achille not only drags Diogene's corpse through the dust as the Homeric Achilles does to Hector, he scatters the limbs in the trees and echoes the imagery of Abel Meeropol's 'Strange Fruit', made most famous in Billie Holiday's 1939 recording of it.

> And then I take Diogene by the heels,
> And drag his bleeding trunk up in the dust,
> Up to the cliff that fall straight to the sea
> Where his tribe mending nets under the almonds,
> I lift his dripping body in the air,
> And swing him spinning down to the white rocks
> [...]
> Hanging like a red fruit from the sea grape trees.[61]

This reads as being more indebted to the *Bacchae* than anything else,[62] yet the evocation of lynchings in the United States is present, if undeveloped, in the imagery of the murdered body in the tree as 'fruit'.

As the play progresses, the classical elements take precedence, to the detriment of the play as a whole, which is slight on characterization, especially of the murderous Achille, rendering it – as the Jamaican poet and playwright Dennis Scott suggested – 'not so much a poetic drama as a dramatic poem'.[63] Yet, this dominance of the Graeco-Roman is not true of the opening, which is introduced by a scene of oral storytelling performed in St Lucian Creole.[64] Taking a break from their work, two roadmenders ask their younger colleague, Annelles, to tell them a story; he obliges and, at their request, begins a less well-known tale. Inserting himself as a character into the story (as the grandson of the prophetic Theresine), Annelles not only embodies the connection between drama and storytelling that Walcott referred to in his recollections of the stories told by his aunt,[65] but also marks the play as a work of *théâtre conté* – to use a term that Chamoiseau coined in *Manman Dlo contre la fée Carabosse* (1977) and Stéphanie Bérard subsequently adopted to refer to work that draws from the form, but not the content, of Caribbean folklore.⁶⁶ As Paul Breslin has argued, in both *Ione* and *Ti-Jean and His Brothers* (discussed below), Walcott also uses this narrative frame to create a Brechtian *Verfremdungseffekt* ('distancing effect') that prompts the audience to engage with the narrative on an ethical, rather than primarily empathetic, level.⁶⁷ The story Annelles tells may be less well-known to his intradiegetic audience, but the snapshots of Greek myth would be familiar to *Ione*'s audiences in theatres around the Caribbean, given the 'sound colonial education' ('The Schooner *Flight*') of many who attended theatre venues such as Kingston's Ward Theatre where the play was first performed in March 1957. Despite its St Lucian setting and its use of creole, Walcott seems to have – as Rae put it – 'fallen fatally in love with the outward conventions of the classical theatre'.⁶⁸

This is particularly striking because it goes against the growing artistic movement towards a 'West Indian National Theatre', which was led by Errol Hill, renowned Trinidadian playwright and scholar, who played the role of Victorin in the first production of *Ione* and who is thanked by Walcott for his 'technical advice with the script'.⁶⁹ Speaking in 1971, Errol Hill declared there to be three stages in the movement from colonial oppression to national identity: 'First comes political freedom; next, economic control; finally, cultural liberation';⁷⁰ the Caribbean, he pronounced, was still at the second stage. The following year, he published his foundational work, *The Trinidad Carnival: Mandate for a National Theatre* (1972), which closed with his vision of how a national theatre might be created:

> Independence does not mean a rejection of existing institutions simply because they are foreign. It does mean an honest reassessment of values that were established under an alien regime and a courageous effort to retain what is good from the past while introducing new ideas and institutions of greater relevance to the present and future. The Trinidad carnival has achieved a synthesis between old and new, between folk forms and art forms, between native and alien traditions.⁷¹

In Hill's idea of 'synthesis', we see the syncretism that is so central to the shaping of a Caribbean canon in the twentieth century. A similar synthesis is begun in Walcott's *Ione*, but remains incomplete. This is to go beyond the maxim that a work of drama requires the collaboration of actors, director, stage designer, audience and many others to become 'finished'; or, as Hill phrased it, adapting the words of set designer Lee Simonson, 'the playwright's script is the intention, the play performed is the work of art, the published play is the corpse'.[72] That remains true of *Ione* but, as I have suggested, one might also see *Omeros*, written more than thirty years later, as finally synthesizing the multiple aspects of *Ione* into a form that creates a new and syncretic whole.

Ti-Jean and His Brothers

Walcott once remarked that 'folk' traditions (a term he deliberates over) have had a greater impact on his drama than his poetry.[73] Keeping in mind Claude Lévi-Strauss' argument that 'we define the myth as consisting of all its versions',[74] it is clear that myth's capacious flexibility means that it is always already syncretic; the same can be seen to be true of folklore. So, it comes as no surprise that some of the most striking syncretisms of the Graeco-Roman and the Caribbean come to the fore in Walcott's drama, even if – as in *Ione* – the fusion is not fully achieved. In *Ti-Jean and His Brothers*,[75] though, Walcott's syncretic, and dramatic, achievement is remarkable, rendering the play an impressive piece of work on a par with much of his later work.

Written only a few months after the first performances of *Ione*,[76] *Ti-Jean and His Brothers* opened at the Little Carib Theatre in Port of Spain in 1958. Walcott regarded the play as 'the most West Indian thing [he] had done',[77] highlighting not only its roots in St Lucian folklore but also its syncretism. *Ti-Jean and His Brothers* retells a Caribbean folktale but begins with a Frog and a Cricket alluding to lines from Aristophanes' *Frogs* (405 BCE) as they repeat the words 'Greek-croak', before the Frog sneezes with the exclamation 'Aeschylus me!' Cementing the syncretism of the modern Caribbean and ancient Greece is the Cricket's observation, 'Creek-crak, it is cold',[78] which refracts the opening words of traditional Caribbean storytelling (Krik? Krak!) and the refrain from the chorus in Aristophanes' *Frogs*, βρεκεκεκὲξ κοὰξ κοὰξ in a way that is reminiscent of Omotoso's imagery of the syncretic kaleidoscope. In both *Ti-Jean* and his later play, *The Odyssey: A Stage Version* (1992), Walcott is unafraid occasionally to use words for their sound rather than sense,[79] here echoing Aristophanes' amphibian refrain and enacting his exhortation from 'What the Twilight Says' (1970) that, 'what is needed is not new names for old things, or old names for old things, but the faith of using the old names anew'.[80] *Ti-Jean and His Brothers*, as Walcott remarked and Breslin has explored, fuses folk and canonical traditions.[81]

In drawing a connection between the ancient Greek comedy and the Caribbean folktale, Walcott contests any hierarchy that prizes drama over folklore or ancient Greek over Caribbean. The eponymous frog chorus of Aristophanes' play are the counterpart to the animal characters that often populate folktales, while the traditional tale of Ti-Jean casts the competition between Aeschylus and Euripides in Aristophanes' play in a new light. For Walcott's tale of Ti-Jean sees the devil (who assumes the guises of the folkloric figure of Papa Bois and a white plantation owner, as well as appearing as himself in the play) test three brothers, of whom Ti-Jean is the youngest, as his name indicates with its abbreviation of 'Petit-Jean'. Like so many folkloric tales of the smallest figure overcoming the most powerful, so too here, Ti-Jean wins the challenge (to make the devil feel 'anger, rage, and human weakness')[82] where his brothers failed.

The connections may be fleeting, but Walcott's explicit allusion to Aristophanes' play at the start encourages us to see the competition between Aeschylus, Sophocles and Euripides as a folkloric trope structured around a tripling of figures;[83] it also highlights the commonalities between Papa Bois and Dionysus, which are only too apt given the latter's association with nature, as seen in his position as god of the vine.[84] So, too, one might draw a parallel between the ending of *The Frogs* and Walcott's play: where Dionysus fetches Aeschylus up from the Underworld to Athens, Ti-Jean's wish – granted by the devil once he succeeds in enraging him – is that the devil's servant, the Bolom (an unborn foetus), be given life. Thus, in both the ancient and the modern play, life is given back as a reward for succeeding at the contest, further highlighting the commonalities between a canonical work of Greek drama and a folkloric tale. In so doing, the play's syncretism rejects imperial hierarchies of value that dismissed folkloric narratives as 'primitive' and hailed ancient Greek drama as a pinnacle of 'civilization'.

'Homecoming: Anse La Raye'

Yet, the syncretism achieved in *Ti-Jean and His Brothers* did not automatically dispel the kinds of division that Walcott articulated in 'A Far Cry from Africa', and if the myths of ancient Greece and the Caribbean could be fused, it did not necessarily follow that a similar synthesis could be easily achieved on a personal level. Such a quandary is explored in Walcott's poem 'Homecoming: Anse La Raye',[85] penned a decade after *Ti-Jean*. In the poem, Walcott enacts an effective literary syncretism made all the more poignant by the poem's theme of dislocation, so that its form achieves what its narrator cannot. Dedicated to his friend, the novelist Garth St Omer, who – like Walcott – would spend much of his career living far from his homeland,[86] the poem begins by recalling their classically inflected education at St Mary's College in Vigie:

> Whatever else we learned
> at school, like solemn Afro-Greeks eager for grades,
> of Helen and the shades
> of borrowed ancestors,
> there are no rites
> for those who have returned.[87]

It is an education that has betrayed their hopes by its model of celebrated homecomings (seen most famously in the *Odyssey* and, more darkly, in the *Agamemnon*) because the poet discovers on his return to St Lucia that 'there are homecomings without home'.[88] Children playing on the beach mistake the poet for a tourist and are disappointed when he gives them nothing, while he is confronted with the reality that his literary success means nothing to them. As the poem closes, it harks back to the 'shades of borrowed ancestors', now understanding that the 'shades' of local ancestors are equally important, as the poet walks through a ghostly scene:

> Dazed by the sun
> you trudge back to the village
> past the white, salty esplanade
> under whose palms, dead
> fishermen move their draughts in shade.[89]

The scene is one of *katabasis*, a journey through the Underworld, which is 'a necessary pre-condition of the writer-hero's successful *nostos*',[90] as Gregson Davis has observed, compellingly arguing that in this poem, as in Césaire's *Cahier d'un retour au pays natal*, the two are conflated: '*nostos* and *katabasis* are collapsed into a single ambivalent experience of local reception, in which a (post)colonial social reality is subsumed under a dominant chthonic imagery'.[91] While the poem seems to achieve its goal, its own kind of *nostos*, in the synthesis of St Lucian and Graeco-Roman elements seen in the shades of the fishermen and the ceremonial welcome offered by 'the coconuts' salt-rusted swords' and 'the seacrabs' brittle helmets', the poet has yet to achieve his spiritual (though not his physical) *nostos*. This facet of the poem would have been even more apparent if Walcott had retained the original title that he intended for the collection, *The Homecoming*, with this poem placed at the centre,[92] just as the katabatic episodes of both the *Odyssey* and the *Aeneid* fall midway through those epics. The eventual title chosen for the collection, *The Gulf* (drawn from another of the poems within it), however, powerfully encapsulates the sense of dislocation from his home that Walcott expresses in 'Homecoming: Anse La Raye'.

'The Schooner *Flight*'

If 'Homecoming: Anse La Raye' depicts a *nostos* of sorts, Walcott's poem 'The Schooner *Flight*' imagines a journey outwards into a kind of exile. The first version was published in 1977 before being revised and included as the opening poem of *The Star-Apple Kingdom* (1979).[93] As in 'Homecoming: Anse La Raye', the autobiographical elements are apparent, with the poem's narrator and protagonist, Shabine, mapping closely onto Walcott himself. A remarkable poem in many ways,[94] Kamau Brathwaite considered it to be Walcott's 'first major nation language effort'.[95] So it is that the poem's syncretism is not only found in the figure of Shabine himself, who declares his 'sound colonial education' and encapsulates the multiple aspects of his heritage with the proclamation, 'either I'm nobody, or I'm a nation';[96] it is also in the poem's form. Examining the three versions published before the poem's appearance in *The Star-Apple Kingdom*, Breslin details how Walcott moved increasingly towards a creole vernacular for the poem.[97] Shabine combines creole language with his 'colonial education', illustrating that the two are not at odds with each other.[98] The divisions that can only pose questions without finding answers in his early poem 'A Far Cry from Africa', here find unity, in large part by Walcott's use of creole in the mouth of the colonially educated Shabine. As Laurence Breiner has observed,

> When Walcott combines a move towards creole language with a move towards the metropolitan language and its literary tradition, he does not imply an opposition, as if there were a need to balance transgressive creole with the weight of that tradition. His impulse is always a creolizing impulse.[99]

Likewise, for all that Shabine reflects Walcott himself and stands as a representative of a Trinidadian collective, his status as a poet-sailor in a mini-epic makes his Odyssean traits clear, as Thieme has noted.[100] The links between the two – sailors, storytellers, adventurers, torn between leaving and returning home – underline the naturalness of their syncretization into one another.

Walcott presents this as a coalescing of elements of equal value, which is not to overlook the contestation that is integral to syncretism in the Caribbean. As Stuart Hall argued, 'Creolization *always* entails inequality, hierarchization, issues of domination and subalternity, mastery and servitude, control and resistance',[101] but Walcott's work, in 'The Schooner *Flight*' as elsewhere, refutes an intrinsic objective quality to those hierarchies.[102] Shabine, then, is not 'indebted' to the ancient Odysseus. The poem's contemplation of the naming of trees highlights this idea, as Shabine reflects on the various names for the trees he sees on the hills of Barbados:

> But cedars, cypresses, or casuarinas,
> whoever called them so had a good cause,
> watching their bending bodies wail like women
> after a storm, when some schooner came home
> with news of one more sailor drowned again.
> Once the sound 'cypress' used to make more sense
> than the green 'casuarinas,' though, to the wind
> whatever grief bent them was all the same,
> since they were trees with nothing else in mind
> but heavenly leaping or to guard a grave;
> but we live like our names and you would have
> to be colonial to know the difference,
> to know the pain of history words contain.[103]

The aetiological myth of Cyparissus, most well-known from Ovid's retelling of it in book 10 of the *Metamorphoses* in which the young Cyparissus accidentally kills his beloved stag and in his grief is transformed into a cypress tree,[104] is what made the younger Shabine believe that that name 'ma[d]e more sense'.

Yet, whatever the name, the trees still bow in the wind like mourners and have been associated with graveyards; it is only the imposition of the culture of the colonizers that encouraged people to believe that that was the more fitting name.[105]

The poem begins with Shabine wracked by his own self-division as he leaves Trinidad at dawn, his abandoned lover still asleep:

> and I look in the rearview mirror and see a man
> exactly like me, and the man was weeping
> for the houses, the streets, that whole fucking island.[106]

While this self that Shabine sees in the rearview mirror is mourning his departure, his other self – the one who attempts to harden his heart against his decision ('I stood like a stone') – is figured as already dead in the eyes of the people of the land he will leave behind; his neighbour, he tells us, 'look through me like I was dead'.[107] In this way, his departure is a betrayal not only of his lover Maria Concepcion but of the people of Trinidad,[108] for whom his wish to leave renders him as good as dead, even if for Shabine, it is also a fresh start, signified by the baptismal 'sea bath' to which he is running.[109]

The movement of the poem, however, will complicate this centrifugal journey, for even while Shabine journeys ever onwards, so too does he grow metaphorically closer to his homeland once more. Resonating with the narrator of Césaire's *Cahier*, Walcott's Shabine also moves from a position of seeing decay and corruption around him and in himself to one in which, having contemplated the history of the region, he celebrates his island and casts himself as a mouthpiece for his people. By the poem's end, he is no longer the divided self of its beginning, longing to leave yet weeping at doing so, and leaving half of himself behind as he goes. Beyond becoming a united self, he has also united others with his poetry: 'I am satisfied | if my hand gave voice to one people's grief'.[110] Yet, despite this trajectory from the private to the public, Walcott's narrator reaches a very different conclusion from Césaire's: while the latter achieves a kind of Odyssean *nostos* in his embrace of his Martiniquan homeland, Shabine's *nostos* lies in 'unhomeliness' of the kind articulated by Homi Bhabha.[111] It is thus not only in its Odyssean motifs that 'The Schooner Flight' prefigures *Omeros*, but also in the particular way in which Walcott Signifies upon Homer, with Shabine's closing acceptance of a perpetual journey as his own version of home ('the flight to a target whose aim we'll never know')[112] reverberating with Achille's sense that, for him, home seemed to 'lay in unsettlement', as well as in the haunting by the Middle Passage that both Achille and Shabine experience.[113] Where the Homeric *Odyssey* raises the question of whether one can ever really 'return' home, Walcott's more Tennysonian narrative for his centrifugal protagonist, syncretizes many aspects of Caribbean history and culture to go beyond Tennyson's Ulysses to assert that home can be a state of perpetual motion.

A Branch of the Blue Nile

Having enacted a compelling artistic syncretism that includes the incorporation of Graeco-Roman elements in *Ti-Jean and His Brothers*, 'Homecoming: Anse La Raye', and 'The Schooner *Flight*', Walcott turned to the question of whether such a practise is wholly desirable in his play, *A Branch of the Blue Nile*.[114] Syncretism's capacity to dismantle binaries imposed by coloniality is a theme of the play, but so too are the difficulties this can pose for those undertaking syncretic work.

A metatheatrical and loosely autobiographical work, first performed in 1983, *A Branch of the Blue Nile* centres around a Trinidadian theatre group rehearsing a production of Shakespeare's *Antony and Cleopatra* alongside a comedy written in Trinidadian Creole by one of the company's actors, Christopher (played by the actor, director and literary critic, Michael Gilkes, in the first production).[115] The 'chain of receptions' is marked, with the intradiegetic director, Harvey, explaining,

> Since the bard had swiped a prose hunk off old Plutarch, and since in old Willy's day the clowns spoke dialect, and since our dialect is so Jacobean, I felt quite justified.[116]

Yet, despite Harvey's apt alignment of Shakespeare's deployment of Plutarch and dialect with the company's use of Shakespeare and nation language, the perceived distance between Shakespeare's works (with all the accretions of canonicity that they bring) and life in modern Port of Spain is also the subject of the play. As with a number of Walcott's other works,[117] *A Branch of the Blue*

Nile, interrogates how – and whether – canonical European culture and contemporary Caribbean culture should be syncretized. For Christopher, there is a gulf between the two that one may have no wish to bridge:

> Look, I stop reading. Why? Because the books I was reading ain't had nothing to do with the life I was living. That goes for plays, too; I ain't care who the arse it is, Shakespeare, Racine, Chekhov, nutten in there had to do with my life, or the life of all them black people out in the hot sun on Frederick Street at twelve o'clock trying to hustle a living.[118]

Beyond the distance at which those literary works stand from life in Port of Spain is the damage Christopher sees them inflicting, as he explains in his accusation of the white director: 'You go make them feel they white. You go teach them self-contempt.'[119] Yet the play we are watching is the play that Christopher goes on to pen: a drama that tells the story of how the theatre group staged Shakespeare's *Antony and Cleopatra* alongside Christopher's own comedy, of the conflicts and the love between the group, and the toll that that those rehearsals took on each of them, as well as the joy it brought. If Harvey, as director, had hoped to bridge the perceived gulf between Shakespeare and the contemporary Caribbean, Christopher – and his extradiegetic counterpart, Walcott – do so by highlighting the costs of that syncretism. *A Branch of the Blue Nile*, which is the title of Christopher's play, too, lays bare the scars of the mended vase (to borrow from Walcott's Nobel Prize acceptance speech again) because to do so and to create a new whole, is to put the canonical European in its place, as just one element that contributes to the creation of Antillean art.[120]

'White Magic'

As *A Branch of the Blue Nile* implies – and in keeping with Walcott's stance throughout his career, even before the syncretism he aimed at was fully achieved – the canonical literature of Europe and Graeco-Roman antiquity has a place in the Caribbean. However, to perceive these aspects as direct analogues to the St Lucian elements, or, worse still, to appreciate the Caribbean only through the Graeco-Roman or European, is both to overlook a great deal and to misunderstand the nature of syncretism. This is even more the case because of the cultural capital that, historically, has been afforded to the cultures of ancient Greece and Rome, especially in formerly colonized countries where they were so closely bound up with the imperial project.

Walcott's 1987 collection of poetry, *The Arkansas Testament*, includes a series of poems that address the ways in which Christianity was similarly imposed by those who attempted to make it usurp indigenous Caribbean religious beliefs.[121] Bringing this thematic thread to a close is 'White Magic', a poem that protests the valorization of European folklore at the expense of the mythology of the Caribbean:

> Dryads and hamadryads were engrained
> in the wood's bark, in papyrus, and this paper;
> but when our dry leaves crackle to the deer-
> footed, hobbling hunter, Papa Bois,
> he's just Pan's clone, one more translated satyr.[122]

Papa Bois, who featured in Walcott's *Ti-Jean and His Brothers* and is a well-known mythical figure across the Caribbean, is here envisaged as reduced to a mere replica of the Greek god Pan. Ironically, the means of Papa Bois' diminution to a satyr is by the very element over which he reigns in the Caribbean: the forests, and by extension, the wood from which paper is made, with the imperial powers claiming the superiority of the written word over the spoken. The colonial theft of a land's resources is succinctly encapsulated in the reduction of Papa Bois to a Pan-figure: imperial powers not only appropriated the Caribbean's natural resources, they also attempted to strip it of its cultural traditions, recasting them as imitations of the European forms they had foisted on the people. Their means of doing so, by claiming priority for the written word over the spoken was the subject of the 1977 play, *Manman Dlo contre la fée Carabosse* by Patrick Chamoiseau,[123] who was much admired by Walcott.[124] It is on this imposed cultural dichotomy that 'White Magic' closes, with the memorable line 'Our myths are ignorance, theirs are literature.'[125] Even while rejecting the colonial mindset that prioritizes the European over the Caribbean, Walcott foregrounds his equal facility with both: the Greek and the Caribbean, the oral and the written, with the written form of his poem being interspersed with Creole terms.

The poem might serve as a reminder, if it were needed, that even while the syncretism of much of Walcott's writing incorporates the Graeco-Roman, the Shakespearean, the St Lucian and the pan-Caribbean, no single aspect should be valued over and above the others. It is the new syncretized whole that Walcott creates that is vital, though two of his next works will pose fresh challenges for that balance, as Walcott embarked on a couple of his most overtly Homeric works.

The Odyssey: A Stage Version

It would be possible to read *Omeros* as, among other things, responding to that bigoted view that 'Our myths are ignorance, theirs are literature'.[126] On the one hand, Walcott's penning of an epic poem for the Caribbean, drawing from St Lucian myth and history, stages a resistance to such prejudice; on the other hand, he could be seen to be capitulating by his sustained engagement with 'their' mythic literature. As we have seen,[127] Walcott's trifold strategy of simultaneity, syncretism, and re-creation refutes the latter charge convincingly, but what was Walcott to do when faced with a task that would take him even closer to Greek epic?

Shortly after the publication of *Omeros*, the Royal Shakespeare Company commissioned Walcott to create a dramatic adaptation of the *Odyssey*; it was staged at The Other Place in Stratford-upon-Avon in the summer of 1992. Initially hesitant about accepting the commission so soon after completing his Homeric *Omeros*, Walcott 'began to experiment with the idea of compressing some of the scenes into lines and essentializing them, and then got excited about the shape of the stage poem'.[128] The term 'stage poem' already gestures to the syncretic nature of a play that recombines genres, characters and intertexts in fresh ways to create a new whole. Such an approach might be regarded as quintessentially Caribbean, in keeping with the syncretism so often associated with the region, but Walcott's play also emphasizes that cultural syncretism was likewise a feature of the ancient Mediterranean.

It is the figure of Eurycleia who most distinctively reflects on this aspect of Greek antiquity in *The Odyssey: A Stage Version*.[129] Emphasizing her Egyptian roots alongside her role in the upbringing of both Odysseus and Telemachus,

Eurycleia remarks that 'Is Egypt cradle Greece till Greece mature'.[130] The echo of the kind of research made famous by Martin Bernal's *Black Athena: The Afroasiatic Roots of Classical Civilization* (1987), but which had previously been put forward by nineteenth-century African American and African Caribbean thinkers, and in the twentieth century by scholars such as George G. M. James and Cheikh Anta Diop, too,[131] is unmistakeable. Given the appropriation of Bernal's work into the culture wars being waged in the early 1990s,[132] this would have been more widely recognized by audience members during the play's initial run than might otherwise have been the case.

Paula Burnett remarks that, 'Walcott, "translating" Martin Bernal's historiography into imaginative terms, revises the Homeric to make visible the contribution of the racial other at the heart of ancient Greece'.[133] This is not an Afrocentric manoeuvre on Walcott's part,[134] but rather an illumination of the syncretic nature of the ancient Mediterranean that is another aspect by which Walcott connects the Aegean and Caribbean archipelagoes.[135] Speaking just before the opening night of his *Odyssey*, Walcott refuted the suggestion that the play was 'a mix' of dialects, pointing out that 'to make it Caribbean, or do it in dialect is very nationalistic'.[136] Instead, he attributes the use of vernacular speech in his play to that which he finds in Homer, remarking that 'the language, the tone you get from the language of Homer, is in itself colloquial'.[137] Eurycleia's language is inflected with Caribbean speech patterns in Walcott's play, bringing together Egypt and the Antilles in a way that is particular to modernity, yet the foundational syncretism of *The Odyssey: A Stage Version* reflects the cultural and linguistic syncretism Walcott finds in the Homeric epic.

The esteem in which the ancient Greeks held the known lands of the African continent is evident in book 4 of Homer's *Odyssey*, when Menelaus' account of his travels around Egypt, Ethiopia and Libya, renders them as societies both more wealthy and more sophisticated than those found in Greece.[138] This shaping influence of Egypt on ancient Greece is an idea that Walcott returned to in a talk he gave at Duke University in 1995; subsequently published as 'Reflections on *Omeros*', in that talk Walcott remarked of Egypt, 'we are talking of a culture older than that of ancient Greece, a culture to which Greece owes a great deal of its mythology, among other things'.[139] The world of Homer's *Odyssey* was always a syncretic one and Walcott's introduction of modern and

Caribbean elements adds to, rather than introduces,[140] that syncretism to the myth.

Despite Walcott's declaration that his *Odyssey* is 'not a mix', the play is integrally syncretic. This is not to contest Walcott's own characterization of his work, but rather to note that syncretism is not simply about 'mixing' aspects together, but rather about combining different elements to create a new whole; as Ortiz remarked of his concept of transculturation, 'it carries the idea of the consequent creation of new cultural phenomena'.[141] The facile idea of a 'melting pot' overlooks crucial creative aspects of syncretism; as Elizabeth Alexander argues in an essay on the artist Romare Bearden,

> African-American culture from the Middle Passage forward is of course broadly characterized by fragmentation and reassemblage, sustaining what can be saved of history while making something new. Collage constructs wholes from fragments in a continual, referential dialogue between the seemingly disparate shards of various pasts and the current moment of the work itself, as well as the future the work might point toward.[142]

The process of 'fragmentation and reassemblage' is equally a feature of much Caribbean culture as a result of the shared experience of the Middle Passage. Walcott reflected on this both in his work and its composition, as we saw of *Omeros* in the Introduction,[143] and as is clear from his recollections of his path to becoming a writer:

> I was going to concentrate purely on trying to develop my painting. While painting, I would find lines coming into my head. I would almost self-destruct them; I'd say, all right, I'll put them down … but with antipoetic vehemence. If they don't work, then I'll just forget it. What kept happening is that the lines would come anyway, perhaps out of that very irritation, and then I would make a very arbitrary collage of them and find they would take some sort of loose shape. Inevitably, of course, you try to join the seams.[144]

Taking the syncretism found in both the ancient Mediterranean and the contemporary Caribbean as a starting point, Walcott pursues a related approach to his dialogue with the ancient *Odyssey*, 'join[ing] the seams'. Christopher Balme's exploration of theatrical syncretism as 'one of the most effective means of decolonizing the stage' is illuminating here.[145] Walcott's *Odyssey*, and much of his writing, can be seen to have a 'decolonizing' drive.

This is not based purely on the fact that Walcott's homeland of St Lucia was formerly colonized; rather, it is a recognition of the impetus of Walcott's work, even while his writing was less adamantly anti-colonial than that of some of his contemporaries. Walcott has expressed his admiration for works from Europe and is in frequent dialogue with them, but he does not overlook their role in the colonial project and the way in which their dominance can be at the expense of Caribbean forms (as we saw with *Omeros*' question, 'Why not see Helen [...] with no Homeric shadow?').[146]

The syncretism of Walcott's *Odyssey*, then, has a decolonizing impetus that is apparent in the foregrounding of Egypt's role in Greece's development (especially given the camouflaging of that connection, which Bernal labelled as 'the Aryan Model') as well as in the play's contestation of the kind of binary oppositions that underpin colonial discourse. Irene Martyniuk rightly observes that 'there are no clear heroes, or monsters, or even colonizers or colonized' in Walcott's *Odyssey*;[147] the play refuses to replicate such dichotomies, creating instead a more complex picture. In doing so, it offers syncretism as an anti-colonial response that goes beyond the mere inversion of colonial binaries, which necessarily always fail to break fully free from the forms they are opposing. When Edward Said noted that cultural identities should be perceived as, 'contrapuntal ensembles, for it is the case that no identity can ever exist by itself and without an array of opposites, negatives, oppositions: Greeks always require barbarians, and Europeans Africans, Orientals, etcetera',[148] he was referring to collective, often national, discourses. Walcott's play condenses this to the level of the individual, with Odysseus coming to recognize at the end of the play that the 'otherness' he had encountered on his journey home is within himself.[149] His final words, referring to the 'monsters' he met, are the recognition that 'We make them ourselves.'[150] One might hear an echo of Homi Bhabha's work on colonial mimicry in these words:[151] not only has Odysseus, as protocolonial traveller,[152] created seemingly monstrous figures by his 'othering' of those he encounters, but by the end of the play, he has recognized both his role in the creation of their monstrosity and their similarity to himself.[153] In Bhabha's terms,[154] he has confronted 'the menace of mimicry' and in so doing, witnessed and acknowledged the disruption of his authority.

Penelope's response to Odysseus' return, which is one of the most striking innovations that Walcott makes to the Homeric epic, consolidates this impression. She reacts with horror to Odysseus' slaughter of the suitors, exclaiming, 'You had to wade this deep in blood?'.[155] Accusing him of turning her home into an 'abattoir',[156] she looks through Odysseus' eyes at the suitors, slaughtered as if they were animals to be consumed, and reveals to him the inhumanity of his own misperceptions. In casting his enemies as 'other' (in this case, as non-human), Odysseus has become monstrous, turning his own home into a slaughterhouse.

One sees here a condensed version of the kind of 'reverse simile' (to use Helene Foley's term) that Lorna Hardwick identifies as existing in Walcott's *Odyssey* at the level of genre, too, and illuminating the relationship developed with ancient Greek epic by some modern Caribbean writers.[157] As Foley explains of the 'reverse similes' in Homer's *Odyssey*, they 'suggest both a sense of identity between people in different social and sexual roles, and a loss of stability, an inversion of the normal'.[158] While Walcott does not deploy overt epic similes within his play, the hallucinations that Odysseus suffers achieve a similar effect by highlighting the commonalities between himself and his enemies while destabilizing the sense of reality. This is especially clear when, after slaughtering the suitors, Walcott's Odysseus sees their corpses stirring and mistakes them for his former Greek comrades, encapsulating both the combat trauma from which he is suffering and the falsity of strategies of 'othering'.[159] That destabilization of reality towards the end of the play is compounded by the fantastical nature of Odysseus' adventures in Homer's epic (especially in books 9–12), which Walcott's version also retells: are we sure that it is only once Odysseus has returned home that he begins to hallucinate, the play asks? And simultaneously, isn't the dichotomy between self and other on the collective scale (Said's 'array of opposites, negatives, oppositions')[160] equally illusory?

Walcott's depiction resonates closely with Aimé Césaire's argument in *Discours sur le colonialisme* (*Discourse on Colonialism*), which Walcott almost certainly knew, given his close familiarity with Césaire's work. As Césaire argues,

> que l'action coloniale, l'enterprise coloniale, la conquête coloniale, fondée sur le mépris de l'homme indigène et justifiée par ce mépris, tend inévitablement à modifier celui qui l'entreprend; [...] le colonisateur, qui, pour se donner bonne conscience, s'habitue à voir dans l'autre *la bête*,

s'entraîne à le traiter en bête, tend objectivement à se transformer lui-même en bête.[161]

colonial activity, colonial enterprise, colonial conquest, which is based on contempt for the native and justified by that contempt, inevitably tends to change him who undertakes it; [...] the colonizer, who in order to ease his conscience gets into the habit of seeing the other man as *an animal*, accustoms himself to treating him like an animal, and tends objectively to transform *himself* into an animal.[162]

Similarly, Walcott's Odysseus becomes that which he had set himself in opposition to, as the play highlights when he hallucinates that the suitors' corpses are the figures of his former comrades rising up.[163] Penelope's horror at the killing of the suitors, then, can be seen as a castigation not only of Odysseus but of the valorization of violence and vengeance that is endemic to heroic traditions more widely,[164] and of the colonial strategy that Césaire terms 'thingification'.[165]

While Penelope questions the ethos of epic heroism, the form of Walcott's play raises related questions surrounding genre. Transposing Homer's epic into drama, Walcott introduces a tragic tone that is absent from the *Odyssey* even while following the narrative of the ancient epic closely. This adaptation of epic narrative into tragic form would not in itself be remarkable, given the close connections between ancient Greek epic and tragedy, if it were not for the ways in which Walcott consciously maximizes its potential. As Hardwick observed, Walcott's *Odyssey* 'provoke[d] both engagement and metatheatrical reflection' in the way it adapted the Homeric epic and 'translated' one genre into another.[166] Rather than merely convert epic forms into dramatic ones, Walcott once again deploys a syncretizing approach. In doing so, he draws on his childhood experience of listening to stories told by his aunt Sidone, and his understandings that 'it wasn't just storytelling; it was dramatization'.[167]

His *Odyssey* opens with the bardic figure of Billy Blue, a poet who evokes both the Homeric 'singer of tales' and oral storytellers from the contemporary Caribbean, of the kind embodied in fiction in the protagonist of Patrick Chamoiseau's *Solibo Magnifique*.[168] But Walcott makes a stronger claim, too, for a blues singer as the internal narrator of his play: for him, it is calypsonians and blues singers who 'contain the history of the race', just as he sees Homer having done in antiquity:

There've been great blind blues singers. The same thing is true of the calypsonian, who is untouchable as a figure, who contains the history of the race, who is its vessel. [...] That is more Homeric than having somebody with a harp and a beard up there, plucking away at a lyre.[169]

The presence of Billy Blue is about creating a compelling *Odyssey* for the contemporary era, rather than about inserting elements from the Americas into the tale for their own sake. Walcott's sense that the Caribbean has such commonalities with ancient Greece is once again key, resonating with Alejo Carpentier's idea of the 'Caribbean Mediterranean' (*Mediterráneo caribe*).[170] Yet, almost despite itself, Carpentier's concept retains a notion of temporal hierarchy that privileges the European even while he destabilizes that hierarchy,[171] whereas Walcott, as we have seen in Chapter 1, refutes such hierarchical understandings of time: for him, there is no 'Caribbean Mediterranean', for all that so much of his work is intricately engaged with the literature of ancient Greece and Rome. Nor does he simply invert the dominance of one region over the other (by claiming, for example, a 'Mediterranean Caribbean'). Rather he sets the two on a par with each other, claiming for the syncretism of the Caribbean not an end-goal of 'assimilation' that has often been part of the discourse of both church and state,[172] but to go beyond that to create something new.[173] Where, in the worlds of Carpentier's work, juxtapositions and binary oppositions are seen to persist despite moves towards syncretism,[174] in Walcott's, syncretism is achieved. As Cécile Chapon has noted, Walcott's vision of the relationship between the Caribbean and Mediterranean is a more 'horizontal' one than Carpentier's; Glissant, meanwhile, seems to oppose the two, yet goes on both to reveal connections and to subvert them.[175]

Billy Blue's prologue in Walcott's *Odyssey* includes a line of transliterated ancient Greek, *Andra moi ennepe mousa polutropon hos mala polla*;[176] and not just any line at that, but the opening line of Homer's *Odyssey*: ἄνδρα μοι ἔννεπε, Μοῦσα, πολύτροπον, ὃς μάλα πολλά. But here Walcott plays with his audience – because the line he includes is syntactically incomplete, missing its verb (πλάγχθη). Not only has Walcott displaced the line from its position of prominence by inserting it five lines down in Billy Blue's opening speech rather than at the very start, he also compels the audience to see that the Greek is being used differently: by leaving the transliterated Greek untranslated and syntactically incomplete, Walcott emphasizes its purpose as sound rather than language.[177]

Billy Blue is not just a theatrical 'character' in *The Odyssey: A Stage Version*. Rather, he functions as what Roger D. Abrahams, in his work on Black folklore in Philadelphia and the anglophone Caribbean, terms a 'man-of-words'.[178] There is an important distinction between the 'man-of-words' and a character on the stage, as Abrahams emphasizes,[179] yet Walcott syncretizes the two in his play.

Billy Blue (played in the original production by Rudolph Walker) reappears later in the play as the Greek Demodocus, and this doubling of characters – which also occurs in the portrayal of Nausicaa/Melantho (Sophie Okonedo), the Cyclops/Arnaeus (Geoffrey Freshwater),[180] and Ajax/Antinous (Jonathan Cake) – highlights the falsity of distinctions imposed between groups of peoples and encourages connection.[181] As well as foreshadowing the realization that Odysseus will reach at the end of the play, this double-casting deploys Brechtian *Verfremdungseffekt*, prompting the audience to engage with the play on a political level too.[182]

The syncretizing approach that Walcott takes to his adaptation of Homer's *Odyssey* can be seen in its intertextuality, its evocation of a myriad of oppressive regimes, and its understanding of time. Drawing on the *Iliad* and Shakespeare's *Troilus and Cressida* (especially in the inclusion of the figure of Thersites),[183] as well as from Horace (filtered through Wilfred Owen),[184] the play takes its place in a 'chain of receptions' that already reveals the connections between epic and drama, and the imbrication of verse and conflict. Walcott's Cyclops in this play is an Orwellian figure, known as the Eye, whose alignment with Greece's far-right Regime of the Colonels (1967–74) is made plain.[185] Like the Homeric Odysseus' description of the Cyclopes as being without agriculture, assemblies, laws, or community (*Odyssey* 9.106–15), so, too, in Walcott's adaptation the Cyclops' land is one with neither art nor history.[186] Yet, the ensuing Homeric plot reveals Odysseus' assessment of the Cyclopes to be inaccurate, and in Walcott, too, the fact that the description echoes colonial misperceptions of the cultures they oppressed, seeing them as places with 'no art, no theatre, no circuses even',[187] encourages the audience to question what they are being told. The play depicts Odysseus as both plunderer of foreign lands and displaced native of Ithaca; the Cyclops is both ruler of his own native land and a despot; as with the play's closing scene, 'self' and 'other' are seen to be not polar opposites but rather to have the potential to exist within an individual.[188]

At the same time, the slippage between the contemporary era and ancient Greece throughout the play exemplifies the simultaneity explored in the previous chapter, even while it leads to one other significant change that Walcott makes to the narrative's ending: in his version, Eurycleia and Penelope prevent the hanging of the enslaved Melantho.[189] Walcott expressed his fear that, in making this radical alteration, he would be doing something similar to what Nahum Tate did when he gave *King Lear* a happy ending in *The History of King Lear* (1681), but ultimately felt that the depletion of cultural codes of *xenia* (guest-friendship/hospitality) in the contemporary world demanded the change, particularly in a work to be performed on stage rather than solely written on the page:

> I wondered when I was doing it if I was sort of giving *King Lear* a happy ending, like this other guy did once. It's the culture, it's because of the severity of ruining hospitality, and of disobedience, that the punishment happens. But it's one thing to write it in a poem; it's another thing to enact it. [...] the ideas of justice that are there in Homer [...] are just not tenable now.[190]

Hardwick has made a compelling case for also seeing the prevention of the hanging of the enslaved women in Walcott's play as 'an affirmation of the desire to recognize history but to avoid becoming its prisoner',[191] in its refusal to enact murders that, throughout the history of slavery in ancient and modern times, have occurred. Walcott received some criticism for his alterations to the ending of the tale,[192] as he had anticipated he might, wryly remarking to Paula Burnett before the play opened that 'the English think Homer belongs to them'.[193] But it is the syncretizing approach Walcott adopts that leads to his alterations which – seemingly paradoxically perhaps, yet entirely in keeping with the ways in which myths are continually adapting – allow his version to be both an original work and an adaptation that sheds light on its ancient predecessor, while continuing to be the 'same' mythic tale. This coheres with Claude Lévi-Strauss' proposition that 'we define the myth as consisting of all its versions; to put it otherwise: a myth remains the same as long as it is felt as such'.[194] Walcott's *Odyssey*, then, is part of that myth even while it alters, synthesizes from other traditions, and innovates: it is both part of the same and something radically new. And it that process of re-creation, developed by Walcott across his body of work, that is the subject of the next chapter.

3

Re-creation

And those who gild cruelty,
who read from the entrails of disembowelled Aztecs
the colors of Hispanic glory
greater than Greece,
greater than Rome,
than the purple of Christ's blood
[...]
those who remain fascinated,
in attitudes of prayer,
by the festering roses made from their fathers' manacles,
[...]
who see a golden, cruel, hawk-bright glory
in the conquistador's malarial eye,
crying, at least here
something happened --
they will absolve us, perhaps, if we begin again

Derek Walcott, *Another Life* (2009: 144)

'If we begin again', ponders the narrator of *Another Life*. Philoctete did exactly that in the penultimate book of *Omeros*, emerging as an Adamic figure reborn by his healing bath:

> and he stood like a boy in his bath with the first clay's
> innocent prick! So she [Ma Kilman] threw Adam a towel.
> And the yard was Eden. And its light the first day's.[1]

The baptismal moment in *Omeros* is a syncretic one that combines, as we saw in the Introduction, the Caribbean, the African, the Graeco-Roman and the

Judaeo-Christian.[2] By retrieving the past into the present and synthesizing the diverse elements of St Lucia's heritage, Ma Kilman creates the cure for Philoctete's seemingly incurable wound and enables him to be reborn. The idea of a 'New World Adam' is a persistent theme in Derek Walcott's oeuvre, but where in earlier works he envisaged this rebirth emerging from an 'amnesia' brought on by the violence of the Caribbean's history, in *Omeros* it also comes from the recovery and incorporation of that history.[3]

A new Crusoe

This Adamic figure in Walcott's writing reappears in several guises throughout his work. If Adam represents the first Man, Walcott's decision to recast him variously as a Robinson Crusoe figure from Daniel Defoe's novel (1719) and a Philoctetes figure from Greek myth highlights his notion of re-creation. If, at first glance, there seems to be an irony in modelling a new Adamic figure on characters from canonical literature because it adds to the sedimentary layers between the first human and his modern instantiation in Walcott's work, it nonetheless harks back to the biblical story in which God created mankind from the earth: before that Adam too, there were previous layers (of earth and divinity). The implication is that every act of creation is an act of re-creation and, combined with Walcott's argument against linear time and in favour of simultaneity (see Chapter 1), it becomes clear why he refutes any suggestion that to engage with what has gone before is to be less original.

The initial appeal for Walcott of Robinson Crusoe lay in the latter's inventiveness and Adamic capacity to name the world around him combined with his isolation that gave the title to the 1965 collection of poetry, *The Castaway*, in which both 'Crusoe's Journal' and 'Crusoe's Island' appear.[4] Nonetheless, the choice of Defoe's protagonist can jar. A trader in enslaved people in the eighteenth-century novel, and one who exhibits the traits of a colonizer and behaves as such, particularly in the treatment of the man he names 'Friday', Walcott's heroizing of this character might seem a wilful dismissal of the historical horrors of colonialism and the slave trade. Walcott's own shifting stance on his figuration of Crusoe is evident in a comparison of his poems 'Crusoe's Island' (1964) and 'Crusoe's Journal' (1965), and his essay

'The Figure of Crusoe' (delivered as a lecture in 1965), with the later play *Pantomime* (first performed in 1978).[5] However, as Patricia Ismond has argued, it is also possible to see Walcott's use of the Crusoe figure as a radical position: 'In choosing to arrogate a position usually identified with the master, Walcott engages in something of a subversive act: he tacitly refuses the condition of servitude and inferiority as the primary term of his identity'.[6] This strategy, though remaining distinctly subterranean in the earlier works, is developed quite overtly in *Pantomime*.

There is another aspect to Walcott's adoption of the figure of Crusoe, too. As he writes in 'Crusoe's Journal' (the almost unavoidable pun of Walcott 'writing' Crusoe's journal being one that Walcott, who seldom let a pun go un-made, likely enjoyed), 'we make his language ours'.[7] Defoe's novel and the figure of Crusoe are part of that 'language' which, alongside other canonical literature including that from ancient Greece and Rome, becomes as much the inheritance and property of the Caribbean as of anywhere else. It constantly takes new forms in the process, as the description of Crusoe as a shapeshifter, 'our ocean's Proteus', makes clear in the poem.[8] So, while one may flinch at Walcott aligning Crusoe with not only Christopher Columbus but also Adam, God and himself, as he does in 'The Figure of Crusoe',[9] it is a position that wholly overturns any claims that to engage with and rework earlier literature is somehow derivative, rather than its own creative process.

The later *Pantomime* sees Walcott return to his consideration of the figure of Robinson Crusoe. He incorporates into the play a celebration of invention and naming that Walcott saw embodied in Defoe's Crusoe, and the role of both Defoe and Crusoe in imperial enterprises, but he refuses to abandon them nonetheless: they can be re-created to become and to signify differently, as his play demonstrates. *Pantomime* enacts on stage what is at stake in the use of Crusoe as a figure in the Caribbean. Set in a Tobago guesthouse run by a white British retired music-hall actor, Harry Trewe, the play begins with Harry proposing that they stage a Christmas pantomime based on Defoe's novel, starring himself and the guesthouse's handyman, Jackson Phillip, a retired calypsonian from Trinidad. Harry's suggestion that they reverse the racially delineated, Caribbean-British roles, so that he plays Friday and Jackson plays Crusoe immediately plunges the play into considerations of colonial mimicry and Bakhtinian carnivalesque.[10] If both mimicry and carnivalesque have the destabilization of binaries at their heart, so, too, do the two forms that the play's protagonists bring together: the presence of the pantomime dame in the British art form destabilizes any expectations of gender binaries,[11] while calypso destabilizes power dynamics since criticism of the ruling classes by the less formally powerful is one of its features.[12] As Breslin notes, both pantomime and calypso 'protect mordant satire behind the shield of convention';[13] they are both politically engaged genres

Within Walcott's *Pantomime*, the silencing and usurpation of Friday's perspective in Defoe's novel is overturned as Jackson, as well as Harry, speaks and directs the action of the play.[14] Moreover, as he encapsulates in the exclamation, 'How do you know that I mightn't choose to call him Thursday? Do I have to copy every ... I mean, are we improvising?',[15] Jackson enacts the kind of re-creation that Walcott advocates, by Signifying upon both Defoe's novel and Harry's pantomime rendition of it, refusing a mimicry that has nothing new within it. When Harry tries to call a stop to the pantomime he has instigated, in which Jackson assumes the character of Crusoe, Jackson's response reverberates as an excoriating retort to those who have denigrated artists from formerly colonized nations as imitative:

> You see, it's your people who introduced us to this culture: Shakespeare, *Robinson Crusoe*, the classics, and so on, and when we start getting as good as them, you can't leave halfway. So, I will continue?[16]

Harry's protestation that Jackson should not continue is met with another moment in which the latter sets out what is at stake and offers another glimpse into the more radical appropriation that Walcott may have had in mind in his 1965 poetic and essayistic engagements with the figure of Robinson Crusoe:

> May I say what I think, Mr Trewe? I think it's a matter of prejudice. I think that you cannot believe: one: that I can act, and two: that any black man should play Robinson Crusoe. [...] Here I am getting into *my* part and you object. This is the story ... this is history. This moment that we are now acting here is the history of imperialism; it's nothing less than that. And I don't think that I can – should – concede my getting into a part halfway and abandoning things, just because you, as my superior, give me orders. People become independent.[17]

Jackson's speech highlights a primary motivating factor behind Walcott's concept of re-creation: the re-creation into new forms of that which has gone before is a contestation of the imperial power dynamics that deem formerly colonized lands 'belated'. Alongside this, as the 'rehearsal' format of *Pantomime* emphasizes, is another dimension of Walcott's capacious notion of re-creation: that the work of theatre is always 'unfinished' because that is a fundamental aspect of the nature of performance. It is constantly 'finished' anew at each performance. Beyond performance, too, it is an understanding that interacts with Helen Tiffin's argument that 'Decolonization is process, not arrival',[18] as well as with the Caribbean's syncretizing approach that embraces the constant recasting of elements into new combinations, as Kole Omotoso's kaleidoscope metaphor emblematizes.[19]

Dream on Monkey Mountain

A central aspect of re-creation, in Walcott's vision, is re-naming, as his adoption of the figures of both Adam and Crusoe signifies. But while those two named other people and things, at the heart of one of Walcott's most well-known plays, *Dream on Monkey Mountain* (first performed in 1967),[20] is the importance of naming the world anew to liberate oneself from the persisting shadow of colonialism. Walcott proposes a route towards what Ngũgĩ wa Thiong'o called 'decolonising the mind',[21] but one which, crucially for Walcott, did not require the rejection of colonial languages. In his essay 'What the Twilight Says: An Overture',[22] published in the same volume as *Dream on Monkey Mountain*, and to which the play is a kind of creative precursor, Walcott suggests a different path:

> What would deliver him from servitude was the forging of a language that went beyond mimicry, a dialect which had the force of revelation as it invented names for things, one which finally settled on its own mode of inflection, and which began to create an oral culture of chants, jokes, folk-songs, and fables; this, not merely the debt of history was his proper claim to the New World.[23]

He emphasizes the syncretism of his approach as he goes on to explain that, 'This did not mean the jettisoning of "culture" but, by the writer's making creative use of his schizophrenia, an electric fusion of the old and the new'.[24] The language of mental illness may jar but is not used quite as loosely as it may sound: Walcott's exploration in both play and essay is of the psychological impact of the kind of division he memorably articulated in 'A Far Cry to Africa'.[25]

Makak, the protagonist of *Dream on Monkey Mountain*, has gone beyond a Du Boisian 'double consciousness' to lose all sight of his own perception of himself;[26] seeing himself only in the way that white society does, he has – in Frantz Fanon's terms – made himself an object.[27] Thus, he has internalized the nickname Makak (the Antillean creole of the French *macaque*, 'monkey') and cannot bear even to see his own reflection:

> People forget me like the mist on Monkey Mountain.
> Is thirty years now I have look in no mirror,
> Not a pool of cold water, when I must drink,
> I stir my hands first, to break up my image.[28]

Makak not only turns from his reflection but splinters it apart, signifying his fragmented sense of self. But if his alignment of himself with the mist on the mountain evokes his sense of being taken for granted, the rest of the speech casts this in a more generative light as Makak encourages his listeners to 'make a white mist | In the mind' to enter the world of his dream with him.[29] The location of the play is specified only as 'a West Indian island';[30] combined with the animal names of many of the characters and the allegorical nature of the play, this evokes oral storytelling traditions of the kind Walcott recalled from his childhood.[31]

Inspired by the apparition of a white female figure who tells him that he is 'from the family of lions and kings',[32] Makak sets out for Africa. This hallucinatory voyage to Africa can be seen as an early forerunner of Achille's journey in *Omeros*, though Walcott's perspective changes markedly in the two decades that separate the works. Where Achille's voyage is a necessary step on the way to reclaiming a full Caribbean identity in *Omeros*, Walcott satirizes Makak's journey 'back to Africa' in *Dream on Monkey Mountain*.[33] Sceptical of Afrocentrism, Walcott depicts Makak's desire to be in Africa as being inspired by White ideology in the form of the Apparition that appears to him. This raises the question of whether such a journey, reminiscent as it is of Marcus

Garvey's 'Back to Africa' movement earlier in the twentieth century as well as the Rastafarian belief in Haile Selassie as God and Ethiopia as their homeland, may spring from White-imposed ideologies and, far from being a journey towards freedom, may only be one still caught in colonial dynamics. As Laurence Breiner has suggested, the play's first epigraph from Sartre's prologue to Fanon's *The Wretched of the Earth* provocatively 'invites the view that black pride remains less a positive statement than the negation of a negation initiated by Europe'.[34] Indeed, the epigraphs to both parts 1 and 2 of the play foreshadow the white Apparition in that Walcott quotes Sartre's introduction to Fanon's work, but Fanon himself is only obliquely (if unmissably) quoted when Makak's friend Moustique brandishes a white mask and exclaims 'black faces, white masks!'.[35]

It is only when Makak recognizes that his vision of a unified, peaceful Africa is an idealized one,[36] and frees himself from the Manichean dualisms of black and white propagated by imperialism,[37] that he can move beyond inverting that model to developing a new, more syncretic one. Beheading the white Apparition and waking from his dream-state,[38] he emerges at the end of the play as a figure who has thrown off the oppressive and illusory notion of an Edenic Africa to instead embrace his Caribbean homeland.

With the idea of a paradisiacal Africa abandoned, Makak is able to begin the process of Adamic renaming, discarding his animalistic nickname and taking up the name of Felix Hobain once more, which he had previously forgotten. But Breslin is surely right to sound a note of warning about any reading of the play that casts it as one of political liberation, and instead to note that, 'What has changed is [Makak's] sense of his place in that world. He still lives within a colonized world, but he no longer has internalized colonial discourse.'[39] In Makak's final speech, he announces,

> Now this old hermit is going back home, back to the beginning, to the green beginning of this world. Come, Moustique, we going home.

And the chorus echo his final words for themselves, 'I going home'.[40] Like *Omeros*' Achille, Makak finds home in the Caribbean rather than in a more Afrocentric proposal; like Philoctete, he does so by going 'back to the beginning' and becoming an 'avatar of Walcott's Caribbean Adam'.[41]

Creative mimicry

That Walcott's considers these reborn figures 'Adamic' could play into the hands of those who wish to deem 'the New World' belated and derivative. But Walcott's notion of mimicry, most powerfully expounded in his 1973 speech, 'The Caribbean: Culture or Mimicry?', overturns this idea, demonstrating that mimicry is generative, adaptive and inventive:

> the degradations have already been endured; they have been endured to the point of irrelevancy. In the Caribbean history is irrelevant, not because it is not being created, or because it was sordid; but because it has never mattered, what has mattered is the loss of history, the amnesia of the races, what has become necessary is imagination, imagination as necessity, as invention.[42]

If mimesis is the representation of reality, and mimicry the representation of a representation, the latter is 'a repetition of something itself repetitious', as Rei Terada has argued, and varies from mimesis primarily in its openness about its 'nonoriginality'.[43]

This is crucial to Walcott's engagement with Graeco-Roman and other canonical literature: far from being overshadowed by the older works, mimicry 'repeats with difference' (to evoke both Gates' Signifying and Bhabha's notion of what is at the heart of the 'menace' of mimicry for colonial powers) to create something new. Such recasting of both mimicry and a perceived lack of history as 'productive hermeneutics',[44] illuminates the creative processes that have led to some of the Caribbean's most distinctive cultural forms, including calypso. As Walcott explained,

> the calypso itself emerged from a sense of mimicry, of patterning its form both on satire and self-satire [...] From the viewpoint of history, these forms originated in imitation if you want, and ended in invention.[45]

This is the process by which Walcott engages with both ancient and modern canonical literature in his work. In its dialogue with art from elsewhere it has been accused of lacking originality, but such charges are often freighted with the legacy of colonialism. As Julia Kristeva articulated in 'The Bounded Text' (1969), every text is 'a permutation of texts, an intertextuality: in the space of a given text, several utterances, taken from other texts, intersect';[46] however, when the intertextuality is developed by a writer from a formerly colonized nation, charges of derivation have more often followed.

The significance of re-creation in Walcott's work is a crucial point of connection between his contemplation of the history of the Caribbean and his engagement with earlier art. Sitting alongside his conceptions of time and syncretism, these three form the major strands that exemplify the ways in which his engagement with Graeco-Roman literature is a facet of Caribbean artistry. Rather than indicating an indebtedness to ancient Greece and Rome, Walcott's oeuvre demonstrates his conviction that antiquity and its literature are realms to which he has as valid a claim as anyone else; there is no debt to be repaid here because the idea of 'ownership' of canonized literature is flawed. This is not to say that classical reception and an engagement with Graeco-Roman antiquity is distinctively Caribbean, of course. Yet, all the same, one might be tempted to argue that the intricate and distinctive concepts of time and syncretism that have been developed by artists and thinkers in the region during the twentieth and twenty-first centuries have equipped it especially well to engage in radically innovative dialogues with antiquity. To this, Walcott adds not only his own particular approaches but also his notion of re-creation that begins anew without forgetting the past:

> The great poetry of the New World does not pretend to such innocence, its vision is not naïve. Rather, like its fruits, its savour is a mixture of the acid and the sweet, the apples of its second Eden have the tartness of experience.[47]

This is neither replication of what went before nor a dilution of it; Walcott, and the poets he deems great, add something new ('the tartness of experience') and begin again.

The Isle is Full of Noises

This process of inventive re-creation is evident in one of Walcott's unpublished plays, *The Isle is Full of Noises*, first performed in 1982, though he had begun work on it seven years earlier.[48] While the tetrad of 'Crusoe's Island', 'Crusoe's Journal', 'The Figure of Crusoe' and *Pantomime* all deploy a refiguration of Defoe's protagonist to embody Walcott's notion of a 'New World Adam', as we have seen,[49] elsewhere the ancient Greek figure of Philoctetes is re-deployed in this way. As with the figure of Crusoe, Philoctetes is reshaped into fresh forms in Walcott's hands; Crusoe's and Philoctetes' roots in the European canon remain of significance, but being syncretized with other aspects, they are refigured anew.

Philoctetes, given only passing mention in the Homeric epics but the subject of Sophocles' eponymous tragedy (409 BCE),[50] might not seem an obvious choice from the whole cast of Greek mythology. Yet this very status, marginal but vital – as the Greeks at Troy were to discover once they received Helenus' prophecy – contributes to Philoctetes' aptness. Philoctetes' bow resonates with the title of Froude's *The English in the West Indies: Or, The Bow of Ulysses* (1888), Signifying upon it to 'repeat with signal difference' (in Gates' terms) the bow of Odysseus as the bow of Philoctetes. As Emily Greenwood has discussed, Froude's metaphor of Ulysses and the bow is triply freighted: England as the absent Ulysses leaving its colonies unprotected from other suitors; England as the only figure who can govern those colonies effectively, being the sole Ulyssean figure who can string the bow; and of course, Froude himself as an intrepid adventurer.[51] Froude's work 'had the unwitting effect of making the reinterpretation, or counter-interpretation, of this myth a vital part of the creative imagination of Anglophone Caribbean literature'.[52] Walcott's ironic use of a quotation from Froude as the epigraph to his poem 'Air' has already been discussed,[53] but in his development of the Philoctetes theme, Walcott gives Omotoso's kaleidoscope of syncretism another turn, and Froude's Ulyssean bow becomes Philoctetes' bow and then, with one more rotation, it becomes Philoctetes' wound, often with the bow now lost.

Prior to *Omeros*, it is in *The Isle is Full of Noises* that the most extensive depiction of a Philoctetes figure occurs; beyond the character, the play also echoes the plot of Sophocles' drama in a number of respects. Walcott began working on it shortly after Pigeon Island in Gros Islet had been connected to the mainland of St Lucia by a man-made causeway.[54] The Philoctetes figure is Sir Lionel Robinson, specified in the cast list as the first Prime Minister of the West Indies Federation, and nicknamed Crusoe. But for a theatre audience, it is the Sophoclean connection that becomes apparent first, before the allusion to Defoe is made explicit. It is heralded by the British Ambassador to the island, Sir Geoffrey Thwaite:

Since that time, Sir Lionel, the great and glowing orator, the lone black wolf of Magdalen College, the author of several books, had lived on Pigeon Island for years as an embittered recluse, because, to put it brutally, he stank. He stank like Philoctetes from a boil, a suppurating wound that drove him into a huge, church-vaulted cave on the lee of Pigeon Island, spear-fishing with the bow of Philoctetes. But in consideration of his own people, he stank to leeward.[55]

In fantastical fashion, the former politician and Oxford-educated writer, seems to have slipped through time and genre into a world virtually unchanged from that of Greek myth, fishing with his bow as Sophocles' protagonist shoots down birds with his in *Philoctetes*.[56] The tone of Walcott's play, alternating between tragic and comic, is glimpsed in Sir Geoffrey's remark about the smell being blown leeward.[57]

Following the Sophoclean precedent, the one sent to coax Sir Lionel out from his cave is Achille's son (here named James), who was baptized by Lionel in the opening scene. As Breslin's illuminating analysis of the play underlines, Achille's reminder to his son that it was Sir Lionel 'whose power drew this archipelago as tight as a bow' doubles the resonances of the bow as it comes to recall not only Philoctetes' but Odysseus'.[58] This affirms the region as home for the wielder of the bow, but reflecting Walcott's concerns about the damage that tourism inflicts on the region and its landscape,[59] it is not Sir Lionel's bow that is wanted so much as the land on which he is living, which the current Prime Minister wishes to turn into a hotel. This is a biting re-envisioning of the Philoctetes myth: if in Sophocles, the prophecy has left it unclear whether it is Philoctetes or his bow that is needed to win the Trojan War, in Walcott's version, neither are needed. The exemplification of an imperialist approach that saw only the land and not its people, wilfully recasting the region as *terra nullius*, is poignantly enacted by Walcott's alteration of the Sophoclean plot in this respect. This underlines the neocolonial predicament of Santa Marta/St Lucia, whereby the changes that had been envisioned were only very partially brought about by independence, since nations remained dependent on foreign capital and political leaders did not always prioritize the needs of the people.[60]

As the location in Gros Islet and the prominence of a wounded Philoctetes indicate, *The Isle is Full of Noises* is fascinating as a precursor to Walcott's later thinking in *Omeros*. In its own right, the play has something of the sense of

Ione's overwrought compression to it and is distractingly self-conscious about its own process. Not only does it feature a singing chorus of 'Unities' (albeit they declare themselves to be 'the Three Unities, Divine, Racial, and Dramatic!' and are led by a calypsonian known as Vox Populi), but Sir Geoffrey remarks towards the end that,

> All had happened in a single day, a single action, in a single place. The classic tragedy had kept its courtesies, the unities had been observed. There was a king, a chorus, a prophetess, a single violent action, an archipelago and the sea, unstained unstainable by human blood, and these parallels, curiously, gave me a dry comfort.

The play's elements of tragic form and Aristotelian unities highlight its neocolonial context since, as David Scott has argued, prior to independence 'anticolonial Romance' with its optimistic vision for the future held sway, but decolonization had ushered in a less glorious future and tragic form had greater resonance.[61] The period during which Walcott was writing *The Isle is Full of Noises* had witnessed these changes, St Lucia having gained independence in 1979 (having been primarily self-governing since being granted Crown Colony status in 1967); Trinidad, where Walcott was living, had become independent in 1962.

The nicknaming of the island's Prime Minister as 'Papa' overtly alludes to the Haitian dictator, François Duvalier, known as Papa Doc, further emphasizing the play's neocolonial setting. This combines with Sir Geoffrey's metatheatrical commentary to produce a Brechtian effect, though there is also a sense in which the remark is not sufficiently integrated to startle the audience into engagement as Brecht's *Verfremdungseffekt* can do, nor to cohere with the play as a whole in the way that the appearance of Agamemnon achieves in Virgilio Piñera's *Electra Garrigó* (first performed in Havana in 1948), for example, when he enters clad in bedsheets with a basin over his head, metatheatrically complaining, 'I wanted to lead a vaguely heroic life, but I'm only well fed and middle class. [...] Tell me, I beg you, tell me. What is my tragedy?'[62] Bruce King has noted that the reviews of the 1982 production of *The Isle is Full of Noises* in Connecticut regarded the play as being 'more symbolism than plot',[63] a characterization which, while problematic for the cohesion of the drama, points to the richness of the ideas that Walcott was juggling in the play.

The play's title, drawn from Caliban's words to Stephano and Trinculo in *The Tempest*, adds another strand to the Philoctetes-Crusoe figure. If Walcott's persistent use of a Crusoe figure seems a problematic choice given the latter's role as an enslaver in Defoe's novel,[64] Carol Dougherty has argued that, within the Greek tradition, Philoctetes 'embodies the themes of isolation, suffering, and the power of the primitive' and functions as a 'Caliban figure'.[65] Walcott's configuration of elements within *The Isle is Full of Noises* suggests he concurred, and by this startling syncretization of the three, he adds to his Crusoe-Philoctetes figure roots in the land. If a combination of the three, and most especially of Crusoe with Caliban, jars, it is nonetheless in keeping with Walcott's perception of the nature of the Caribbean and the divided identities of many of its people, which he explores in so many of his works.[66]

Crusoe's role as one who re-names the world is exemplified most starkly by his belief that he has the right to 'name' Friday, a manoeuvre replicating that of his role as a trader in enslaved people. Shakespeare's Caliban significantly does not 'name' the world, but he does reveal all the aspects of the island to Prospero before coming to regret that he has done so (Act 1.ii.333–41). In Aimé Césaire's 1969 adaptation, *Une Tempête*, which Walcott almost certainly knew, the role of naming became prominent when Caliban (echoing Malcolm X) declares,

> Appelle-moi X. Ça vaudra mieux. Comme qui dirait l'homme sans nom. Plus exactement, l'homme dont on a *volé* le nom. Tu parles d'histoire. Eh bien ça, c'est de l'histoire, et fameuse! Chaque fois que tu m'appeleras, ça me rappellera le fait fondamental, que tu m'as tout volé et jusqu'à mon identité! Uhuru![67]

> Call me X. That would be best. Like a man without a name. Or, to be more precise, like a man whose name has been stolen. You talk about history ... Well, that's history, and everyone knows it! Every time you summon me it reminds me of a basic fact, the fact that you've stolen everything from me, even my identity! Uhuru![68]

Walcott's idea of Adamic re-naming acknowledges the need for a recognition of the history of un-naming but rejects the potential of staying in that liminal space in favour of taking on the Adamic role of renaming. As he explained in 'What the Twilight Says',

What is needed is not new names for old things, or old names for old things, but the faith of using the old names anew.⁶⁹

It is this concept, the possibility that old names could be given new meaning, that is also vital to his reconceptualization of the notion of mimicry.

'The Spoiler's Return'

Walcott's poem, 'The Spoiler's Return', published in *The Fortunate Traveller*,⁷⁰ encapsulates Walcott's notion of 'originat[ing] in imitation [...] and end[ing] in invention',⁷¹ revelling both in its engagement with canonical European works and its specifically Caribbean creativity. The eponymous Spoiler of the poem alludes to Theophilus Philip, a renowned Trinidadian calypsonian known as the Mighty Spoiler, who died in 1960. His 'return' in Walcott's poem is to the land of the living, which is itself a riff on the narrative of the Mighty Spoiler's hit song, 'Bed Bug' (1953). In the calypso, the singer imagines being reincarnated as a bed bug so that he can bite the flesh of women he desires; in Walcott's hands, this sexualized joke is transposed into a meditation on the process of artistic creation without losing sight of the poem's calypso roots. 'Bed Bug' begins,

> Yes, I heard when you die, after burial
> You have to come back as some insect or animal.

The singer may choose to return as a bed bug, but Walcott's joke is to have him come back as a poet still, nudging the reader to see poetry as a parasitic endeavour. However, the primarily negative connotations conjured by the adjective 'parasitic' are recast in the poem: as Walcott's Spoiler proclaims, 'I decompose, but I composing still.'⁷² Beyond the play on words, this evokes – as Michael Dash has observed – 'the kind of intertextuality and interrelating that Walcott sees as the defining mode of the Creole sensibility', and which questions the notion of the solitary originality of the artist.⁷³

Walcott's poem opens as follows:

> I sit high on this bridge in Laventille,
> watching that city where I left no will

> but my own conscience and rum-eaten wit,
> and limers passing see me where I sit,
> ghost in brown gabardine, bones in a sack,
> and bawl: 'Ay, Spoiler, boy! When you come back?'
> And those who bold don't feel they out of place
> to peel my limeskin back, and see a face
> with eyes as cold as a dead macajuel,
> and if they still can talk, I answer: 'Hell.'
> I have a room there where I keep a crown,
> and Satan send me to check out this town.[74]

The polyphony and creative mimicry of the poem are both instantly striking: syncretizing Creole with 'Standard English', the literary with the colloquial, the poem stitches together its engagement with Trinidadian calypso and Roman and neoclassical satire. As Walcott commented when he read from the poem in October 1980, it could be seen as being composed in either calypso metre or heroic couplets.[75] In achieving this syncretism, the poem both argues against a qualitative distinction between calypso and the satire of literary canons and creates a new form out of the synthesis between the two.

It is the achievement of this syncretism that Helen Vendler, in her *New York Review of Books* assessment of *The Fortunate Traveller*, fails to appreciate.[76] She sees artifice in the combination of the two where one can recognize instead a code-switching that is finely honed in the Caribbean and in many other multilingual societies. It is almost ironic that a review which takes as its opening gambit, 'Derek Walcott is a poet, now over fifty, whose voice was for a long time a derivative one,'[77] should go on to chastise that poet for doing something that Vendler finds too original. Of 'The Spoiler's Return' she remarks that 'A macaronic aesthetic, using two or more languages at once, has never yet been sustained in poetry at any length ... the mixed diction has yet to validate itself as a literary resource with aesthetic power.'[78] It is hard not to hear a racist distinction being drawn in what Vendler sees as an 'unhappy disjunction' in Walcott's combination of 'his explosive subject' (which she terms 'the black colonial predicament') and 'his harmonious pentameters, his lyrical allusions, his stately rhymes, his Yeatsian meditations', as John Figueroa so trenchantly satirized in his poem 'Problems of a Writer who does not Quite ...', published in response to Vendler's review just a few months later:

> Watch dis pentameter ting, man.
> Dat is white people play!
>
> Wha de hell yu read Homer --[79]

Given Walcott's characterization of calypso as being patterned on 'satire and self-satire', 'The Spoiler's Return' can be seen to locate itself at the point where two 'chains of receptions' (the calypso and the Roman satire) meet and overtly to insert itself into these traditions:

> Nothing ain't change but color and attire,
> So back me up, Old Brigade of Satire,
> Back me up, Martial, Juvenal, and Pope
> (to hang theirself I giving plenty rope).[80]

The Old Brigade here is both a reference to a group of calypsonians from Spoiler's time known by that name, and a logical term for the poets of the past that Walcott lists, contributing to the poem as a 'complex mosaic' that displays 'dialectical continuities across cultures and periods *and* within the utterances of a particular speech act or literary text'.[81] The remarkable dexterity with which Walcott achieves this is highlighted when, after quoting from the Mighty Spoiler's calypso, Walcott appends two lines from 'Bed Bug' to a verse by the seventeenth-century poet, John Wilmot, second Earl of Rochester. They join almost seamlessly, an effect achieved by the closeness of the metre, as Breslin has identified: 'The calypso couplet, since it can be heard either as accentual tetrameter or iambic pentameter, slips unobtrusively into Rochester's frame, continuing not only his thought but, to a surprising degree, his manner.'[82] While the poem Signifies upon the Mighty Spoiler's song 'Bed Bug' and Rochester's neoclassical satire, its allusions to Juvenal bring to mind Samuel Johnson's famous 'mimicry' of the Roman poet in *London: A Poem in Imitation of the Third Satire of Juvenal* (1738). Walcott and Johnson both, then, write works that 'originated in imitation', if – as Walcott remarked – one wishes to term artistic engagement in that way, and 'ended in invention'.

That creole languages are the medium of calypso adds another layer to Walcott's pronouncement of it as a satiric form because, as Terada has pointed out, creole languages are always 'alluding to other languages and ringing changes upon them',[83] just as satire does to other forms. But the creolization of language is not limited to the Caribbean, as Figueroa has argued in his analysis of Walcott's poem. For Figueroa, himself well-known for engaging with Graeco-Roman literature in his poetry, what Walcott does with language in a poem like 'The Spoiler's Return' can be seen in Virgil's *Aeneid* too. Focusing on the opening line of book 2 and the closing line of book 3 of the *Aeneid*, which encircle Aeneas' tale of Troy and his wanderings, Figueroa argues that both Virgil and Walcott achieve their effects through 'the juxtaposition of various registers of a language, and various varieties within that language, and the variations on the suprasegmental aspects of language'.[84]

'The Spoiler's Return', dedicated to the novelist Earl Lovelace who had recently published his carnival novel, *The Dragon Can't Dance* (1979) and cited by Walcott as one of his favourite works on account of its directness,[85] creates a startlingly new poem by drawing on that which has gone before, syncretizing those elements and developing an innovative creative work. This exemplifies Walcott's notion, articulated in 'The Muse of History', that 'maturity is the assimilation of the features of every ancestor',[86] but it is a hard-won process and one that requires the ability to step beyond even this syncretism to engage in a process of re-naming, as his later poem 'A Latin Primer' will explore.[87]

'The Hotel Normandie Pool'

However, before Walcott pens 'A Latin Primer', another poem published in *The Fortunate Traveller*, 'The Hotel Normandie Pool',[88] offers a different aspect to the re-creation that is so important to Walcott's work. The poet finds himself, on New Year's morning, in Port of Spain, the city that had been his home for more than two decades. But in the wake of divorce, Walcott is staying in a hotel and feels no less exiled than Ovid, banished to Tomis.

Subdivided into three sections, the theme of Ovid as Walcott's double is prefigured in visual form by the Roman numerals used to label them, as Rei Terada has observed, so that the solitariness of Part I is mirrored in Part II by the turn to Ovid, with whom Walcott identifies.[89] Walcott is like a second Adam, regarding himself as a re-creation of the ancient Roman poet, both men disparaged on opposing sides for their poetry and the variety of their work, as the imagined Ovid articulates:

> 'And where are those detractors now who said
> that in and out of the imperial shade
> I scuttled, showing to a frowning sun
> the fickle dyes of the chameleon?
> Romans' – he smiled – 'will mock your slavish rhyme,
> the slaves your love of Roman structures, when,
> from Metamorphoses to Tristia,
> art obeys its own order.'[90]

Like Ovid in this portrayal, Walcott too had been criticized for writing in 'the imperial shade' of canonical European literature.[91] He, too, had written in different styles and genres, risking the charge that he is as changeable as the chameleon, who alters either to camouflage itself or attract attention. And he, too, had been castigated for his 'love of Roman structures', both by metropolitan elites who saw it as uninventive mimicry and by those previously oppressed by the metropole, who saw it as a fawning assimilation; neither recognizing that, for Walcott, 'art obeys its own order'.

In figuring himself as an Ovid-like character, Walcott departs from his more usual identification with Odysseus and in doing so, seems to have lost hope that he will ever achieve a *nostos*. Like Ovid, Walcott wishes to end his exile and reach a metropolitan centre, but whereas this would have been a homecoming for the Roman poet, for Walcott it entails a physical distance that he already feels at the emotional level. It is not only his personal isolation brought on by what he terms 'the disfiguring exile of divorce' that has led to the poet's sense of solitude, therefore;[92] nor even solely the kind of dislocation that he articulated in 'Homecoming: Anse La Raye',[93] though his sense of being in exile even when in his adopted home city resonates with that poem's understanding that 'there are homecomings without home'.[94] But further, as Emily Greenwood has observed, it is the sense that he is 'on the wrong side of prevailing cultural politics and aesthetics',[95] which he aligns with the diminished role of Classics when he laments 'the lovely Latin lost to all our schools'.[96]

'A Latin Primer'

A few years later, Walcott continues to reassess his view of 'lovely Latin'. Recollecting his time as a Latin teacher in the 1950s, Walcott is troubled by his role, as his poem 'A Latin Primer', published in *The Arkansas Testament* (1988), explores:[97]

> The discipline I preached
> made me a hypocrite;
> their lithe black bodies, beached,
> would die in dialect.[98]

It is not only the pupils he is teaching who suffer under this colonial prioritization of Latin, but the narrator himself who, having received a similar education, struggles to find his own voice. Devaluing the world around him, the young narrator cannot conceive that the Caribbean people and landscape may be his guide, and so he turns to the literature of the European canon to garner inspiration:

> so I shook all the help
> my young right hand could use
> from the sand-crusted kelp
> of distant literatures.[99]

The ambiguity of these lines foreshadows the poem's ending. At the poem's opening, Walcott is shaking the 'distant literatures' to dislodge the help they can offer him so that he may use it, and from these he adopts 'the frigate bird my phoenix' as his guide.[100] But in the shaking of the 'sand-crusted' books, one might also envisage Walcott brushing the sand off his hands and more freely deciding only to keep that which he chooses (the kelp, perhaps, instead of its sand too). This is the point that is reached by the end of the poem when 'trying to find [his] voice', he spots a frigate flying through the sky and thinks not of books but of St Lucia, where the bird is

> named with the common sense
> of fishermen: sea scissors,
> *Fregata magnificens,*
>
> *ciseau-le-mer*, the patois
> for its cloud-cutting course.[101]

Encapsulated in these lines is not only Walcott's appreciation of creole languages and the way in which they are developed by the people of the Caribbean, but also that the Creole name can sit alongside the Latin one, gesturing towards the syncretism that is vital to so much of his work as we saw in Chapter 2.

The possibility of re-creation and Adamic renaming, then, is born from the appreciation of and revalorization of that which has been deemed 'nothing',[102] syncretized with other elements. It is this process that the poem comes to celebrate, enacted in so much of Walcott's work, which will take him – as the poem's closing lines indicate – beyond the achievements of European literature:

> beyond the sheep-nibbled columns
> of fallen marble trees,
> or the roofless pillars once
> sacred to Hercules.[103]

There is an echo here, too, of Walcott's earlier poem 'Ruins of a Great House',[104] where the 'leprosy of Empire' was still figured in the scattered stones of the house but was only a passing phase, Greece's marble a 'deciduous beauty'.[105]

Omeros on screen

Walcott extends this notion of continual process and re-creation even to his own work, as is evident from an examination of the film script and storyboards that he created for a planned production of *Omeros*.[106] When he reworked his poem for the screen, it is not so much a process of circular return, but rather a forward-moving spiral,[107] so that the film would have not only translated the poem to a new medium but also moved it in a new direction.

Many drafts of Walcott's film script of *Omeros*, that he began writing in 1994, are held among his papers at the Thomas Fisher Rare Book Library at the University of Toronto.[108] One is particularly striking for the way in which it embodies the notion of the 'unfinished': it opens with an explicit pronouncement of its intention to engage creatively with the published version of *Omeros*. The narrator and Plunkett are sat chatting on the latter's verandah, two books on a table nearby: *Omeros* itself and the historical account that Plunkett worked on throughout the poem, now published as *The Battle for Another Helen*. The narrator speaks the opening lines:

> Now that I've read your book, and you've read mine, Major Plunkett
> I've come to this frightening conclusion, sir. We were both wrong.[109]

This can be heard as an even starker iteration of the narrator's reflections immediately prior to his recognition that the St Lucian Helen could be seen 'with no Homeric shadow'.[110] Signalling his intention to set the record straight – or at least to offer a new, alternative version – the film script proceeds to diverge in a number of other ways from the published poem, exemplifying Walcott's idea of continual re-creation (Figures 3.1 and 3.2).

Figure 3.1 Unpublished storyboard created by Derek Walcott, based on his poem *Omeros*, printed by permission of Farrar, Straus and Giroux on behalf of the Walcott Estate. All rights reserved.

Figure 3.2 Unpublished storyboard created by Derek Walcott, based on his poem, *Omeros*, and intersplicing scenes from the Trojan War with those on Gros Islet. Printed by permission of Farrar, Straus and Giroux on behalf of the Walcott Estate. All rights reserved.

Such rewriting is fascinating not only for its meta-commentary on Walcott's artistic process, but also for its suggestion that part of the fault in the books of the narrator and Plunkett may lie in their fixed, written form. Although film enables the permanent record of a performance, the medium itself straddles the unrepeatability of performance and the perpetual reiteration offered by film and recording technology, and it is striking that Walcott uses filmic language in several moments in the poem. The film script gives him the opportunity to develop this even further, as Jean Antoine-Dunne has shown. Analysing another of the draft scripts, in which Hector's death is still intercut with ancient Troy and scenes of tourism in East Africa (as in the published poem),[111] but with another reverberation added as Hector's face is superimposed on that of the enslaver whom Achille kills in Africa, Antoine-Dunne observes that Walcott thereby emphasizes his sense that tourism is a kind of 'neo-enslavement' and 'achieve[s] a quite overt sense of the simultaneity of Greek, African, and Antillean history and myth through the use of superimposition'.[112] One might also note that this doubling of Hector with the African enslaver is of a kind with the doubling that Walcott developed throughout his stage version of the *Odyssey* just a couple of years earlier.[113]

Another facet of continual re-creation that the very existence of the draft film scripts underlines is the way in which a move from written poetry to performance is also a move from sole to communal authorship. Walcott's film scripts are the work of his hand alone, but if the film had been made, they would have become an overtly communal creation, shaped also by the director, the actors and so many others who would have worked on and impacted the film.

At the same time, because film scripts – unlike play texts – are seldom published, the film itself would take the place of the written version. Not the place of Walcott's published *Omeros*, but of the film script which, as those opening lines alert us, is a different work of art altogether, thereby highlighting the continual regeneration of art.

The Prodigal

This is, for Walcott, a perpetual renewal made possible by the processes of syncretism, as we have seen, and which, paradoxically, locates itself on the same temporal plane as that which preceded it. The criticisms that have attended Walcott's engagement with canonical literature are familiar not only from discourse on postcolonial literature but also reiterate a disparagement of adaptations as being somehow lesser than 'original' works, which has persisted since the Romantic era despite the myopia of such a view.[114] As Linda Hutcheon argues, 'an adaptation is a derivation that is not derivative – a work that is second without being secondary'.[115] Creativity, then, has always been a part of both adaptation and reception,[116] but for Walcott, reflecting on the processes and the narratives of creativity, re-creation forms a central component of his work and is fundamental to his reception of Graeco-Roman antiquity and canonical literature more broadly. Thirty years after the publication of his essay, 'The Caribbean: Culture or Mimicry?', Walcott reiterates his argument in poetic form as he exclaims in the (untitled) thirteenth poem of *The Prodigal* (2004), 'no, the point is not comparison or mimicry',[117] but rather to see the world afresh even where connections present themselves. As Walcott expresses it in that same poem, in words voiced by the trees of the Caribbean, that echo *Omeros*' plaintive question 'Why not see her as the sun saw her, with no Homeric shadow',

> The dawn would be fresh, the morning bliss,
> if the light would break on your glaucous eyes
> to see us without a simile.[118]

Yet, much of *The Prodigal* is devoted to comparing the Caribbean with other places Walcott had travelled and lived: Gros Islet with modern Rome in the collection's fourth poem,[119] for example, or Choiseul with Venice.[120] So, it comes as no surprise that, even as Walcott exhorts us to look at the Caribbean 'without a simile', our 'glaucous eyes' seem to be his eyes too, made hazy by the glaucoma that he is more vulnerable to as a result of the diabetes he laments in his final collection, *White Egrets*,[121] but also Athene's eyes, whose most famous epithet is as the 'grey-eyed' (γλαυκῶπις – *glaukopis*) goddess.

Walcott's decision to title his 2004 collection, *The Prodigal*, indicates his intention that this would be his final book, with the prodigal son returning home,[122] even though (as he could not have known at the time), *White Egrets* would follow six years later. Towards the end of the collection, he captures this sense not only of finality, but of re-creation that had been so crucial throughout his career:

> In what will be your last book make each place
> as if it had just been made, already old.
> but new again from naming it.[123]

Walcott's strategy of re-naming and his process of re-creation, whether of canonical literature or more broadly, is an indication of the ways in which he was in dialogue with other artists, as was personified in his conversation with Ovid in 'The Hotel Normandie Pool' and with Homer in *Omeros*.[124] But it was not only long-dead poets with whom Walcott was in conversation: despite the solitariness of a poet's craft, Walcott did not compose in closeted solitude. As we have seen from the ways in which he is in dialogue with the works of other Caribbean writers and thinkers, including Édouard Glissant, Wilson Harris and Aimé Césaire, his work is also the craft of community.[125] It is in the context of this kind of collective enterprise that Walcott's work exists.[126] This is not to discount the force of the individual ego or the singling out that awards and prizes confer, especially ones as prestigious as the Nobel Prize. Nor is it to claim that Walcott always saw himself as part of this collective: his preoccupations with his sense of a divided identity and a feeling of being in a kind of Ovidian exile indicate that he did not. But it is what the work itself strives for, contributing to the literature of a region, and the creation of an ever-evolving canon for the Caribbean: what we might term a 'classical Caribbean'.

Epilogue

Towards the end of *Another Life*, Derek Walcott pictures his children playing by the creek of the Rampanalgas River on the north-east coast of Trinidad:

> that child who puts the shell's howl to his ear,
> hears nothing, hears everything
> that the historian cannot hear, the howls
> of all the races that crossed the water,
> the howls of grandfathers drowned
> in that intricately swivelled Babel.[1]

Here are different ways of knowing. The young boy launching a child's coconut-shell boat into the water, setting it to sail across the Atlantic Ocean, is not troubled by the weight of History; he does not seek to reverse the Middle Passage as Achille tried to do in his hallucinatory dream. Yet, the boy hears the human cries and knows this history, not from the linear accounts of books but in each moment of the present as he holds a shell to his ear. As in Walcott's reconceptualization of time, the boy and his ancestors exist simultaneously. Calendrical time is insufficient for the Caribbean, and the historian, thinking that linear time predominates, knows of, but 'cannot hear', the cries of those who experienced the Middle Passage. The 'Babel' of the transatlantic crossing became syncretized in the Caribbean in creole languages and in culture, creating new ways of speaking that make possible the creative artistry of the region.

These ways of knowing shape Derek Walcott's engagement with the ancient Mediterranean in unique respects. The literature of ancient Greece and Rome pervades his writing throughout his career, in shifting and altering ways, never fully receding nor overwhelming the work either. Always, it is in dialogue with other aspects, syncretizing with elements from other times and places in ways that are drawn specifically from the culture of the Caribbean. Far from being a series of self-conscious intertexts, classical reception is integral both to Walcott's creative aesthetic and his vision of Caribbean culture. If the postcolonial model of 'writing back' has predominated, Walcott's work can be seen as a remarkable exemplum of such interaction; but his writing also encourages us to think again, and to recognize that he engages with Graeco-Roman literature not only to 'write back', but to 'write forward' to a new condition of Caribbean modernity. And in so doing, he contributes to the creation of a classical Caribbean.

This classical Caribbean is 'classical' in a triple sense, as we have seen. In its dialogue with Graeco-Roman antiquity and the ways in which the history and literature of the ancient Mediterranean came to have a place in the Caribbean, it engages with the discipline that has traditionally been called 'Classics'. In its engagement with canonical literature more widely, with literary 'classics' (lower-case 'c') from Shakespeare to Eliot, Baudelaire to Joyce, it is in conversation with classic literature that occupies a place within literary canons, especially the one known as 'the Western canon', and it situates itself in dialogue with them. In its self-conscious assertion of its own place as canonical, achieved in part by the two strategies above, as well as by its narratives of Caribbean history and its written deployment of primarily oral creole languages, it proclaims itself as a new canon that stands on a par with other literary canons.

As a result, Derek Walcott's explorations of simultaneity, syncretism and re-creation in turn illuminate the reception of the ancient Graeco-Roman world beyond his own oeuvre, making an important contribution to classical reception theory. Those three themes prompt reconsideration of the notions of tradition, literary origins and the process of 'reception' itself: Walcott's conceptualization of time and simultaneity rethinks the linearity of 'the classical tradition'; his understanding of syncretism refutes a search for a singular source, replacing it with plurality and emphasizing the transformation that ensues when different elements are synthesized; and his concept of re-creation priorities the active engagement of reception, sidelining any concerns that the term 'reception' still implies passivity.[2]

Walcott's understanding of time, which asserts simultaneity in place of linearity even while emphasizing that it is the horrors of historical colonialism that produced the 'amnesia' of the Caribbean, destabilizes notions of 'the classical tradition'. In place of the proclamation that opens Gilbert Highet's *The Classical Tradition: Greek and Roman Influences on Western Literature* (1949), that 'Our modern world is in many ways a continuation of the worlds of Greece and Rome' and 'we are the grandsons of the Romans, and the great-grandsons of the Greeks',[3] Walcott urges a recognition of simultaneity. Not because he ignores history but because he understands that such a narrative of linearity is underwritten by colonial discourse.

Even leaving aside the Eurocentrism of Highet's gaze, announced in the book's subtitle, his perspective is unapologetically one that seeks to trace a genealogy of influence from Graeco-Roman antiquity. It is T. S. Eliot's conception of 'tradition', which contrasts with Highet's in many ways,[4] that resonates more soundly with Walcott's thinking, for Eliot argues in his 1919 essay, 'Tradition and the Individual Talent', that tradition 'cannot be inherited', that it requires 'a perception, not only of the pastness of the past, but of its presence', and an understanding that all literature 'has a simultaneous existence and composes a simultaneous order'.[5] Walcott's conception of time echoes this idea of the co-existence of simultaneity and historical impact, adding to Eliot's notion the understanding that linear theories of time are bound up with coloniality. Given the pervasiveness of coloniality,[6] it is no surprise that this has implications for engagements with the Graeco-Roman world beyond those in postcolonial art and literature. Madhavi Menon, for example, has drawn from postcolonial discourse to identify the need for a 'temporal version of decolonization – what may be termed dechronolization' in queer theory, while Sebastian Matzner has applied the notion of 'queer unhistoricism' to classical reception.[7]

While syncretism has particular resonance in the Caribbean and, in the wake of colonialism, enslavement and forced diaspora, has become a feature of modern Caribbean culture, Derek Walcott's pursuit of artistic syncretism has implications for classical reception theory more broadly. Specifically, Walcott's work demands a comparative approach that seeks out not only the ways in which he engages with Graeco-Roman antiquity but with other literary works too, and reflects on these within their new context. Doing so highlights the constellation of influences and inspirations at play within his writing, drawing attention to how they reshape each other into new forms when Walcott combines them, as well as to the ways in which his engagement with them is one of 'repetition with difference', all the more confidently so as his career progresses. In turn, this highlights what Emily Greenwood has referred to as the 'omni-local' of both modern and ancient texts, which have always been 'local' in the sense that they are created in a particular context.⁸ Furthermore, as Greenwood articulates, 'the omni-local substitutes a horizontal, two-way relationship in place of a vertical, hierarchical tradition'.⁹ Walcott's syncretic approach, then, can be seen to destabilize notions of 'tradition' in a way that is akin to the destabilization enacted by his notion of simultaneity.

Finally, Walcott's development and valorization of the idea of 're-creation' serves as a reminder that reception is a creative process. The persistent, if convincingly debunked,¹⁰ idea that works which respond to others are somehow less creative than those designated 'original' is refuted by Walcott's notion of re-creation. Instead, he draws attention to the innovations wrought by the passage of time and context, to the impact that 'the tartness of experience' brings,¹¹ and to the artist's own creative endeavour even when engaging with that which has gone before. Walcott encourages his readers and audience to focus on the alterations as much as the similarities, the innovations as much as the echoes, the modern context as much as the ancient, in a way that proves to be an apt model for classical reception more widely.

Derek Walcott's engagement with Graeco-Roman antiquity is a persistent feature of his writing, and one that has a significant role to play in his development of a classical Caribbean. This new canon of Caribbean literature to which he offers his own work is not unshifting, its borders and its contents are not fixed; unlike many other bodies of classic works, however, it is not invested in proclaiming that it is unchanging. Instead, in keeping with the understanding that syncretism is always an ongoing process, and that re-creation is key to art, it embraces transformation. The role of Walcott's reception of the literature of ancient Greece and Rome in his creation of a classical Caribbean does not so much depend on the canonicity of Graeco-Roman literature, though undoubtedly that was a part of its appeal, but rather on the manner in which Walcott syncretizes ancient art with other elements, recasts them anew, and overturns colonial ways of knowing by proclaiming the simultaneity of his work and that of antiquity. It is these approaches, which in Walcott's hands are tied so closely to the history, art and culture of the Caribbean, that give the worlds of ancient Greece and Rome a prominent and mutually transformative place within Walcott's classical Caribbean.

Notes

Introduction

1. Ricks (1989), vii.
2. Walcott (1976), 35–49 at 39. On Walcott's use of language in this poem, see McDougall (1992).
3. See Cobham-Sander (2013), 108–12, on the ways in which several aspects of this poem are reprised in *Omeros*, not least the figure of Ma Kilman who first appears in 'Sainte Lucie' and the exploration of poetic form and language.
4. Hall (2008), 387–8; Lianeri and Zajko (2008), 2–3.
5. Hall (2008), 387.
6. With ideas of modern imperialism at their core, the question has been posed again by J. M. Coetzee in a lecture first delivered in 1991, and by Ankhi Mukherjee. See Coetzee (2002), 1–19; and Mukherjee (2014).
7. See Brathwaite (1963). For a reflection on responses to Walcott in the Caribbean, see Morris (1968).
8. Cobham-Sander (2016), 2.
9. Walcott (1998), 223.
10. Bernabé, Chamoiseau and Confiant (1993), 14; 76.
11. Walcott (1998), 36.
12. Ibid.
13. Ibid., 38.
14. Carpentier (1967), 114.
15. On the literary dialogue between Walcott, Brathwaite and Naipaul, which sits alongside their rivalry, see Cobham-Sander (2016), 133–239.
16. Walcott (1962), 60–1.
17. Greenwood (2016).
18. Cf. Césaire ([1950] 2000), 32: 'what, fundamentally, is colonization? To agree on what it is not: neither evangelization, nor a philanthropic enterprise, nor a desire to push back the frontiers of ignorance, disease, and tyranny, nor a project undertaken for the greater glory of God, nor an attempt to extend the rule of law.'
19. Walcott (2014).
20. Barkan and Bush (1995a), 2.

21 On infantilization as a trope of colonialist discourse, see, for example, Said ([1978] 1995), 36–42; and Shohat and Stam (2014), 137–41.
22 McClintock (1992), 85.
23 Sauvy (1952).
24 See Majeed (1999), 89–98; and Vasunia (2005). As Vasunia (2005), 37, notes: 'Greek and Latin authorized and participated in imperial culture, and also intersected, in metropolitan and colonial contexts, with issues such as race, class, and gender.'
25 Goff (2005a), 11.
26 Lorna Goodison's *I Am Becoming My Mother* (1986) includes the poems 'The Mulatta and the Minotaur' (31) and 'The Mulatta as Penelope' (25), discussed in Baugh (1990), as well as another *Odyssey*-inflected poem, 'Homecoming' (21). Nonetheless, it is important to keep in mind Emily Greenwood's argument that Caribbean women writers who had a classical education have often chosen not to deploy it, which Greenwood regards 'not as the marginalization of Caribbean women with respect to Classics, but rather as the marginalization of Classics in Caribbean women's writing' (2010), 11–12, at 11.
27 Césaire (2017).
28 For a cultural history of the Cyclops, see Aguirre and Buxton (2020).
29 Wynter (1997).
30 McConnell (2013), 39–69.
31 Fabian ([1983] 2014); Chakrabarty (2000), 7: 'Historicism thus posited historical time as a measure of the cultural distance (at least in institutional development) that was assumed to exist between the West and the non-West'; McClintock (1992).
32 Bhabha (1994); Gilroy (1993).
33 Glissant (1999); Brathwaite (1971); see also Dash (1998).
34 Harris (1999b); Gates (1988); Alexander (2007b).
35 See further, Introduction n.89.
36 Rose (1993), 170–7. This is not to overlook the importance of their work on 'the implied reader' for understanding how parody functions.
37 Walcott (1965a), 36–7; Walcott (1976), 3; Walcott ([1973] 2009).
38 Walcott (1997a), 232.
39 Walcott ([1987] 1988), 39.
40 McConnell (2013), 107–34, offers an earlier iteration of a few of the readings of *Omeros* explored here.
41 See, for example, Quint (1993).
42 Walcott (1997a), 232. Cf. Valentin Mudimbe's wry comment on Sartre's 'Black Orpheus' essay: '[Senghor] had asked Sartre for a cloak to celebrate negritude; he was given a shroud'-Mudimbe (1988), 85.

43 As Taplin (1991), 218 notes, *Omeros* displays an ambivalence towards epic, 'a simultaneous embracing and fending off'.
44 Quoted by Bruckner (1990), 13; reprinted in Hamner (1997), 396. On 'seven seas' in *Omeros*, and Walcott's stance on epic here, see McConnell (2013), 110–12.
45 Gates (2014), 56.
46 Ibid., 113. Playwright Suzan-Lori Parks, who has also engaged with Graeco-Roman literature in a number of her works, likewise draws on jazz when describing her own technique of 'Rep and Rev' (repetition and revision). See Parks (1995a), 8–10.
47 Gates (1988), xxiv.
48 Gates (2014), 5.
49 Bhabha (1984), 128.
50 Gates (2014), 123.
51 Walcott (1974). For discussion of this essay and Walcott's reconceptualization of mimicry, see Chapter 1, 45 and 60 and Chapter 3, 110–11.
52 On oral Signifying, see Abrahams (1970) and Mitchell-Kernan (1971), whose work underpins Gates' literary theory.
53 Gates (1988), xxii.
54 Fumagalli (2001), 281: in conversation with Fumagalli, Walcott remarked, 'What is important [in poetry] is not the language so much as the tone of the language. [...] What I hope I have never done is go away from the sound of my own language.'
55 Walcott (1990), 283; Farrell (1999), 278–9.
56 As Nepaulsingh (1993), 205, exhorts us, extrapolating from Barbara Webb's analysis of Carpentier's *Los pasos perdidos* (itself a text that is in dialogue with the *Odyssey*), 'Let *Omeros* be what it is, the masterwork, and let Homer serve.'
57 Davis (2016), 464.
58 On Walcott's engagement with Dante throughout his oeuvre, see Fumagalli (2001), with particular reference to *Omeros* at 187–223.
59 Sampietro (n.d.).
60 See Abani (2006).
61 On the continuation of calypso's subversive strand, see 'Calypso Songs' (1951).
62 Walcott (1990), 286.
63 Breslin (2001), 245.
64 On parody, see Hutcheon (1985) and Rose (1993). Hutcheon (1985), 32, 37, citing Deleuze's 1968 work, *Différence et Répétition*, describes parody as 'repetition with difference'.
65 Walcott (1998), 36.
66 Rose (1993), 51.

67 See Chapter 1.
68 Davis (1997).
69 Callimachus, fr.1.21–4; Virgil, *Eclogue* 3.3–5.
70 Davis (1997), 328: 'he is not so much renouncing "epic" as redefining it'.
71 Walcott (1990), 149.
72 Cobham-Sander (2016), 168, and 182.
73 Walcott, quoted in Sampietro (n.d.), where he explains the nature of this 'rough-texture'. See also Taplin (1991), 214 and 225 n. 3.
74 Sampietro (n.d.). Walcott's idea that adapting Homer into Caribbean-inflected 'rough-textured' *terza rima* is true to the ancient poetry's essence brings to mind J. H. Kells' suggestion in his 1973 edition of Sophocles' *Electra* that an Anglo-Irish idiom could be 'more faithful to the tone of the Greek', cited in Macintosh (1994), xviii.
75 Brathwaite ([1984] 2011), 10.
76 Ibid., 13.
77 Ibid. Walcott and Brathwaite have often been cast in contradistinction to each other, though as so often with neat dichotomies, the contrast can prove reductive – on which, see Ismond (1971). At any rate, in *History of the Voice*, Brathwaite cites three of Walcott's poems ('The Schooner *Flight*', 'Blues' and 'Sainte Lucie') as examples of nation language, Brathwaite ([1984] 2011), 10, 41–2, 49. Cobham-Sander (2016), 167–201, has explored the influence of Brathwaite's work on *Omeros*, in particular.
78 Brathwaite ([1984] 2011), 14.
79 Sampietro (n.d.).
80 Walcott (1990), 15.
81 Taplin (1991), 218.
82 See Eastman (2015), 808.
83 Walcott (1990), 271. See also Walcott (1997a), 232–4. As Whitaker (1996), 98 notes, the aptness of the ancient Greek parallels deployed by Plunkett and the narrator is questioned early in the poem (*Omeros*, 31 and 32).
84 See, for example, *Iliad* 5.302–4 and 20.285–7.
85 Dacier (1711), xix.
86 Rose (1975).
87 Sampietro (n.d.).
88 Tempest (2013), 4. See Macintosh and McConnell (2020), 45–8.
89 Gates (2014), 134, elaborates on the figure of the Signifying Monkey and the different forms this trope can take, corresponding to parody (motivated) and pastiche (unmotivated): 'Signifyin(g) revision is a rhetorical transfer that can be motivated or unmotivated. Motivated Signifyin(g) is the sort in which the Monkey delights; it functions to redress an imbalance of power, to clear a space, rhetorically.'

90 Walcott (1990), 320.
91 Moretti (2000), 65, emphasis in original.
92 Walcott (1990), 17.
93 Ibid., 224–6.
94 Ibid., 64. On this metaphor, see Hardwick (1997), 331. Hardwick reads these lines as being the thoughts of the narrator rather than of Plunkett, which is also possible; to my ear, the use of 'them' signifies Plunkett's perspective, yet the recently returned narrator does feel dislocated from the St Lucian people at this stage of the poem and the indeterminacy of the focalization may be seen as an exemplification of the poem's insistence on celebrating the commonalities between people, rather than the divisions.
95 Taplin (1991), 220–1.
96 Walcott (1990), 275.
97 Ibid., 144.
98 James (1954); Diop (1974); Bernal (1987); Amin (2009), 165–9.
99 Walcott (1998), 37.
100 Ibid., 37.
101 Glissant (1999), 62. See Chapter 1, 39 and Breslin (2001), 5–6.
102 Walcott (1998), 39.
103 Harris (1999a), 177–87. On this, see Greenwood (2007).
104 On the ways in which *The Mask of the Beggar* responds to Homer, see McConnell (2013), 181–210.
105 Greenwood (2007), 196.
106 Walcott, quoted in Burnett (2000b), 114.
107 See Fabian ([1983] 2014) on the 'denial of coevalness' in the context of anthropological work.
108 Walcott (1997a), 241.
109 Walcott (1998), 40.
110 Ibid., 41. Chapter 3 explores this concept of recreation throughout Walcott's work.
111 See Figure 3.1.
112 Walcott (1990), 131.
113 Ibid., 319.
114 Hardwick (2000), 105–8. On this episode within *Omeros*, see also McConnell (2013), 124–31.
115 Cobham-Sander (2013), 101; Brathwaite (1973), especially chapters 4 ('The Return') and 5 ('Crossing the River') of the middle poem of the trilogy, *Masks*. On *Masks*, see Rohlehr (1977/1978).
116 Walcott (1990), 148.

117 Van Sickle (1999), 23–4. Walcott (1990), 148: just before Achille falls, 'the one thought thudding in him was, I can deliver | all of them [...] I could change their whole future, even the course of the river | would flow backwards.'
118 See Davis (2007), 206, on the way Walcott's earlier poem, 'Homecoming: Anse La Raye' (1969) anticipates this episode, and Chapter 2, 85–7 for further discussion of that poem.
119 Walcott (1997a), 237.
120 Walcott (1990), 129–30, 155.
121 Ibid., 155–6.
122 On the ways in which tourism and photography were rooted in colonialism and impacted the lives of the inhabitants of Caribbean islands, see Thompson (2006).
123 Walcott (1990), 3. The destructive nature of tourism is strikingly condemned later in the poem (289) when 'the traitors | who, in elected office, saw the land as views | for hotels' are discovered in one of the rings of hell through which Omeros leads the narrator. On the role of tourism in *Omeros* and the way in which the reader comes to be merged with the figure of a tourist, see Melas (2007), 133–54; 164–9.
124 Walcott (1997a), 241.
125 Breslin (2001), 248.
126 Walcott (1990), 137.
127 Patterson (1982), 55.
128 On the practice of imposing Graeco-Roman names on enslaved people in the anglophone Caribbean, see Williamson (2017) and (2020).
129 Patterson (1982).
130 Walcott, speaking at the University of West Indies (UWI), Mona in Jamaica, in May 1988. Recording held at UWI Mona's Library of the Spoken Word.
131 Walcott (1990), 138.
132 Ibid., 283.
133 Walcott (1998), 39.
134 Walcott (1990), 139.
135 Hardwick (2000), 107.
136 Callahan (2003), 89.
137 See Patterson (1982), 5–6, on what he terms 'a genealogical isolate'.
138 See Peradotto (1990) on the importance of naming in the *Odyssey*.
139 Horkheimer and Adorno (2002), 48.
140 Etymologically, *kleos* ('glory' or 'renown') is derived from the verb *kluein* ('to hear'). See Nagy (2007), 56. For Walcott, it is those whose names are no longer heard that deserve *kleos*.

141 Cf. the line cited earlier from Walcott (1990), 149: 'But they crossed, they survived. There is the epical splendour.'
142 Froude (1888), 347.
143 Walcott (1969), 36–7. For discussion of 'Air', see Chapter 1, 56–7.
144 Naipaul ([1962] 2001), 20.
145 Walcott was very familiar with Césaire's *Cahier* and even worked on a translation of it that remains unpublished, see King (2000), 236.
146 Césaire ([1939] 2017), 126, 127. See also, Chapter 1, 56–7. Walcott quotes these lines in his 1964 essay, 'Necessity of Negritude', see Walcott ([1964] 1997), 21, and riffs on them early in *Omeros* (22), as Melas (2007), 140–1 notes.
147 Rodman (1974), 240.
148 On the first and third of these, see Greenwood (2007), 200–2.
149 Horkheimer and Adorno (2002), 53.
150 The contrast set up in *Omeros* between Achille's continued career as a fisherman and Hector's effort to secure a more stable income by becoming a driver, confirms Achille's less capitalist leanings. Cf. Walcott (1990), 231.
151 Homer, *Odyssey* 9.355–412. Odysseus hides his famous trait of cunning (*mētis*) in his negative pseudonym, when by that sleight of syntax whereby οὐ changes to μή in the conditional, his pseudonym Οὖτις changes to his characteristic μῆτις.
152 Walcott (1990), 272–7, 318.
153 Ibid., 271.
154 Hardwick (2000), 99. Cf. Clifford (1988), 15. Drawing on Lévi-Strauss' idea of the 'filth' that the Western world has 'thrown into the face of mankind' (Lévi-Strauss 2011: 38), Clifford's articulation is strikingly similar to Walcott's, as he observes that that 'filth' 'appears as raw material, compost for new orders of difference. It is also filth.'
155 Goff and Simpson (2007), 244–70, 244.
156 Hall (2015), 23.
157 Walcott (1990), 151.
158 On the ways in which Achille's *katabasis* engages with but ultimately rejects Afrocentrism, see McConnell (2013), 119–22.
159 Walcott (1990), 141.
160 Ibid., 140.
161 Ibid., 142.
162 Benítez-Rojo (1996), 12.
163 Walcott (1990), 164.
164 Walcott ([1964] 1997), 22–3.
165 Hall (1990), 226.
166 Sampietro (n.d.).

167 See, for example, Walcott (1990), 25–6.
168 McConnell (2013), 120–1.
169 Walcott (1990), 306–9.
170 Ibid., 307.
171 Ibid., 289.
172 Ibid., 289–94. On Plunkett's and the narrator's *katabaseis*, see Ciocia (2000), 92–8; and Goff and Simpson (2007), 246–50.
173 See Friedman (2007), 463–4, on the ways in which Walcott deliberately evokes Odysseus' return home in that of the narrator.
174 See Introduction, 19ff.
175 Walcott (1990), 28.
176 Ramazani (2001), 71.
177 Walcott (2009), 144.
178 Walcott (1998), 38.
179 Walcott (1990), 19.
180 Ramazani (2001), 49–71.
181 Césaire ([1950] 2000), 35.
182 See Ramazani (2001), 49–71.
183 On Walcott's consideration of indigeneity in *Omeros* and *The Ghost Dance* (first performed in 1989, and published in Walcott, 2002: 115–246), see Casteel (2011).
184 Walcott (1990), 318.
185 Lévi-Strauss (1955), 435; Davis (1997), 329.
186 See above, p. 10.
187 See Meador (2000), 72–3, for a translation of the hymn.
188 Walcott (1990), 17–18. In the name 'St Omere', Walcott also evokes his friend, the painter Dunstan St Omer.
189 See, for example, Bowra (1952), 10–13.
190 Walcott (1990), 139.
191 Ibid., 235–48. This syncretism is also apparent in the way that Ma Kilman's name echoes that of the Iliadic Machaon, son of Asclepius, even while Ma Kilman first appears in Walcott's work in 'Sainte Lucie' (1976). As Farrell (1999), n. 29, discusses, it would be wrong, therefore, to see only Homeric roots in her name and actions.
192 Walcott (1990), 248.
193 Breslin (2001), 251. See further, Chapter 3 in this volume.
194 Walcott (1990), 272–7.
195 Ibid., 143, 275.
196 Ibid., 277.
197 Ibid., 248.

198 Ibid.
198 Walcott, quoted in Rodman (1974), 240; Figueroa (1991), 193, 195, 206.
200 Walcott (1990), 28.
201 Ramazani (2001), 50.
202 Walcott (1990), 319.
203 Walcott (1997a), 229. See Tynan (2011), 78–88, on Bearden and Walcott, and Walcott's lauding of Bearden in the sixth poem of *White Egrets* (2010), dedicated to August Wilson.
204 Alexander (2007b), 36. See further, Chapter 2, 95.
205 Walcott (1998), 9.
206 Hamner (1993), 86.
207 Walcott (1990), 14.
208 Breiner (2005), 40.
209 Cf. Okpewho (2002), 36, who regards *Omeros* as 'placing Creole speech and culture on equal footing with the dominant colonialist style'. While Creole speech does not seem to me to be on an equal footing in the poem, when combined with culture as Okpewho does here, the observation is apt.
210 Walcott (1990), 15–16.
211 Kamau Brathwaite, in a talk, 'West Indian Poetry, a Search for Voices' (14 March 1965), quoted in Ismond (1971), 62.
212 Cobham-Sander (2013). See Introduction, n.115, for the way in which Brathwaite's *Masks* serves as a source-text for Achille's journey.
213 Walcott (1990), 18.
214 Beecroft (2015), 6.
215 Callahan (2003), 20.
216 Ibid., 22–3.
217 Walcott (1998), 36.
218 Ibid.
219 Breslin (2001), 103.
220 Walcott (1998), 43.
221 Ibid., 47.
222 On this passage of *Omeros*, see Farrell (1999), 281–3.
223 Walcott (1990), 320.
224 Farrell (1999), 282.
225 *Odyssey* 11.489–91.
226 Wilson (2018), 295.
227 Walcott (1990), 47–8.
228 Stanford (1987), 387, notes that the most likely translation of ἐξ ἁλὸς is 'away from, out of range of, the sea', but goes on to observe that both Aeschylus and

Sophocles read it differently: as a 'death coming from the sea'. Although Stanford is sceptical of the way in which this interpretation could be the 'gentle death' that Teiresias prophesies – given that it is a death caused by a wound from a fish bone that causes sepsis – this not only embodies the same ambiguity that Walcott retains, but also resonates with Philoctete's wound from a rusty anchor.

229 Froude (1888), 10: 'If ever the naval exploits of this country are done into an epic poem – and since the *Iliad* there has been no subject better fitted for such treatment or better deserving it – the West Indies will be the scene of the most brilliant cantos.'

Chapter 1

1 Walcott (1998).
2 See Webb (1992), who focuses on myth and history in the fiction of Alejo Carpentier, Wilson Harris and Édouard Glissant, and also Scott (2004), 39, and *passim*, who argues that in his renowned history of the Haitian Revolution, *The Black Jacobins*, C. L. R. James ([1938] 2001) should be seen as 'a storyteller – a mythmaker'.
3 Walcott (2002a), 1–107.
4 Goody and Watt (1963), 311. See also Griffin (2006).
5 Goody and Watt (1963).
6 Fabian ([1983] 2014), 32 and *passim*; see below, 41–4.
7 'The Caribbean: Culture or Mimicry?' was first delivered as a talk at the University of Miami American Assembly on the United States and the Caribbean in April 1973 and is published as Walcott (1974). In conversation with Paul Breslin, Walcott specified that 'The Muse of History' was finished in 1970 or early 1971, placing it even more closely in the era of the Black Power Revolution.
8 See Kaufmann (2006), on the risks of scholars and readers 'colonizing' texts.
9 What Martin Bernal termed the 'Aryan Model', which took hold in the first half of the nineteenth century and denied the Egyptian and Phoenician influences on ancient Greece, as well as the Fascist appropriation of Graeco-Roman antiquity are two prominent examples of such moments in the discipline's history. On these, see, respectively, Bernal (1987) and Roche (2018).
10 Glissant (1981), 133; Glissant (1999), 65.
11 Harris (1999a), 180, emphasis in original. See also Harris (2008).
12 Goffe (2022), especially 110 and 112–13.
13 Trouillot ([1995] 2015), 7, emphasis in original.

14 Ibid., 7–8.
15 Henry (2000), 15: '[In Afro-Caribbean art, religion and philosophy] there are strong tendencies towards reconceptualizing the fragments of broken traditions, creolizing the differences between them, and projecting transformative alternatives.' As will be apparent, these three are also the notions underpinning this book's three core chapters, with the understanding that the Middle Passage enacted a break in time for those who underwent it; cf. Sharpe (2016).
16 The phrase 'clock time' is intended to evoke Anderson (2006), 24, when he draws from and adapts Walter Benjamin's idea of Messianic time: 'to borrow again from Benjamin, an idea of "homogenous, empty time," in which simultaneity is, as it were, transverse, cross-time, marked not by prefiguring and fulfilment, but by temporal coincidence, and measured by clock and calendar'. It is worth bearing in mind, however, that, in his adoption of the phrase, Anderson overlooks Benjamin's 'profound ambivalence' towards this narrative of modernity, as Bhabha (1990a), 311 points out.
17 Fabian ([1983] 2014).
18 Said ([1978] 1995); Fabian ([1983] 2014).
19 Fabian ([1983] 2014), xxxiii; xli.
20 Ibid., xli.
21 Gough (1968), 12.
22 Fabian ([1983] 2014), 21: 'If one compares uses of Time in anthropological *writing* with the ones in ethnographic *research* he discovers remarkable divergence,' emphasis in original.
23 Ibid., 29–30.
24 Ibid., 31–2.
25 Appadurai (1996), 30.
26 Benítez-Rojo (1996), 11.
27 For example, 'What the Twilight Says: An Overture', in Walcott (1970), 3–40; Walcott (1974); Walcott (1998), 36–64; and Harris (1999b), especially 'Quetzalcoatl and the Smoking Mirror', 'History, Fable and Myth in the Caribbean and Guianas' and 'The Unfinished Genesis of the Imagination'.
28 Greenwood (2010), 18.
29 Glissant (1965), 128. For a bilingual edition of *Les Indes*, see Glissant ([1955] 1992), where these lines appear at 56 (English) and 156 (French).
30 These lines are quoted and discussed by Sylvia Wynter, who offers her own translation of them, in Wynter (1989), 644. Wynter argues (646) that the new way of knowing developed by Glissant, following Frantz Fanon, and which Wynter defines as 'a shift from ontogeny to sociogeny, from *l'Être* to *l'étant*' should have an

impact on knowledge formation beyond the Caribbean, functioning as 'the gift of the New World to the Old'.
31. Walcott's poem, 'The Map of the Antilles', first published in 1960 and collected in *In a Green Night* two years later, echoes Glissant's idea: 'men invent those truths which they discover'. See Chapter 1, 51-2.
32. Dash (1995), 52.
33. Glissant (1981), 159.
34. Glissant (1999), 93.
35. See 'Histoire, temps, identité' in Glissant (1981), 158-9, at 158, translated as 'History, Time, Identity' in Glissant (1999), 92-3, at 93: 'Cette contradiction entre un vécu par quoi la communauté récuse d'instinct l'unicité usurpatrice de l'Histoire et un pensé officiel par quoi elle y consent passivement à travers l'idéologie "représentée" par ses élites: voici en quoi la recherche d'identité devient pour certains peuples incertaine et ambiguë. L'ambigu n'est pas à tout coup la marque d'une tare.' ('There is a contradiction between a lived experience through which the community instinctively rejects the intrusive exclusiveness of a single History and an official way of thinking through which it passively consents in the ideology "represented" by its elite. Ambiguity is not always the sign of some shortcoming.')
36. Britton (2020).
37. Walcott (1990), 282-4, when the narrator moves from pretended indifference to Homer's works to admitting '"I have always heard | your voice in that sea, master"' (283). The word 'master' here evokes the history of slavery but provocatively re-signifies it at this moment as a mark of literary status.
38. See Chakrabarty (2000) and in particular, his conceptualization of the 'time-knot' (111-13).
39. Pollard (2004), 46.
40. Gates (1988). See Introduction, 11 and 35-6, for a discussion of Signifying in the context of Walcott's work.
41. Greenwood (2010), 40-1.
42. While *Henri Christophe* was his first play to be published (by Advocate in Bridgetown, Barbados in 1950), Walcott had written and staged several plays while still in his teens. See King (2000), 73-6.
43. Walcott (2002), 1-107.
44. Carpentier ([1949] 2017), xvii.
45. Breslin (2008).
46. The history of Walcott's homeland of St Lucia exemplifies this, having been passed back and forth between the French and the British several times before the Treaty of Paris in 1814 ceded the island to the British. These changes brought not only alterations of language (French and English) and religion (Catholicism and

Anglicanism), but even the abolition of slavery under the French in 1794 and its reinstatement by the British the following year, before it was finally abolished in 1834. Such battles over the possession of the island are one of the reasons why it came to be known as 'Helen of the West Indies', after the ancient Greek Helen of Troy.
47 Walcott (1974), 6.
48 James ([1938] 2001), xviii.
49 Buck-Morss (2009), 42.
50 Walcott (1998), 37, and quoted as this chapter's epigraph.
51 Trouillot ([1995] 2015), 96. See also Daut (2015) on late-eighteenth to mid-nineteenth-century narratives in which the events of the Haitian Revolution were, as she argues in a development of Trouillot's work, 'perhaps less "silenced" in literal terms than they were incessantly narrated in a particularly "racialized" way that had the ultimate effect of subordinating the position of the Haitian Revolution to the French and American revolutions' (3).
52 Trouillot ([1995] 2015), 70–107.
53 Walcott (1974), 9.
54 Baugh (2005); Walcott (2009), 75.
55 Walcott (2002a), 121. The four figures are Christopher Columbus, Walter Raleigh, Toussaint L'Ouverture and George William Gordon, representing a trajectory from colonialism to resistance in the Caribbean.
56 Baugh (2005), 52.
57 Walcott (1970b), 12.
58 Ibid., 11.
59 Scott (2004), 36.
60 Walcott (2002a), 10.
61 Breslin (2008), 225–6.
62 Ibid., 234.
63 Walcott (2002a), 11.
64 Ibid., 46–7. The historical massacre this speech retells took place from January to April 1804.
65 Ibid., 47.
66 Euripides, *Bacchae* 734–68.
67 Ibid. 735–42.
68 Gibbons and Segal (2009), 271–2.
69 Kaisary (2014), 142.
70 See Chapter 2, 79–84, for a discussion of *Ione*.
71 Walcott (2002a), 14.
72 James ([1938] 2001), 299.
73 Walcott (2002a), 7, 56.

74 Walcott (1970b), 11. On *Henri Christophe* and its Jacobean aspects in particular, see Thieme (1999), 45–51; and Breslin (2001), 75–82.
75 Walcott (1970b), 13.
76 See Baugh (2005), 46–7, on Walcott's term 'heraldic men' and the ways in which it is in keeping with Walcott's changing perspective on history.
77 Walcott (2002a), 410. See Daut (2021) on the often overlooked influence of Baron de Vastey and other nineteenth-century Haitian historians on the work of Michel-Rolph Trouillot.
78 Bongie (2005), 105.
79 See, for example, Kaisary (2014), 135–56.
80 Breslin (2001), 78.
81 Walcott (1970b), 12.
82 Walcott (2002a), 19.
83 Bongie (2005), 72–4. I part from Bongie, however, in seeing Walcott's anachronisms as careless or in reading his depiction of 'the postrevolutionary condition in terms of a monotonously linear succession of rulers' (ibid.: 91).
84 See Chapter 1, 65–8.
85 Glissant ([1961] 1998).
86 Kaisary (2014), 109–20.
87 Walcott ([1958] 1961).
88 Cf. Walcott ([1970c] 1997): 'it is almost death to the spirit to try to survive as an artist under colonial conditions, which haven't really changed with our independent governments'.
89 Walcott (1962), 55.
90 Ibid.
91 Ibid.
92 Gonzalo Fernández de Oviedo, *Historia general y natural de las Indias* (1535), book 2, chapter 3. See also Lupher (2006), 214–19.
93 See Introduction, 17.
94 Walcott (1962), 55.
95 Walcott (1990), 64. See Introduction, 16.
96 Walcott (1965a), 36–7.
97 See Introduction, 23.
98 Walcott (1965a), 36.
99 Ibid.
100 Ibid., 37.
101 Ibid., 36. Walcott presumably has in mind the mosaic at the Villa Romana del Casale in Sicily, but the attribution to Pompeii conjures up the imagery of heat's destructive power.

102 Gates (2014), 56.
103 Walcott (1965a), 36.
104 Shakespeare (2017), 279 (III. iv.105–6).
105 Ibid., 164.
106 On Walcott's persistent concern with 'nothingness', especially in *Another Life* (1973), *The Gulf* (1969) and *In a Green Night* (1962), see Figueroa (1974).
107 Walcott (1965a), 37.
108 Baugh (2006), 51.
109 Walcott (1998), 9.
110 Ovid, *Metamorphoses* 1.452–67.
111 Thieme (1999), 81. See also Izevbaye (1980), 75–7.
112 On Walcott's adoption and adaptation of the figure of Robinson Crusoe in this essay and elsewhere, see Chapter 3, 104–7.
113 Walcott ([1965b] 1997), 39. See Baugh (2012), 71, on the way Walcott engages with, and recasts, Ralph Waldo Emerson's vision of history as being constituted of the actions of a few great men. On Walcott's refiguration of Crusoe in the poems 'Crusoe's Journal' and 'Crusoe's Island' in *The Castaway*, the essay 'The Figure of Crusoe', and the plays, *The Isle is Full of Noises* and *Pantomime*, see Chapter 3, 104–7 and 111–16.
114 Greenwood (2010), 178–80, offers a bleaker reading of the poem, seeing the ravages of the trees' transatlantic translation – rather than their endurance and survival – as being at its heart.
115 Walcott (1965a), 37.
116 Walcott (1969), 36–7.
117 Ibid. See Introduction, 23.
118 Okpewho (2002), 31.
119 Walcott (1969), 36.
120 For a contrasting reading, see Baugh (2006), 49, in which he argues that Walcott depicts Nature as 'eras[ing] and transcend[ing] history'.
121 Césaire ([1939] 2017), 126 and 127. It is worth noting that Davis dedicates his translation of *Cahier* to Walcott, in gratitude for the inspiration he drew from Walcott's own translation of the poem's refrain 'petit matin' (xv), offered in Walcott (1997b), reprinted in Walcott (1998), 219.
122 Césaire ([1939] 2017), 252.
123 Walcott (2009).
124 Baugh (1978), 28.
125 Thieme (1999), 231 n. 14, quoting from Walcott (2009), 31.
126 Walcott (2009), 16.
127 Ibid., 236: notes on chapter 3 at 236.

128 Walcott (2009), 17–18, ll.352–63.
129 Ibid., 17–20, ll.413, 368, 442.
130 Ibid., 20, ll.461–2.
131 Ibid., 22, ll.503–5.
132 On *The Odyssey: A Stage Version*, see Chapter 2, 93–101.
133 Hardwick (2007), 65.
134 See Chapter 1, n.7.
135 Walcott (1998), 36.
136 Ibid., 62. For an example of the criticism levelled at Walcott, see the scathing review of his 1965 play, *Batai*, by Trinidadian playwright and scholar, Errol Hill, in 'No Tears for Narcissus', *Sunday Guardian*, 7 March 1965. Hill describes the play as an 'unmitigated calamity', remarking that Walcott is 'buttered up by the culture of Athens. For his *Batai* script parades a host of classical allusions that include Aeneas, Dido, Cassandra, Minerva, Juno and Venus, Anchises and a Sybil. Only Narcissus is missing.' The reproach must also be read, however, in light of the personal relationship between the two and Walcott's own negative review of the revised script of Hill's *Man Better Man* which he deemed to be 'doggerel' before even seeing it performed – see Rohlehr (1985), 30.
137 See also D'Aguiar (1991), 165: 'the bias in the idea of an unknowable past or a grand past belonging to another world is neutralised'.
138 Glissant (1981), 133.
139 Translation by Dash in Glissant (1999), 65.
140 The talk went on to be published as Baugh (2012), having originally been published in two parts in *Tapia* on 20 and 27 February 1977, at 6–7 and 6, 7, 11, respectively, available online: https://dloc.com/UF00072147/00265 and https://dloc.com/UF00072147/00264 (accessed 7 October 2022).
141 Glissant (1981), 132.
142 Translation by Dash in Glissant (1999), 64.
143 Walcott (1998), 37; Glissant (1981), 138: 'Remarquons que, donné de la conscience historique en formation, le Mythe préfigure l'histoire autant qu'il en répète nécessairement les accidents qu'il a transfigurés, c'est-à-dire qu'il est à son tour producteur d'histoire.' Translated by Dash in Glissant (1999), 71: 'We should note that, given the formative process of a historical consciousness, myth anticipates history as much as it inevitably repeats the accidents that it has glorified; that means it is in turn a producer of history.'
144 Glissant (1981), 132.
145 Translation by Dash in Glissant (1999), 64.
146 This methodology is embodied in the history of Pound's phrase itself, which he openly adopted from an anecdote about the first king of the Shang dynasty,

Ch'eng T'ang, who was said to have had the phrase inscribed on a basin. See North (2013), 162–5.
147 Walcott (1998), 62, cf. 36: 'maturity is the assimilation of the features of every ancestor', quoted in Introduction, 3.
148 Walcott (1974), 9.
149 On Carnival, see Hill ([1972b] 1997).
150 Walcott (1974), 10.
151 Ibid., 7.
152 On *Epitaph for the Young*, see Chapter 2, 74–6.
153 Henriksen (2006), xxii.
154 Glissant (1981), 256.
155 Glissant (1999), 146.
156 Dash (1998), 16.
157 Breslin (1987), 172, observes that modernist literature's status as 'already an adversary literature' was one of its appeals for Walcott.
158 On Joyce's intermittent inclusion of the Homeric scheme, see Ellman (1977), 568–70. On Joyce and Graeco-Roman antiquity, see most recently, Flack (2020).
159 Eliot ([1923] 1975), 177.
160 Ibid., 178.
161 See Seeger (2018) on the non-linear conception of time articulated in Joyce's *Ulysses* and *Finnegan's Wake* and Walcott's *Omeros* and *Tiepolo's Hound*.
162 Thelwell (1987), 222. One of the epigraphs to Thelwell's essay is attributed to Walcott, though without full details of citation: 'A writer dies inside when he betrays, like a paid spy, the rhythm of his race.'
163 Burnett (2000a), 98.
164 Pollard (2004), 45–50.
165 Eliot ([1919] 1975), 38.
166 Pollard (2004), 9 and *passim*.
167 See Gikandi (1992), 8–9, on Walcott's rejection of this European model of history.
168 Walcott (1997a), 241.
169 Walcott (1974), 8–9; Naipaul ([1962] 2001), 20.
170 For discussion of the Caribbean and modernity, including in Walcott's *Tiepolo's Hound*, see Fumagalli (2009), the subtitle of which presumably takes inspiration from Walcott's analogy of history as Medusa.
171 Walcott (1998), 37.
172 Ibid., 37.
173 Ibid., 38.
174 Ibid.

175 Borges ([1951] 1999), 420–7, 420: 'we read that we Argentines possess a classic poem, *Martín Fierro*, and that this poem should be for us what the Homeric poems were for the Greeks'. On Borges' engagement with the Graeco-Roman world, see Jansen (2018).
176 For an excellent exploration of mimicry in Walcott's work, see Terada (1992). As she explains at the start (2): 'for Walcott mimicry, with all its ambivalent freight, replaces mimesis as the ground of representation and culture'. See further, Chapter 3, 110–11.
177 Walcott (1998), 38.
178 King (2000), 333: the versions entitled 'Sour Grapes' were published in *American Poetry Review*, 1.5 (January–February 1976); and *London Magazine*, 15.6 (February–March 1976).
179 Aesop, 'The Fox and the Grapes' (no. 15 in Perry Index).
180 Walcott (1976), 3.
181 Greenwood (2005), 134.
182 On the ways in which 'Sea Grapes' and *Omeros* are in intertextual dialogue with each other, see Greenwood (2005), 136–41.
183 Ibid., 135.
184 Thomas (1991), 85–6. On the themes of obsession and responsibility as motifs within both the *Iliad* and *Odyssey*, see Greenwood (2005), 143 n.13.
185 Baugh (2006), 223.
186 Horkheimer and Adorno (2002), 47.
187 Ibid., 52–4.
188 Ibid., 35.
189 Ibid., 4: 'For the Enlightenment, only what can be encompassed by unity has the status of an existent or an event; its ideal is the system from which everything and anything follows.'
190 Ibid., 1–2: 'Enlightenment, understood in the widest sense as the advance of thought, has always aimed at liberating human beings from fear and installing them as masters. [...] What human beings seek to learn from nature is how to use it to dominate wholly both it and human beings. Nothing else counts.'
191 Walcott (1976), 3.
192 On the publication history of *Cahier*, which renders 1939 the date of only the earliest, rather than the definitive, edition, see Arnold (2004) and (2008).
193 See McConnell (2013), 7–9, 39–69.
194 Walcott (1981), 25–7.
195 See Chapter 1, 51–2.
196 Walcott (1981), 25.

197 Thieme (1999), 167; Borges ([1939] 1998) originally published in *Sur*, 56 (May 1939): 7–16.
198 Gikandi (1992), 6.
199 Joyce, *Ulysses* ([1922] 1992), 48.
200 Walcott (1996b).
201 Joyce ([1922] 1992), 48.
202 Walcott (1996b), 23, emphasis added. Equally, it would be wrong to read too much into this alteration because the published essay is transcribed from a recording of Walcott's talk at York University in Toronto (18 January 1989), and although often meticulous about checking proofs, the alteration may have been made by the transcriber rather than Walcott himself. The possibility that he quoted the phrase without checking is occluded by the precise page reference being given, though again, this could be the hand of the transcriber.
203 Walcott (1996b), 23.
204 Walcott (1979), 25–8.
205 Walcott (1979), 25. Man-made monumentality is also a subject of Walcott's 'Names', published in Walcott (1976), 32–4; see Greenwood (2010), 50–1.
206 White (1996), 158.
207 Posmentier (2020), 108–12.
208 Walcott (1990) 325.
209 See Chapter 1, 59.
210 Walcott (1979), 8. On 'The Schooner *Flight*', see Chapter 2, 87–90.

Chapter 2

1 For a succinct potted history of the use of the term 'syncretism', including its revalorization in the twentieth century, see Balme (1999), 7–13; and in the context of religious studies especially, Shaw and Stewart (1994).
2 Benítez-Rojo (1996), 12. Cf. See García Canclini (2005), xxiv–xxxiv, who, in his exploration of Latin American modernity, opts for the term 'hybridity', regarding it as more able to encompass his concern with technology and the social processes of modernity; for García Canclini, 'syncretism', *contra* Benítez-Rojo, is still primarily related to systems of belief.
3 Clifford (1988), 173. As Greenwood (2010), 251 notes, there is an ironic echo of Shelley's 'We are all Greeks' in Clifford's pronouncement.
4 Stewart (1999), 40–1.
5 Glissant (1981), 250–1.

6 Glissant (1999), 140–1.
7 Balme (1999), 8.
8 JanMohamed (1985), 85.
9 Ortiz (1995), 97–103.
10 Ibid., 102–3. See Pérez Firmat (1989), 22–3, on *transculturación*'s highlighting of the process of transition, rather than the synthesis of cultures itself.
11 Benítez-Rojo (1996), 9.
12 Omotoso (1982), 12. Bernabé, Chamoiseau and Confiant (1993), 8/28, write of the 'kaleidoscopic totality' ('totalité kaléidoscopique') of the region.
13 Here I depart from Gregory D. Alles' conception of syncretism, explored in relation to Walcott's work. Alles (2001), 442, sees syncretism as involving the combination of disparate traditions but does not regard invention and innovation as aspects of it.
14 Dash (1998), 5.
15 On the way in which this is an ever-unfinished process, see Hall (1990), 235: 'Diaspora identities are those which are constantly producing and reproducing themselves anew, through transformation and difference.'
16 Walcott (1998), 69.
17 Brathwaite (1975), 1.
18 Benítez-Rojo (1996), 189.
19 Glissant (1999), 142; Glissant (1981), 252. See Dash (1996) on the way in which Walcott's work develops an 'aesthetic of renascence and metamorphosis', as Dash terms it, drawing on Wilson Harris' work (49).
20 Walcott (1990), 325.
21 Walcott (1948).
22 Walcott ([1949] 2002–3).
23 Ismond (2001), 25–6.
24 See Breslin (2001), 63.
25 Walcott ([1949] 2002–3), 21.
26 Sixty years later, in the eponymous poem of *White Egrets* (2010), 6–10, Walcott alluded to Eumaeus once again, now featuring as 'a third companion' to Walcott and his friend, the poet Joseph Brodsky, figuring as 'the unutterable word' death. In the poem, Walcott recalls Brodsky's astonishment upon spotting a white egret that seemed to him a bird from a Hieronymus Bosch artwork, 'a sepulchral egret or heron'.
27 Hirsch (1996), 53.
28 Walcott ([1949] 2002–3), 35–8.
29 Ibid., 35.
30 See further, Fumagalli (2002–3).
31 Walcott ([1949] 2002–3), 36.

32 Alleyne (1949), 267.
33 Brown (1991a), 21.
34 King (2000), 101. The poem was first published in *Public Opinion*, 15 December 1956, 7.
35 Walcott (1998), 69; Walcott (1990), 28; Walcott (1986), 209–312. On the latter, see Chapter 2, 90–1.
36 Walcott (1962), 18.
37 Breslin (2001), 61.
38 See ibid., 60–2, for an illuminating reading of the way poetic style embodies the poem's shifting sentiments.
39 Walcott (1962), 18.
40 On the way in which this dynamic underpins Walcott's oeuvre, see Ismond (2001), 17–18, 41–2.
41 Brathwaite, quoted in Ismond (1971), 62; see Introduction, 33.
42 Hill (1965); see Chapter 1, n.136.
43 Brand (1984–5).
44 Walcott ([1970c] 1997), 50.
45 See Laplantine and Nouss (1997), 10, and 15 on the way that syncretism (*métissage*, in their terms) includes confrontation.
46 On Walcott's use of English metre in this poem and elsewhere, and the way in which it suggests a greater adherence to the British elements of his identity in 'A Far Cry from Africa', see Roberts (2002–3).
47 Walcott (1962), 19–20. Originally published in *New World Writing: Tenth Mentor Selection* (New York: New American Library, 1956), 159–60.
48 Walcott (1962), 20.
49 Ibid.
50 Ibid., 19.
51 Horace, *Satires* 1.4.62.
52 Most (1992).
53 See Brand (1984–5), and on Dionne Brand's critical intertextual engagement with 'Ruins of a Great House' in her poem and short story, both entitled 'St Mary's Estate', published in 1978 and 1988, respectively, see Gingell (1994).
54 On 'A Far Cry from Africa', see Chapter 2, 76–8.
55 Walcott (1962), 20.
56 Ismond (2001), 41.
57 Walcott (n.d.).
58 Wetmore, Jr. (2003), 222, disagrees with this last assessment, seeing in *Ione*, a 'refusal to allow the source material to dominate the new creation'.
59 Rae ([1957] 1997), 113.

60 Derek Walcott, 'Modern Theatre', *Daily Gleaner*, 25 March 1957. Held in the Derek Walcott Special Collections at the University of the West Indies, Mona (Envelope 21).
61 Walcott (n.d.).
62 Euripides, *Bacchae* 1135–8:

> πᾶσα δ' ἡματωμένη
> χεῖρας διεσφαίριζε σάρκα Πενθέως.
>
> κεῖται δὲ χωρὶς σῶμα, τὸ μὲν ὑπὸ στύφλοις
> πέτραις, τὸ δ' ὕλης ἐν βαθυξύλῳ φόβῃ

> And all with bloodied hands were playing games
> By tossing hunks of the flesh of Pentheus.
> His corpse lies scattered among the rugged rocks
> And deep within the forest in thick foliage (Trans. Gibbons and Segal, 2009: 288)

63 Scott (1968), 77. Dennis Scott's adaptation of the Clytemnestra story, *The Crime of Anabel Campbell*, premiered a couple of years after this interview in 1970, and is published in Noel (1985), 24–42.
64 The published text of *Ione* offers an English translation of the Creole passages in parenthesis, although these may not have been voiced at performances where the Creole was delivered.
65 See Chapter 2, 98.
66 Bérard (2009), 117–18.
67 Breslin (2001), 90.
68 Rae ([1957] 1997), 113.
69 Walcott (n.d.), dedication page. For a discussion of the ways Hill's advocacy of the traditions of carnival contrast with Walcott's rejection of Afrocentrism, see Omotoso (1982), *passim*, especially 51, 79, 161.
70 Hill (1972a), 15.
71 Hill ([1972b] 1997), 115. Despite the overarching sentiment of this pronouncement, the binary of 'folk' and 'art' forms is uncomfortable, indicating Hill's own separation of the two – a bias that may also be seen in his depiction of Diable Papa in *Man Better Man*, the initial prose version of which was first performed, like *Ione*, in 1957. On the latter, see further, Canfield (2001).
72 Hill (1972a), 9–10.
73 Walcott (1996a), 270–1.
74 Lévi-Strauss (1955), 435.
75 Walcott (1970b), 81–166.

76 King (1995), 17, mentions that Walcott wrote *Ti-Jean and His Brothers* over the course of just three days while staying in New York in September 1957.
77 Walcott (1970a).
78 Walcott (1970b), 85.
79 See Chapter 2, 99.
80 Walcott (1998), 9.
81 Walcott (1970a), 7; Breslin (2001), 90–6.
82 Walcott (1970b), 99.
83 Walcott (1998), 21, discusses the folkloric persistence of the figure of three in his essay, 'What the Twilight Says': 'The true folktale concealed a structure as universal as the skeleton, the one armature from Br'er Anancy to King Lear. It kept the same digital rhythm of three movements, three acts, three moral revelations, whether it was the tale of three sons or of three bears, whether it ended in tragedy or happily ever after.'
84 On Dionysus' close association with trees, see Frazer (2009), 396–7.
85 Walcott (1969), 50–1.
86 In 1969, St Omer had already spent several years teaching in France and Ghana before returning to St Lucia and then leaving to pursue a PhD at Princeton University, New Jersey, in the United States.
87 Walcott (1969), 50.
88 Ibid., 51.
89 Ibid.
90 Davis (2007), 204.
91 Ibid., 206. As Davis also notes, the hallucinatory nature of this vision of 'dead fisherman' seen when 'dazed' by the sun, will recur in *Omeros* in the scenes of Achille's sunstroke-induced vision of journeying to Africa.
92 King (2000), 236.
93 Walcott (1979), 3–20. An audio recording of Walcott performing the poem at the University of the West Indies, Mona, in 2006 is available at the Library of the Spoken Word at the University of the West Indies, Mona.
94 For illuminating analyses, see Breslin (2001), 189–214; Ismond (2001), 229–48; Thieme (1999), 162–4.
95 Brathwaite ([1984] 2011), 10.
96 Walcott (1979), 4.
97 Breslin (2001), 189–94.
98 Breiner (2005), 36–7.
99 Ibid., 40.
100 Thieme (1999), 162–3.
101 Hall (2015), 16, emphasis in original.

102 Despite this equality of 'value' endorsed by Walcott's writing, Olaniyan (1995), 114–15, rightly observes that it is to European traditions that Walcott most often turns, even if Olaniyan slightly overstates the case in seeing this as 'thoroughly ideological'.
103 Walcott (1979), 12.
104 Ovid, *Metamorphoses* 10.106–42.
105 On the significance of naming within Walcott's work, see Chapter 3.
106 Walcott (1979), 4.
107 Ibid., 3. As Breslin (2001), 195, points out, this imagery of death is consolidated by the idea of Shabine seeing himself in the rearview mirror as if he is already a figure of the past, and by the driver of that route taxi exclaiming to him that this time, '"you really gone!"'
108 On the personal level, the poem is wracked with guilt over Shabine's abandonment of his wife and children, whom he left to be with Maria Concepcion before likewise abandoning her.
109 Walcott (1979), 4.
110 Ibid., 19.
111 Bhabha (1994), 9. On 'unhomeliness' in postcolonial poetry, see Ramazani (2001), 12–18.
112 Walcott (1979), 19.
113 Ibid., 140. This alteration to the Homeric conception of home might be seen to be foreshadowed in another moment in the poem that engages with Graeco-Roman mythology, as Shabine dreams 'of three old women | featureless as silkworms, stitching my fate' (ibid.: 16) who he desperately tries in vain to usher out of his house, attempting to reject the future spun by the three Fates.
114 Walcott (1986), 209–312.
115 The story of Antony and Cleopatra features in Walcott's poem 'Egypt, Tobago', too (Walcott 1979: 29–32).
116 Walcott (1986), 268.
117 Stone (1994), 127, identifies three other plays of Walcott's that also 'rais[e] the question of compatibility between the classical and the creole': *Remembrance* (first performed in 1977), *Pantomime* (1978) and *Steel* (1991, unpublished).
118 Walcott (1986), 246.
119 Ibid., 247.
120 For a Bakhtinian reading of the play's polyphony, see Breslow (1989). Like Thieme (1999), 139 and 228 n.107, I see Christopher as having written two plays (his comedy and the play we are watching), rather than the three that Breslow identifies (the third being the tape-recorded transcription from which, in my reading of the play, Christopher writes his play, *A Branch of the Blue Nile*).

121 Thieme (1999), 178.
122 Walcott (1988), 38.
123 Chamoiseau (1982). On the play's engagement with Greek myth, see McConnell (2020).
124 Walcott (1997b).
125 Walcott (1988), 39.
126 Ibid.
127 See Introduction.
128 Burnett (2000b), 113.
129 First performed in July 1992, the playscript was published the following year by Faber and Faber as Walcott (1993).
130 Ibid., 9.
131 James (1954); and Diop (1974). See further, including on the nineteenth-century African American precursors to Bernal's work, Berlinerblau (1999), 133–46; and on the Haitian intellectual, Joseph Auguste Anténor Firmin, see Delices (2021) and Hawkins (2024), 78–98.
132 See Adler (2016), 113–72.
133 Burnett (2000a), 281.
134 Burian (1999), 72.
135 On the correspondences and similarities between the Caribbean and the Mediterranean, see also Lewis (1983), 16–20.
136 Burnett (2000b), 118.
137 Ibid., 119.
138 *Odyssey* 4.80–91, 126–7, 227–32.
139 Walcott (1997a), 234.
140 This is a point missed by many of the more negative reviews of the play, which sometimes objected to such syncretism of ancient and modern, European and Caribbean, perceiving it as leading to a 'lack of coherence' (Nightingale, 1992), or regarding it as a 'misguided melange of Homer and West Indian patois' (Gussow 1992).
141 Ortiz (1995), 102–3.
142 Alexander (2007b), 36.
143 See Introduction, 31ff.
144 Hirsch (1986), reprinted in Baer (1996), 120, ellipsis in original.
145 Balme (1999), 2.
146 Walcott (1990), 271.
147 Martyniuk (2005), 188.
148 Said (1994), 60.

149 On this aspect of Walcott's play, as well as its counterpart in Homer's epic, see Burian (1999), 77.
150 Walcott (1993), 160.
151 Bhabha (1984).
152 On the Homeric Odysseus as a protocolonial figure, see Malkin (1998), especially 3–5.
153 However, unlike in Bhabha's theorization, much of the colonial mimicry that Walcott's Odysseus comes to perceive, is in his mind, reflecting Walcott's concern with the psychological in this play.
154 Bhabha (1984), 127, at 129: 'the excess or slippage produced by the *ambivalence* of mimicry (almost the same, *but not quite*) does not merely "rupture" the discourse, but becomes transformed into an uncertainty which fixes the colonial subject as a "partial" presence'; 'The *menace* of mimicry is its *double* vision which in disclosing the ambivalence of colonial discourse also disrupts its authority', emphasis in the original.
155 Walcott (1993), 153. By contrast, in Homer's *Odyssey* Eurycleia assures Penelope that she would have been delighted by the sight of Odysseus surrounded by the corpses of the suitors:

> ἰδοῦσά κε θυμὸν ἰάνθης
> αἵματι καὶ λύθρῳ πεπαλαγμένον ὥς τε λέοντα.

> You would have been
> thrilled if you saw him, like a lion, drenched
> in blood and gore.
> (*Odyssey* 23.47–48, trans. Wilson 2018: 496).

156 Walcott (1993), 153.
157 Foley (1978); Hardwick (2007), 61–2.
158 Foley (1978), 8.
159 On combat trauma as a latent theme of the ancient epic that has received significant attention in recent decades, and the ways in which Odysseus' hallucinations in Walcott's play can be regarded as a symptom of combat trauma, see McConnell (2012).
160 Said (1994), 60, cited above in Chapter 2, 96.
161 Césaire (1955), 21, emphasis in original.
162 Césaire ([1950] 2000), 41, emphasis in original.
163 Walcott (1993), 151.
164 Burian (1999), 77.
165 Césaire ([1950] 2000), 42.

166 Hardwick (2000), 113–25, 118.
167 Walcott (1996a), 270. See also Hirsch (1996), 57: 'I was lucky to be born as a poet in a tradition that uses poetry as demonstration, as theater.'
168 Chamoiseau (1988).
169 Walcott, quoted in Burnett (2000b), 116.
170 Carpentier (1967), 114.
171 Chapon (2017), 462–7.
172 Stewart (1999), 49.
173 Ortiz (1995), 103, offers the coinage, 'neoculturation', for this aspect of syncretism.
174 See further, Miller (2001).
175 Chapon (2017).
176 Walcott (1993), 1.
177 Ibid. See Macintosh and McConnell (2020), 119–20.
178 Abrahams (1983).
179 Ibid., xxxi: 'the personae taken by the men-of-words in each case differ from those of stage characters, and the qualities of these enactments differ precisely because they are not theatrical but engage the audience in an entirely different manner'.
180 See Hardwick (1997), 337, on the double-casting of the Cyclops with the swineherd Arnaeus (rather than one of the suitors, for example) illustrating, again, that the self and other are closer than such projections like to admit.
181 Fiorindi (2011). As Burian (1999), 80, remarks, 'Billy Blue's embodiment of Phemius and Demodocus is emblematic of the openness and dynamism of the synthesis towards which Walcott moves us.'
182 See Hamner (2001), 387, on the way this Brechtian aspect highlights the intertextual nature of Walcott's play.
183 Walcott (1993), 2–6 and 93; McConnell (2013), 135–42.
184 Walcott (1993), 60 and 62.
185 Ibid., 62: 'This is the era of the grey colonels.'
186 Ibid., 61–2. See Giannopoulou (2006), 7, on the way that the ideas from 'The Muse of History' (see Chapter 1, 58–64) resonate through the Philosopher's pronouncement that, 'With History erased, there's just the present tense,' rendering it a celebration rather than a lament.
187 Walcott (1993), 62.
188 Davis (1995), 36.
189 Walcott (1993), 155.
190 Burnett (2000b), 117.

191 Hardwick (2007), 64.
192 Nightingale (1992); and Taylor (1992). See further, Reed (2018).
193 Burnett (2000b), 118.
194 Lévi-Strauss (1955), 435.

Chapter 3

1 Walcott (1990), 248.
2 See Introduction, 29–30.
3 Ramazani (2001), 58–60.
4 Walcott (1965a), 51–3, 54–7.
5 Walcott (1980), 89–170; Walcott (1965a), 51–3 and 54–7; Walcott ([1965b] 1997). See Okpewho (2002), 40 n. 2.
6 Ismond (2001), 48.
7 Walcott (1965a), 51.
8 Ibid.
9 Walcott ([1965b] 1997).
10 On colonial mimicry, see Bhabha (1984); on the carnivalesque, see Bakhtin (1984).
11 See MacQueen-Pope (1957), 456, who highlights pantomime's connection with the Roman festival of the Saturnalia, which he describes as 'a topsy-turvey affair when the world went upside down, when women dressed as men and men as women, when slaves became the masters and masters waited on their slaves'; and Ardener (2016).
12 Rohlehr (2001).
13 Breslin (2001), 120.
14 Vásquez (2012), 129.
15 Walcott (1980), 126.
16 Ibid., 124.
17 Ibid., 125.
18 Tiffin (1987), 17.
19 See Chapter 2, 71–2.
20 Walcott (1970b), 207–326.
21 Ngũgĩ ([1952] 1986).
22 Walcott (1970b), 3–40.
23 Ibid., 17.
24 Ibid.
25 See Chapter 2, 76–8.

26 Du Bois ([1903] 2003), 9.
27 Fanon (1986), 112: 'completely dislocated, unable to be abroad with the other, the white man, who unmercifully imprisoned me, I took myself far off from my own presence, far indeed, and made myself an object'.
28 Walcott (1970b), 226. Breslin (2001), 138, rightly notes that Makak is 'a sort of anti-Narcissus'.
29 Walcott (1970b), 226.
30 Ibid., 210.
31 See Chapter 2, 98.
32 Walcott (1970b), 236.
33 See Terada (1992), 26–7, on Walcott's shifting attitude to Africa over the course of his career.
34 Breiner (1991), 80.
35 Walcott (1970b), 271.
36 Ibid., 305.
37 Olaniyan (1995), 104–9.
38 On the gendered violence of this moment, and the way in which, throughout much of Walcott's (earlier) work, his depictions of women are 'full of clichés, stereotypes, and negativity', and 'the White man seems less culpable in Walcott's world' in comparison to White women, see Savory Fido (1986), 110, 117 and *passim*; and Olaniyan (1995), 109.
39 Breslin (2001), 155.
40 Walcott (1970b), 326.
41 Breslin (2001), 154.
42 Walcott (1974), 6.
43 Terada (1992), 1.
44 Griffith (2020), 305.
45 Walcott (1974), 9.
46 Reprinted in Kristeva (1980), 36–63, at 36.
47 Walcott (1998), 40–1.
48 King (2000), 325, 411.
49 See Chapter 3, 104–7.
50 Homer, *Iliad* 2.716–8; and *Odyssey* 3.190 and 8.219–20.
51 Greenwood (2007), 193–5.
52 Ibid., 195.
53 See Introduction, 23 and Chapter 1, 56–7.
54 Although the play is set on the fictional island of Santa Marta, the naming of 'Pigeon Island', a real version of which sits just north of Gros Islet in St Lucia, ensures that Walcott's homeland is kept in the forefront of one's mind, even while

the play's exploration of tourism and corruption is seen to be relevant to many islands across the region.

55 Derek Walcott, *The Isle is Full of Noises*. Script held in the Derek Walcott Collection at the Alma Jordan Library, University of the West Indies at St Augustine, Trinidad, Box 5, Folder 8, p. 5. A version of the script is now also available online via Alexander Street Press.

56 Sophocles (1990), 42–4, ll. 287–92.

57 Later in the play, Sir Geoffrey identifies himself with Ovid in exile, missing Sussex as Ovid longed for Rome, only to be corrected by his wife who has little time for such self-pitying self-aggrandizement: 'You weren't exiled. You're an ambassador. They don't exile ambassadors. They appoint them.' (Alexander Street Press version, p. 19.) In 'The Hotel Normandie Pool' (*The Fortunate Traveller*, 1981), written during the period of time that Walcott was developing *The Isle is Full of Noises*, he again evokes Ovid's exile, this time identifying with it himself.

58 Walcott, *The Isle is Full of Noises*, 3; Breslin (2001), 247.

59 See Introduction, 20, on this theme in *Omeros*.

60 Cf. Walcott ([1970c] 1997), 45: 'it is almost death to the spirit to try to survive as an artist under colonial conditions, which haven't really changed with our independent governments'.

61 Scott (2004). Analysing the alterations C. L. R. James made to the 1963 edition of *The Black Jacobins*, in particular to the opening of 'The War of Independence' chapter, Scott argues that James reframes Toussaint's story 'as one of tragedy rather than one of Romance' and recasts him as a figure 'of tragic suffering rather than one of revolutionary heroism', Scott (2004), 133–4.

62 Piñera (2008), 187. Piñera's play was first performed in Havana in 1948; see Andújar (2015).

63 King (2000), 412.

64 See Chapter 3, 104–5.

65 Dougherty (1997), 342.

66 See Chapter 2.

67 Césaire (1969), 28 (Act I, scene ii).

68 Césaire (1992), 15.

69 Walcott (1998), 9.

70 Walcott (1981), 53–60.

71 Walcott (1974), 9.

72 Walcott (1981), 53.

73 Dash (1996), 50.

74 Walcott (1981), 53.

75 King (2000), 394.

76 Vendler (1982).
77 Ibid., 23.
78 Ibid., 26. Vendler's objection to multilingualism coheres with Edward Said's characterization in *Culture and Imperialism* of her vision of literature more broadly, when he singles her out as a prominent proponent of novels as '*simply* the product of lonely genius', dislocated from their social context. See Said (1994), 87, emphasis in original.
79 Figueroa (1982), 84.
80 Walcott (1981), 54.
81 Thieme (1999), 20–1, 23.
82 Breslin (2001), 218.
83 Terada (1992), 109.
84 Figueroa (1995), 161.
85 Hutchinson (2015), 175.
86 Walcott (1998), 36. See further, Introduction, 3–4.
87 On 'A Latin Primer', see Chapter 3, 120–2.
88 Walcott (1981), 63–70. The poem was first published in the *New Yorker* in January 1981.
89 Terada (1992), 136.
90 Walcott (1981), 69.
91 See Chapter 2, 77–8.
92 Walcott (1981), 65.
93 See Chapter 2, 85–7.
94 Walcott (1969), 51.
95 Greenwood (2010), 109.
96 Walcott (1981), 66; Greenwood (2010), 109.
97 Walcott (1988), 21–4.
98 Ibid., 23. See Greenwood (2010), 81, for a comparison of 'A Latin Primer' with Howard Fergus' 'At Grammar School' and Tony Harrison's 'Classics Society', all of which reflect on the incongruity of Classics within their local environments.
99 Walcott (1988), 21.
100 Baugh (2006), 181.
101 Walcott (1988), 23–4.
102 See Chapter 1, 53–7.
103 Walcott (1988), 24.
104 See Chapter 2, 78–9. 'Ruins of a Great House' was written around the same time that 'A Latin Primer' refers back to. See King (2000), 100–1, for a trip that Walcott took to Guava Ridge (Jamaica) with the poet John Figueroa, who was his tutor on

the Diploma in Education that he was studying for at the University of the West Indies, Mona, and which inspired 'Ruins of a Great House'.
105 Walcott (1962), 19.
106 See also MᶜConnell (2018) for a discussion of these alongside Isaac Julien's *Paradise Omeros* and the Globe Theatre's staging of Walcott's poem.
107 The evocation of Haiti's Spiralist literature is productive here, not least in what Kaiama L. Glover calls its 'interplay of repetition and deviation', which brings to mind Henry Louis Gates, Jr.'s later notion of Signifying as 'repetition, with a signal difference'. See Glover (2010), viii.
108 The film was due to be produced by PBS but the project was never completed.
109 Manuscript Collection 136, Box 13, Folder 29, Derek Walcott Papers held at the Thomas Fisher Rare Book Library, University of Toronto.
110 Walcott (1990), 270–1.
111 Ibid., 230.
112 Antoine-Dunne (2013), 147. Walcott's later poem 'The Acacia Trees', published in *White Egrets* (2010), 11–13, at 11, makes the idea of tourism as new kind of slavery explicit: 'these new plantations | by the sea; a slavery without chains, with no blood spilt'.
113 On this doubling in Walcott's *Odyssey*, see Chapter 2, 100.
114 On adaptation, see Hutcheon with O'Flynn (2013) and Elliott (2020).
115 Hutcheon with O'Flynn (2013), 9.
116 For a précis of the creative processes of reception, see Willis (2018), 41–4.
117 Walcott (2005), 75.
118 Ibid., 76.
119 Ibid., 23–9, 28–9.
120 Ibid., 66.
121 Walcott (2010), 6: 'your tired eyes | behind two clouding lenses [...] | the quiet ravages of diabetes'.
122 On the collection's sense of unhomeliness, despite Walcott's protestations, see Erickson (2009).
123 Walcott ([2004] 2005), 99.
124 See Chapter 3, 119–20 and Chapter 1, 44 and n.37.
125 See Dash (1998), 101, on the way this sense of a collective relates to syncretism and creolization in the Caribbean:
'not only did the creole model depend on the collective as opposed to the individual, it also was less interested in direct challenges to the system than in cultural resistance within a context of domination. For the proponents of creolization, it is less the externally driven explicit rebellion of the maroon that is noteworthy; it is rather the internal, psychic processes that allowed groups not

only to endure but to actively engage in a more subtle, re-creative response to a hegemonic system'.

126 Walcott's final collection, in particular, seems to acknowledge this, with its poems for August Wilson, John Hearne, Lorna Goodison, Robert Antoni and Aimé Césaire – see Walcott (2010), 14, 75, 76, 85, 87.

Epilogue

1 Walcott (2009), 143.
2 For example, Goldhill (2002), 297, discussing those who have adopted Greekness as a facet of their cultural identity: '"Reception" is too blunt, too *passive* a term for the dynamics of resistance and appropriation,' emphasis in original.
3 Highet ([1949] 2015), 1.
4 Silk, Gildenhard and Barrow (2014) seek to reclaim the term 'the classical tradition', but their embrace of 'value' as a defining factor of 'the classical tradition' that is absent from 'reception' encapsulates why the term remains problematic for postcolonial engagements with Graeco-Roman antiquity, given the entanglement of notions of value with coloniality. See ibid., 5: 'whereas "classical" and "tradition" tend to prompt consideration of value, "reception" does not'; on the ways in which the two terms should be recognized as overlapping rather than starkly opposed, see Budelmann and Haubold (2008).
5 Eliot ([1919] 1975), 38.
6 On coloniality and the ways in which it refers to structures of power that grew out of colonialism but reach far beyond it, both temporally and in terms of the aspects of life that it governs, see Quijano (2000).
7 Menon (2006), 839; Matzner (2016).
8 Greenwood (2016).
9 Ibid., 43.
10 See, for example, Hutcheon with O'Flynn (2013).
11 Walcott (1998), 41.

Bibliography

Abani, Chris (2006), *The Myth of Fingerprints: Signifying as Displacement in Derek Walcott's Omeros*. Unpublished PhD diss., University of Southern California, Los Angeles.

Abrahams, Roger D. (1970), *Deep Down in the Jungle: Negro Narrative Folklore from the Streets of Philadelphia*, 2nd edn. New York: Aldine de Gruyter.

Abrahams, Roger D. (1983), *The Man-of-Words in the West Indies: Performance and the Emergence of Creole Culture*. Baltimore, MD, and London: Johns Hopkins University Press.

Adler, Eric (2016), *Classics, the Culture Wars, and Beyond*. Ann Arbor, MI: University of Michigan Press.

Aguirre, Mercedes, and Richard Buxton (2020), *Cyclops: The Myth and Its Cultural History*. Oxford: Oxford University Press.

Alexander, Elizabeth (2007a), *Power and Possibility: Essays, Reviews, and Interviews*. Ann Arbor, MI: University of Michigan Press.

Alexander, Elizabeth (2007b), 'The Genius of Romare Bearden', in *Power and Possibility: Essays, Reviews, and Interviews*, 33–44. Ann Arbor, MI: University of Michigan Press.

Alles, Gregory D. (2001), 'The Greeks in the Caribbean: Reflections on Derek Walcott, Homer and Syncretism', *Historical Reflections/Réflexions Historiques*, 27 (3): 425–52.

Alleyne, Keith (1949), '*Epitaph for the Young: A Poem in XII Cantos* by Derek Walcott', *Bim*, 3 (11): 267–72.

Amin, Samir (1989), *Eurocentrism*, Russell Moore (trans.). London: Zed Books.

Anderson, Benedict (2006), *Imagined Communities: Reflections on the Origins and Spread of Nationalism*, revd edn. London and New York: Verso.

Andújar, Rosa (2015), 'Revolutionizing Greek Tragedy in Cuba: Virgilio Piñera's *Electra*', in Kathryn Bosher, Fiona Macintosh, Justine McConnell and Patrice Rankine (eds), *The Oxford Handbook of Greek Drama in the Americas*, 361–79. Oxford: Oxford University Press.

Antoine-Dunne, Jean (2013), '"Overtones of the Visual Imagination": Or "Just Like the Movies"', in Jean Antoine-Dunne (ed.), *Interlocking Basins of a Globe: Essays on Derek Walcott*, 135–55. Leeds: Peepal Tree Press.

Appadurai, Arjun (1996), *Modernity at Large: Cultural Dimensions of Globalization*. Minneapolis, MN, and London: University of Minnesota Press.

Ardener, Shirley (2016), 'The English Christmas Pantomime: Toying with History, Playing with Gender, Laughing at Today', in Lidia Dina Sciama (ed.), *Humour, Comedy and Laughter: Obscenities, Paradoxes, Insights and the Renewal of Life*, 137–58. New York and Oxford: Berghahn.

Arnold, A. James (2004), 'Césaire's *Notebook* as Palimpsest: The Text before, during, and after World War II', *Research in African Literatures*, 35 (3): 133–40.

Arnold, A. James (2008), 'Beyond Postcolonial Césaire: Reading *Cahier d'un retour au pays natal* Historically', *Forum for Modern Language Studies*, 44 (3): 258–75.

Baer, William, ed. (1996), *Conversations with Derek Walcott*. Jackson, MS: University Press of Mississippi.

Bakhtin, Mikhail (1984), *Rabelais and His World*, Hélène Iswolsky (trans.). Bloomington, IN: Indiana University Press.

Balme, Christopher B. (1999), *Decolonizing the Stage: Theatrical Syncretism and Post-Colonial Dram*. Oxford: Clarendon Press.

Barkan, Elazar, and Ronald Bush (1995a), 'Introduction', in Elazar Barkan and Ronald Bush (eds), *Prehistories of the Future: The Primitivist Project and the Culture of Modernism*, 1–19. Stanford, CA: Stanford University Press.

Barkan, Elazar, and Ronald Bush, eds (1995b), *Prehistories of the Future: The Primitivist Project and the Culture of Modernism*. Stanford, CA: Stanford University Press.

Baugh, Edward (1978), *Derek Walcott: Memory as Vision: Another Life*. London: Longman.

Baugh, Edward (1990), 'Lorna Goodison in the Context of Feminist Criticism', *Journal of West Indian Literature*, 4 (1): 1–13.

Baugh, Edward (2005), 'Of Men and Heroes: Walcott and the Haitian Revolution', *Callaloo* 28 (1): 45–54.

Baugh, Edward (2006), *Derek Walcott*. Cambridge: Cambridge University Press.

Baugh, Edward (2012), 'The West Indian Writer and His Quarrel with History', *Small Axe*, 16, no. 2 (38): 60–74.

Beecroft, Alexander (2015), *An Ecology of World Literature: From Antiquity to the Present Day*. London and New York: Verso.

Benítez-Rojo, Antonio (1996), *The Repeating Island: The Caribbean and the Postmodern Perspective*, 2nd edn, James E. Maraniss (trans.). Durham, NC, and London: Duke University Press.

Bérard, Stéphanie (2009), *Théâtres des Antilles: Traditions et scènes contemporaines*. Paris: L'Harmattan.

Berlinerblau, Jacques (1999), *Heresy in the University: The Black Athena Controversy and the Responsibilities of American Intellectuals*. New Brunswick, NJ, and London: Rutgers University Press.

Bernabé, Jean, Patrick Chamoiseau and Raphaël Confiant (1993), *Éloge de la créolité / In Praise of Creoleness*, Mohamed B. Taleb Khyer (trans.), bilingual edn. Paris: Gallimard.

Bernal, Martin (1987), *Black Athena: The Afroasiatic Roots of Classical Civilization*, vol. 1. London: Free Association Books.

Bhabha, Homi (1984), 'Of Mimicry and Man: The Ambivalence of Colonial Discourse', *October*, 28 (Spring): 125–33.

Bhabha, Homi K. (1990a), 'DissemiNation: Time, Narrative, and the Margins of the Modern Nation', in Homi K. Bhabha (ed.), *Nation and Narration*, 291–322. Abingdon: Routledge.

Bhabha, Homi K., ed. (1990b), *Nation and Narration*. Abingdon: Routledge.

Bhabha, Homi K. (1994), *The Location of Culture*. London: Routledge.

Birbalsingh, Frank, ed. (1996), *Frontiers of Caribbean Literature in English*. London and Basingstoke: Macmillan.

Bongie, Chris (2005), '"Monotonies of History": Baron de Vastey and the Mulatto Legend of Derek Walcott's *Haitian Trilogy*', *Yale French Studies*, 107: 70–107.

Borges, Jorge Luis ([1939] 1998), 'Pierre Menard, Autor del *Quijote*', *Sur*, 56 (May 1939), 7–16, Andrew Hurley in Borges (trans.), *Collected Fictions*, 88–95. New York: Penguin.

Borges, Jorge Luis ([1951] 1999), 'The Argentine Writer and Tradition' (1951), reprinted in Eliot Weinberger (ed.) and Esther Allen, Suzanne Jill Levine and Eliot Weinberger (trans.), in Borges, *Selected Non-Fictions*, 420–7. New York and London: Penguin Viking.

Bowra, C. M. (1952), *Heroic Poetry*. London: Macmillan.

Brand, Dionne (1984–5), 'The Caribbean', *Poetry Canada Review*, 6 (2): 26.

Brathwaite, Edward (Kamau) (1963), 'Review of *In a Green Night* by Derek Walcott', *The Voice of St Lucia*, 13 April, 4.

Brathwaite, Edward (Kamau) (1971), *The Development of Creole Society in Jamaica, 1770–182*. Oxford: Oxford University Press.

Brathwaite, Edward (Kamau) (1973), *The Arrivants: A New World Trilogy*. Oxford: Oxford University Press.

Brathwaite, Edward Kamau (1975), 'Caribbean Man in Space and Time', *Savacou*, 11–12 (September): 1–11.

Brathwaite, Edward Kamau ([1984] 2011), *History of the Voice: The Development of Nation Language in Anglophone Caribbean Poetry*. London: New Beacon Books.

Breiner, Laurence A. (1991), 'Walcott's Early Drama', in Stewart Brown (ed.), *The Art of Derek Walcott*, 69–81. Glamorgan: Seren Books.

Breiner, Laurence A. (2005), 'Creole Language in the Poetry of Derek Walcott', *Callaloo*, 281 (1): 29–41.

Breslin, Paul (1987), '"I Met History Once, But He Ain't Recognise Me": The Poetry of Derek Walcott', *TriQuarterly*, 68 (Winter): 168–83.

Breslin, Paul (2001), *Nobody's Nation: Reading Derek Walcott*. Chicago, IL, and London: University of Chicago Press.

Breslin, Paul (2008), '"The First Epic of the New World": But How Shall It Be Written?', in Doris L. Garraway (ed.), *Tree of Liberty: Cultural Legacies of the Haitian Revolution in the Atlantic World*, 223–47. Charlottesville, NC, and London: University of Virginia Press.

Breslow, Stephen P. (1989), 'Trinidadian Heteroglossia: A Bakhtinian View of Derek Walcott's Play *A Branch of the Blue Nile*', *World Literature Today*, 63 (1): 36–9.

Britton, Celia (2020), 'History as Neurosis: Psychoanalysis and Marxism in Édouard Glissant's *Le Discours antillais*', *French Cultural Studies*, 31 (3): 199–209.

Brown, Stewart (1991a), 'The Apprentice: *25 Poems, Epitaph for the Young, Poems* and *In a Green Night*', in Stewart Brown (ed.), *The Art of Derek Walcott*, 13–33. Bridgend: Seren Books.

Brown, Stewart, ed. (1991b), *The Art of Derek Walcott*. Bridgend: Seren Books

Bruckner, D. J. R. (1990), 'A Poem in Homage to an Unwanted Man', *New York Times*, 9 October, 13, reprinted in Robert D. Hamner (ed.), *Critical Perspectives on Derek Walcott*, 396. Boulder, CO, and London: Lynne Rienner, 1997.

Buck-Morss, Susan (2009), *Hegel, Haiti, and Universal History*. Pittsburgh, PA: University of Pittsburgh Press.

Budelmann, Felix, and Johannes Haubold (2008), 'Reception and Tradition', in Lorna Hardwick and Christopher Stray (eds), *A Companion to Classical Receptions*, 13–25. Malden, MA, and Oxford: Blackwell.

Burian, Peter (1999), '"You Can Build a Heavy-Beamed Poem out of This": Derek Walcott's *Odyssey*', *Classical World*, 93 (1): 71–81.

Burnett, Paula (2000a), *Derek Walcott: Politics and Poetics*. Gainesville, FL: University Press of Florida.

Burnett, Paula (2000b), '"Walcott, Man of the Theatre": An Interview with Derek Walcott', *The Caribbean Writer*, 14: 113–19.

Callahan, Lance (2003), *In the Shadows of Divine Perfection: Derek Walcott's Omeros*. New York and London: Routledge.

'Calypso Songs Use Biting Satire to Criticise Colonial Rule' (1951), *Freedom*, 1, no. 2 (February): 6.

Canfield, Rob (2001), 'Theatralizing the Anglophone Caribbean, 1492 to the 1980s', in A. James Arnold (ed.), *A History of Literature in the Caribbean, Volume 2: English- and Dutch-Speaking Regions*, 285–326. Amsterdam and Philadelphia, PA: John Benjamins.

Carpentier, Alejo (1967), 'De lo real maravilloso americano', *Tientos y diferencias*, 103–21. Montevideo: Acra.

Carpentier, Alejo ([1949] 2017), *The Kingdom of This World*, Pablo Medina (trans.). New York: Farrar, Straus and Giroux.

Casteel, Sarah Phillips (2011), '"One Elegy from Aruac to Sioux": The Absent Presence of Indigeneity in Derek Walcott's Poetry and Drama', *Canadian Review of Comparative Literature / Revue Canadienne de Littérature Comparée*, 38 (1): 106–18.

Césaire, Aimé ([1939] 2017), *Cahier d'un retour au pays natal / Journal of a Homecoming*, N. Gregson Davis (trans.), with introduction, commentary, and notes by F. Abiola Irele. Durham, NC, London: Duke University Press.

Césaire, Aimé ([1950] 2000), *Discourse on Colonialism*, Joan Pinkham (trans.), with an introduction by Robin D. G. Kelley. New York: Monthly Review Press.

Césaire, Aimé (1955), *Discours sur le colonialisme*. Paris: Présence Africaine.

Césaire, Aimé (1969), *Une Tempête*. Paris: Éditions du Seuil.

Césaire, Aimé (1992), *A Tempest*, Richard Miller (trans.). New York: Theatre Communications Group.

Chakrabarty, Dipesh (2000), *Provincializing Europe: Postcolonial Thought and Historical Difference*. Princeton, NJ, and Oxford: Princeton University Press.

Chamoiseau, Patrick (1982), *Manman Dlo contre la fée Carabosse*. Paris: Éditions Caribéennes.

Chamoiseau, Patrick (1988), *Solibo Magnifique*. Paris: Gallimard.

Chapon, Cécile (2017), 'Méditerranée / Caraïbe: du canon à l'archipel', *Revue de littérature comparée*, 364 (4): 459–77.

Ciocia, Stephania (2000), 'To Hell and Back: The Katabasis and the Impossibility of Epic in Derek Walcott's *Omeros*', *Journal of Commonwealth Literature*, 35 (2): 87–103.

Clifford, James (1988), *The Predicament of Culture: Twentieth-Century Ethnography, Literature, and Art*. Cambridge, MA, and London: Harvard University Press.

Cobham-Sander, Rhonda (2013), '"Any Enemy So Was a Compliment": Walcott, Brathwaite, and the Formal Possibilities of Creole', in Jean Antoine-Dunne (ed.), *Interlocking Basins of a Globe: Essays on Derek Walcott*, 100–22. Leeds: Peepal Tree Press.

Cobham-Sander, Rhonda (2016), *I and I: Epitaphs for the Self in the Work of V.S. Naipaul, Kamau Brathwaite and Derek Walcott*. Kingston: University of the West Indies Press.

Coetzee, J. M. (2002), *Stranger Shores: Essays 1986–1999*. London: Vintage.
D'Aguiar, Fred (1991), 'Ambiguity without a Crisis? Twin Traditions, the Individual and Community in Derek Walcott's Essays', in Stewart Brown (ed.), *The Art of Derek Walcott*, 155–68. Bridgend: Seren Books.
Dacier, Anne (1711), *L'Iliade*, Paris: Rigaud.
Dash, J. Michael (1995), *Edouard Glissant*. Cambridge: Cambridge University Press.
Dash, J. Michael (1996), 'Psychology, Creolization, and Hybridization', in Bruce King (ed.), *New National and Post-Colonial Literatures: An Introduction*, 45–58. Oxford: Clarendon Press.
Dash, J. Michael (1998), *The Other America: Caribbean Literature in a New World Context*. Charlottesville, NC: University Press of Virginia.
Daut, Marlene L. (2015), *Tropics of Haiti: Race and the Literary History of the Haitian Revolution in the Atlantic World, 1789–1865*. Liverpool: Liverpool University Press.
Daut, Marlene L. (2021), 'Beyond Trouillot: Unsettling Genealogies of Historical Thought', *Small Axe*, 25, no. 1 (64): 132–54.
Davis, C. B. (1995), '"There is No 'I' after the 'Eye'" – The Cyclops as Dramatized by Euripides and Derek Walcott', *Text and Presentation: Journal of the Comparative Drama Conference*, 16: 32–8.
Davis, Gregson (1997), '"With No Homeric Shadow": The Disavowal of Epic in Derek Walcott's *Omeros*', *South Atlantic Quarterly*, 96 (2): 321–33.
Davis, Gregson (2007), '"Homecomings without Home": Representations of (Post) colonial *nostos* (Homecoming) in the Lyric of Aimé Césaire and Derek Walcott', in Barbara Graziosi and Emily Greenwood (eds), *Homer in the Twentieth Century: Between World Literature and the Western Canon*, 191–209. Oxford: Oxford University Press.
Davis, Gregson (2016), 'Forging a Caribbean Literary Style: "Vulgar Eloquence" and the Language of Césaire's *Cahier d'un retour au pays natal*', *South Atlantic Quarterly* 115 (3): 457–67.
Delices, Patrick (2021), 'At the Center of World History, before Diop, there was Firmin: Great Scholars on the Black African Origin of the Ancient Egyptians and Their Civilization', in Celucien L. Joseph and Paul C. Mocombe (eds), *Reconstructing the Social Sciences and Humanities: Anténor Firmin, Western Intellectual Tradition, and Black Atlantic Tradition*, 147–70. New York: Routledge.
Diop, Cheikh Anta (1974), *The African Origin of Civilization: Myth or Reality*, Mercer Cook (trans. and ed.). Westport, CT: Lawrence Hill.
Dougherty, Carol (1997), 'Homer after *Omeros*: Reading a H/Omeric Text', *South Atlantic Quarterly*, 96 (2): 335–57.
Du Bois, W.E.B. ([1903] 2003), *The Souls of Black Folk*, with an introduction and notes by Farah Jasmine Griffin. New York: Barnes & Noble.

Eastman, Helen (2015), 'Talking Greeks with Derek Walcott', in Kathryn Bosher, Fiona Macintosh, Justine McConnell and Patrice Rankine (eds), *The Oxford Handbook of Greek Drama in the Americas*, 807–16. Oxford: Oxford University Press.

Eliot, T. S. ([1919] 1975), 'Tradition and the Individual Talent', in Frank Kermode (ed.), *Selected Prose of T.S. Eliot*, 3–44. London: Faber & Faber.

Eliot, T. S. ([1923] 1975), '*Ulysses*, Order, and Myth', in Frank Kermode (ed.), *Selected Prose of T.S. Eliot*, 175–8. London: Faber & Faber.

Eliot, T.S. ([1944] 1975), 'What is a Classic?', in Frank Kermode (ed.), *Selected Prose of T.S. Eliot*, 115–31. London: Faber & Faber.

Elliott, Kamilla (2020), *Theorizing Adaptation*. Oxford: Oxford University Press.

Ellman, Richard (1977), 'Joyce and Homer', *Critical Inquiry*, 3 (3): 567–82.

Erickson, Peter (2009), 'The Power of Prodigality in the Work of Derek Walcott and Harry Berger', in Nina Levine and David Lee Miller (eds), *A Touch More Rare: Harry Berger, Jr. and the Arts of Interpretation*, 165–81. New York: Fordham University Press.

Euripides (1960), *Bacchae*, E. R. Dodds (ed.), 2nd edn, Oxford: Clarendon Press.

Fabian, Johannes ([1983] 2014), *Time and the Other: How Anthropology Makes Its Object*. New York: Columbia University Press.

Fanon, Frantz (1986), *Black Skin, White Masks*, Charles Lam Markmann (trans.). London: Pluto Press.

Fanon, Frantz (2001), *The Wretched of the Earth*, Constance Farrington (trans.). London: Penguin.

Farrell, Joseph (1999), 'Walcott's *Omeros*: The Classical Epic in a Postmodern World', in Margaret Beissinger, Jane Tylus and Susanne Wofford (eds), *Epic Traditions in the Contemporary World: The Poetics of Community*, 270–96. Berkeley, CA: University of California Press.

Figueroa, John (1974), 'A Note on Derek Walcott's Concern with Nothing', *Revista / Review Interamericana*, 4 (3): 422–8.

Figueroa, John (1982), 'Problems of a Writer who does not Quite . . .', *Ambit*, 91: 84–5.

Figueroa, John (1991), '*Omeros*', in Stewart Brown (ed.), *The Art of Derek Walcott*, 193–213. Bridgend: Seren Books.

Figueroa, John J. (1995), 'Creole in Literature: Beyond Verisimilitude: Texture and Varieties: Derek Walcott', *The Yearbook of English Studies*, 25: 156–62.

Fiorindi, Lisa Pike (2011), 'Derek Walcott's *The Odyssey: A Stage Version*: An Examination of the Function of Metaphor', *Wasafiri*, 26 (3): 20–4.

Flack, Leah Culligan (2020), *James Joyce and Classical Modernism*. London: Bloomsbury.

Foley, Helene P. (1978), '"Reverse Similes" and Sex Roles in the *Odyssey*', *Arethusa*, 11 (1–2): 7–26.

Frazer, James George (2009), *The Golden Bough: A Study in Magic and Religion*, abridged with an introduction and notes by Robert Fraser. Oxford: Oxford University Press.

Friedman, Rachel D. (2007), 'Derek Walcott's Odysseys', *International Journal of the Classical Tradition* 14 (3–4): 455–80.

Froude, James Anthony (1888), *The English in the West Indies: Or, The Bow of Ulysses*. London: Longmans, Green & Co.

Fumagalli, Maria Cristina (2001), *The Flight of the Vernacular: Seamus Heaney, Derek Walcott, and the Impress of Dant*. Amsterdam: Rodopi.

Fumagalli, Maria Cristina (2002–3), '*Epitaph for the Young*: Culture or Mimicry', in Maria Cristina Fumagalli (ed.), *Agenda: Special Issue on Derek Walcott*, 39 (1–3): 51–76.

Fumagalli, Maria Cristina (2009), *Caribbean Perspectives on Modernity: Returning Medusa's Gaze*. Charlottesville, NC, and London: University of Virginia Press.

García Canclini, Néstor (2005), *Hybrid Cultures: Strategies for Entering and Leaving Modernity*, Christopher L. Chiappari and Silvia L. Lopez (trans.). Minneapolis, MN, and London: University of Minnesota Press.

Gates, Jr., Henry Louis (1988), *The Signifying Monkey: A Theory of African-American Literary Criticism*. New York and Oxford: Oxford University Press.

Gates, Jr., Henry Louis (2014), *The Signifying Monkey: A Theory of African-American Literary Criticism*, Twenty-Fifth Anniversary Edition. New York: Oxford University Press.

Giannopoulou, Zina (2006), 'Intertextualising Polyphemus: Politics and Ideology in Walcott's *Odyssey*', *Comparative Drama*, 40 (1): 1–28.

Gibbons, Reginald and Charles Segal (2009), *Bacchae [Bakkai]*, reprinted in Peter Burian and Alan Shapiro (eds), *The Complete Euripides, Volume IV: Bacchae and Other Plays*, 199–346. Oxford: Oxford University Press.

Gikandi, Simon (1992), *Writing in Limbo: Modernism and Caribbean Literature*. Ithaca, NY, and London: Cornell University Press.

Gilroy, Paul (1993), *The Black Atlantic: Modernity and Double Consciousness*. London and New York: Verso.

Gingell, Susan (1994), 'Returning to Come Forward: Dionne Brand Confronts Derek Walcott', *Journal of West Indian Literature* 6 (2), 43–53.

Glissant, Édouard (1965), *Poèmes*. Paris: Éditions du Seuil.

Glissant, Édouard (1981), *Le Discours antillais*. Paris: Éditions du Seuil.

Glissant, Édouard ([1955] 1992), *The Indies*, Dominique O'Neill (trans.), followed by the original poem in French, *Les Indes*. Toronto: Éditions du Gref.

Glissant, Édouard ([1961] 1998), *Monsieur Toussaint*. Paris: Gallimard.

Glissant, Édouard (1999), *Caribbean Discourse: Selected Essays*, J. Michael Dash (trans.). Charlottesville, NC: University Press of Virginia.

Glover, Kaiama L. (2010), *Haiti Unbound: A Spiralist Challenge to the Postcolonial Canon*. Liverpool: Liverpool University Press.

Goff, Barbara (2005a), 'Introduction', in Barbara Goff (ed.), *Classics and Colonialism*, 1–24. London: Duckworth.

Goff, Barbara, ed. (2005b), *Classics and Colonialism*. London: Duckworth.

Goff, Barbara, and Michael Simpson (2007), *Crossroads in the Black Aegean: Oedipus, Antigone, and Dramas of the African Diaspora*. Oxford: Oxford University Press.

Goffe, Tao Leigh (2022), 'Stolen Life, Stolen Time: Black Temporality, Speculation, and Racial Capitalism', *South Atlantic Quarterly*, 121 (1): 109–30.

Goldhill, Simon (2002), *Who Needs Greek? Contests in the Cultural History of Hellenism*. Cambridge: Cambridge University Press.

Goodison, Lorna (1986), *I Am Becoming My Mother*. London: New Beacon Books.

Goody, Jack, and Ian Watt (1963), 'The Consequences of Literacy', *Comparative Studies in Society and History*, 5 (3): 304–45.

Gough, Kathleen (1968), 'Anthropology and Imperialism', *Monthly Review*, 19 (11): 1–27.

Graziosi, Barbara, and Emily Greenwood, eds (2007), *Homer in the Twentieth Century: Between World Literature and the Western Canon*. Oxford: Oxford University Press.

Greenwood, Emily (2005), '"Still Going On": Temporal Adverbs and the View of the Past in Walcott's Poetry', *Callaloo*, 28 (1): 132–45.

Greenwood, Emily (2007), 'Arriving Backwards: The Return of *The Odyssey* in the English-Speaking Caribbean', in Lorna Hardwick and Carol Gillespie (eds), *Classics in Post-Colonial Worlds*, 192–210. Oxford: Oxford University Press.

Greenwood, Emily (2010), *Afro-Greeks: Dialogues between Anglophone Caribbean Literature and Classics in the Twentieth Century*. Oxford: Oxford University Press.

Greenwood, Emily (2016), 'Reception Studies: The Cultural Mobility of Classics', *Daedalus* 145 (2): 41–9.

Griffin, Benjamin (2006), 'Moving Tales: Narrative Drift in Oral Culture and Scripted Theater', *New Literary History*, 37 (4): 725–38.

Griffith, Glyne (2020), 'Forging the Critical Canon', in Raphael Dalleo and Curdella Forbes (eds), *Caribbean Literature in Transition, 1920–1970*, vol. 2, 293–307. Cambridge: Cambridge University Press.

Gussow, Mel (1992), 'Critic's Notebook: Beggary Abounding Onstage, but Not Off, at Stratford-on-Avon', *New York Times*, 29 July, 15.

Hall, Edith (2008), 'Putting the Class into Classical Reception', in Lorna Hardwick and Christopher Stray (eds), *A Companion to Classical Receptions*, 386–97. Oxford: Blackwell.

Hall, Stuart (1990), 'Cultural Identity and Diaspora', reprinted in Jonathan Rutherford (ed.), *Identity: Community, Culture, Difference*, 222–37. London: Lawrence & Wishart.

Hall, Stuart (2015), 'Creolité and the Process of Creolization', reprinted in Encarnación Gutiérrez Rodríguez and Shirley Anne Tate (eds), *Creolizing Europe: Legacies and Transformations*, 12–25. Liverpool: Liverpool University Press.

Hamner, Robert D. (1993), *Derek Walcott*, 2nd edn. New York: Twayne.

Hamner, Robert (2001), 'Creolizing Homer for the Stage: Walcott's *The Odyssey*', *Twentieth-Century Literature*, 47 (3): 374–90.

Hamner, Robert D., ed. (1997), *Critical Perspectives on Derek Walcott*. Boulder, CO, and London: Lynne Rienner.

Hardwick, Lorna (1997), 'Reception as Simile: The Poetics of Reversal in Homer and Derek Walcott', *International Journal of the Classical Tradition*, 3 (3): 326–38.

Hardwick, Lorna (2000), *Translating Words, Translating Cultures*. London: Duckworth.

Hardwick, Lorna (2007), 'Singing across the Faultlines: Cultural Shifts in Twentieth-Century Receptions of Homer', in Barbara Graziosi and Emily Greenwood (eds), *Homer in the Twentieth Century: Between World Literature and the Western Canon*, 47–71. Oxford: Oxford University Press, 2007.

Hardwick, Lorna, and Carol Gillespie, eds (2007), *Classics in Post-Colonial Worlds*. Oxford: Oxford University Press.

Harris, Wilson (1999a), 'Quetzalcoatl and the Smoking Mirror: Reflections on Originality and Tradition', in Wilson Harris, *Selected Essays of Wilson Harris: The Unfinished Genesis of the Imagination*, Andrew Bundy (ed.), 177–87. London and New York: Routledge.

Harris, Wilson (1999b), *Selected Essays of Wilson Harris: The Unfinished Genesis of the Imagination*, introduced by Andrew Bundy (ed.). London and New York: Routledge.

Harris, Wilson (2003), *The Mask of the Beggar*, London: Faber & Faber.

Harris, Wilson E. (2008), 'History, Fable and Myth in the Caribbean and Guianas', *Caribbean Quarterly*, 54 (1–2): 5–38.

Hawkins, Tom (2024), *Hacking Classical Forms in Haitian Literature*. London: Routledge.

Henriksen, Line (2006), *Ambition and Anxiety: Ezra Pound's* Cantos *and Derek Walcott's* Omeros *as Twentieth-Century Epics*. Amsterdam: Rodopi.

Henry, Paget (2000), *Caliban's Reason: Introducing Afro-Caribbean Philosophy*. New York and London: Routledge.

Highet, Gilbert ([1949] 2015), *The Classical Tradition: Greek and Roman Influences on Western Literature*, with a new foreword by Harold Bloom. Oxford: Oxford University Press.

Hill, Errol (1965), 'No Tears for Narcissus', *Sunday Guardian*, 7 March.

Hill, Errol (1972a), 'The Emergence of a National Drama in the West Indies', *Caribbean Quarterly*, 18 (4): 9–40.

Hill, Errol ([1972b] 1997), *The Trinidad Carnival: Mandate for a National Theatre*. London: New Beacon Books.

Hirsch, Edward (1986), 'Derek Walcott, The Art of Poetry No. 37', *Paris Review*, 101 (Winter): 196–230, reprinted in William Baer ed. (1996), *Conversations with Derek Walcott*, 95–121. Jackson, MS: University Press of Mississippi.

Hirsch, Edward (1996), 'An Interview with Derek Walcott', in William Baer (ed.), *Conversations with Derek Walcott*, 50–63. Jackson: University Press of Mississippi.

Homer (1963a), *Odyssey*, D. B. Munro and T. W. Allen (eds), 2nd edn. Oxford: Clarendon Press.

Homer (1963b), *Iliad*, D. B. Munro and T. W. Allen (eds), 3rd edn. Oxford: Clarendon Press.

Horkheimer, Max, and Theodor W. Adorno (2002), *Dialectic of Enlightenment: Philosophical Fragments*, Gunzelin Schmid Noerr (ed.) and Edmund Jephcott (trans.). Stanford, CA: Stanford University Press.

Hutcheon, Linda (1985), *A Theory of Parody: The Teachings of Twentieth-Century Art Forms*. New York: Methuen.

Hutcheon, Linda, with Siobhan O'Flynn (2013), *A Theory of Adaptation*, 2nd edn. London and New York: Routledge.

Hutchinson, Ishion (2015), 'A Voice at the Edge of the Sea: An Interview with Derek Walcott', *Virginia Quarterly Review*, 91 (1): 172–5.

Ismond, Patricia (1971), 'Walcott versus Brathwaite', *Caribbean Quarterly*, 17 (3–4): 54–71.

Ismond, Patricia (2001), *Abandoning Dead Metaphors: The Caribbean Phase of Derek Walcott's Poetry*. Kingston: University of the West Indies Press.

Izevbaye, D. S. (1980), 'The Exile and the Prodigal: Derek Walcott as West Indian Poet', *Caribbean Quarterly*, 26 (1–2): 70–82.

James, C. L. R. ([1938] 2001), *The Black Jacobins*. London: Penguin.

James, George G. M. (1954), *Stolen Legacy: The Greeks were not the Authors of Greek Philosophy, but the People of North Africa, Commonly Called the Egyptians*. New York: Philosophical Library.

JanMohamed, Abdul R. (1985), 'The Economy of Manichean Allegory: The Function of Racial Difference in Colonialist Literature', *Critical Inquiry*, 12 (1): 59–87.

Jansen, Laura (2018), *Borges' Classics: Global Encounters with the Graeco-Roman Past*. Cambridge: Cambridge University Press.

Joyce, James ([1922] 1992), *Ulysses*. London: Everyman's Library.

Kaisary, Philip (2014), *The Haitian Revolution in the Literary Imagination: Radical Horizons, Conservative Constraints*. Charlottesville, NC, and London: University of Virginia Press.

Kaufmann, Helen (2006), 'Decolonizing the Postcolonial Colonizers: Helen in Derek Walcott's *Omeros*', in Charles Martindale and Richard F. Thomas (eds), *Classics and the Uses of Reception*, 192–203. Oxford: Blackwell Publishing.
Kermode, Frank, ed. *Selected Prose of T.S. Eliot*. London: Faber & Faber.
King, Bruce (1995), *Derek Walcott and West Indian Drama*. Oxford: Clarendon Press.
King, Bruce (2000), *Derek Walcott: A Caribbean Life*. Oxford: Oxford University Press.
Kristeva, Julia (1980), *Desire in Language: A Semiotic Approach to Literature and Art*, Leon S. Roudiez (ed.) and Thomas Gora, Alice Jardine and Leon S. Roudiez (trans.). Oxford: Blackwell.
Laplantine, François, and Alexis Nouss (1997), *Le Métissage*. Paris: Flammarion.
Lévi-Strauss, Claude (1955), 'The Structural Study of Myth', *Journal of American Folklore* 68 (270): 428–44.
Lévi-Strauss, Claude (2011), *Tristes Tropiques*, John Weightman and Doreen Weightman (trans.). London: Penguin.
Lewis, Gordon K. (1983), *Main Currents in Caribbean Thought: The Historical Evolution of Caribbean Society in Its Ideological Aspects, 1492–1900*. Baltimore, MA, and London: Johns Hopkins University Press.
Lianeri, Alexandra, and Vanda Zajko (2008), 'Still Being Read after So Many Years: Rethinking the Classic Through Translation', in Lianeri and Zakjo (eds), *Translation and the Classic: Identity as Change in the History of Culture*, 1–23. Oxford: Oxford University Press.
Lupher, David A. (2006), *Romans in a New World: Classical Models in Sixteenth-Century Spanish America*. Ann Arbor, MI: University of Michigan Press.
Macintosh, Fiona (1994), *Dying Acts: Death in Ancient Greek and Modern Irish Tragic Drama*. Cork: Cork University Press.
Macintosh, Fiona, and Justine McConnell (2020), *Performing Epic or Telling Tales*. Oxford: Oxford University Press.
MacQueen-Pope, W. (1957), 'The Story of Pantomime', *Journal of the Royal Society of Arts*, 105, no. 5002 (26 April): 456–8.
Majeed, Javed (1999), 'Comparativism and References to Rome in British Imperial Attitudes to India', in Catharine Edwards (ed.), *Roman Presences: Receptions of Rome in European Culture, 1789–1945*, 88–109. Cambridge: Cambridge University Press.
Malkin, Irad (1998), *The Returns of Odysseus: Colonization and Ethnicity*. Berkeley and Los Angeles, CA: University of California Press.
Martindale, Charles (1993), *Redeeming the Text: Latin Poetry and the Hermeneutics of Reception*. Cambridge: Cambridge University Press.
Martindale, Charles, and Richard F. Thomas, eds (2006), *Classics and the Uses of Reception*. Oxford: Blackwell Publishing.

Martyniuk, Irene (2005), 'Playing with Europe: Derek Walcott's Retelling of Homer's *Odyssey*', *Callaloo*, 2 (1): 188–99.

Matzner, Sebastian (2016), 'Queer Unhistoricism: Scholars, Metalepsis, and Interventions of the Unruly Past', in Shane Butler (ed.), *Deep Classics: Rethinking Classical Reception*, 179–201. London: Bloomsbury.

McClintock, Anne (1992), 'The Angel of Progress: Pitfalls of the Term "Post-Colonialism"', *Social Text*, 31–2: 84–98.

McConnell, Justine (2012), '"You Had to Wade this Deep in Blood?": Violence and Madness in Derek Walcott's *The Odyssey*', *Intertexts*, 16 (1): 43–56.

McConnell, Justine (2013), *Black Odysseys: The Homeric Odyssey in the African Diaspora since 1939*. Oxford: Oxford University Press.

McConnell, Justine (2018), 'Performing Walcott, Performing Homer: *Omeros* on Stage and Screen', in Fiona Macintosh, Justine McConnell, Stephen Harrison and Claire Kenward (eds), *Epic Performances from the Middle Ages into the Twenty-First Century*, 404–17. Oxford: Oxford University Press.

McConnell, Justine (2020), 'The Contest between Créolité and Classics in Patrick Chamoiseau's Stage Plays', in Rosa Andújar and Konstantinos Nikoloutsos (eds), *Greeks and Romans on the Latin American Stage*, 171–83. London: Bloomsbury.

McDougall, Russell (1992), 'Music, Body, and the Torture of Articulation in Derek Walcott's "Sainte Lucie"', *ARIEL: A Review of International English Literature*, 23 (2): 65–83.

Meador, Betty de Shong (2000), *Inanna, Lady of Largest Heart: Poems of the Sumerian High Priestess Enheduanna*. Austin, TX: University of Texas Press.

Melas, Natalie (2007), *All the Difference in the World: Postcoloniality and the Ends of Comparison*. Stanford, CA: Stanford University Press.

Menon, Madhavi (2006), 'Reply to letter of Carolyn Dinshaw and Karma Lochrie', *PMLA*, 121 (3): 838–9.

Miller, Paul B. (2001), 'Blancas Y Negras: Carpentier and the Temporalities of Exclusion', *Latin American Literary Review*, 29 (58): 23–45.

Mitchell-Kernan, Claudia (1971), *Language Behavior in a Black Urban Community*. Berkeley, CA: University of California, Language-Behavior Research Laboratory.

Moretti, Franco (2000), 'Conjectures on World Literature', *New Left Review*, 1 (January–February): 54–68.

Morris, Mervyn (1968), 'Walcott and the Audience for Poetry', *Caribbean Quarterly*, 14 (1–2): 7–24.

Most, Glenn W. (1992), '*Disiecti membra poetae*: The Rhetoric of Dismemberment in Neronian Poetry', in Ralph Hexter and Daniel Selden (eds), *Innovations of Antiquity*, 391–419. New York and London: Routledge.

Moyer, Ian, Adam Lecznar, and Heidi Morse, eds (2020), *Classicisms in the Black Atlantic*. Oxford: Oxford University Press.

Mudimbe, V. Y. (1988), *The Invention of Africa: Gnosis, Philosophy, and the Order of Knowledge*. Bloomington and Indianapolis, IN: Indiana University Press.

Mukherjee, Ankhi (2014), *What is a Classic? Postcolonial Rewriting and Invention of the Canon*. Stanford, CA: Stanford University Press.

Nagy, Gregory (2007), 'Homer and Greek Myth', in Roger D. Woodard (ed.), *The Cambridge Companion to Greek Mythology*, 52–82. Cambridge: Cambridge University Press.

Naipaul, V. S. ([1962] 2001), *The Middle Passage: Impressions of Five Colonial Societies*. London: Picador.

Naipaul, V. S. (2011), *The Mimic Men*. London: Picador.

Nepaulsingh, Colberg I. (1993), 'Review of *Myth and History in Caribbean Fiction: Alejo Carpentier, Wilson Harris, and Edouard Glissant* by Barbara J. Webb', *Caribbean Studies*, 26 (1–2): 196–206.

Ngũgĩ wa Thiong'o ([1952] 1986), *Decolonising the Mind: The Politics of Language in African Literature*. Woodbridge: James Currey.

Nightingale, Benedict (1992), 'Homer Minus the Old Magic', *The Times*, 4 July.

Noel, Keith, ed. (1985), *Caribbean Plays for Playing*, London and Kingston: Heinemann.

North, Michael (2013), *Novelty: A History of the New*. Chicago, IL, and London: University of Chicago Press.

Okpewho, Isidore (2002), 'Walcott, Homer, and the "Black Atlantic"', *Research in African Literatures*, 33 (1): 27–44.

Olaniyan, Tejumola (1995), *Scars of Conquest/Masks of Resistance: The Invention of Cultural Identities in African, African-American, and Caribbean Drama*. New York and Oxford: Oxford University Press.

Omotoso, Kole (1982), *The Theatrical into Theatre: A Study of the Drama and Theatre of the English-Speaking Caribbean*. London and Port of Spain: New Beacon.

Ortiz, Fernando (1995), *Cuban Counterpoint: Tobacco and Sugar*, Harriet de Onís (trans.). Durham, NC, and London: Duke University Press.

Ovid (2004), *Metamorphoses*, R. J. Tarrant (ed.). Oxford: Clarendon Press.

Parks, Suzan-Lori (1995a), 'From *Elements of Style*', *The America Play and Other Works*, 6–18. New York: Theatre Communications Group.

Parks, Suzan-Lori (1995b), *The America Play and Other Works*. New York: Theatre Communications Group.

Patterson, Orlando (1982), *Slavery and Social Death: A Comparative Study*. Cambridge, MA, and London: Harvard University Press.

Peradotto, John (1990), *Man in the Middle Voice: Name and Narration in the Odyssey.* Princeton, NJ: Princeton University Press.

Pérez Firmat, Gustavo (1989), *The Cuban Condition: Translation and Identity in Modern Cuban Literatur.* Cambridge: Cambridge University Press.

Piñera, Virgilio (2008), *Electra Garrigó*, Margaret Carson (trans.), in Diana Taylor and Sarah J. Townsend (eds), *Stages of Conflict: A Critical Anthology of Latin American Theater and Performance*, 173–95. Ann Arbor, MI: University of Michigan Press.

Pollard, Charles W. (2004), *New World Modernisms: T.S. Eliot, Derek Walcott, and Kamau Brathwaite.* Charlottesville, NC, and London: University of Virginia Press.

Posmentier, Sonya (2020), *Cultivation and Catastrophe: The Lyric Ecology of Modern Black* Literature. Baltimore, MD: Johns Hopkins University Press.

Quijano, Aníbal (2000), 'Coloniality of Power, Eurocentrism, and Latin America', *Nepantla: Views from the South*, 1 (3): 533–80.

Quint, David (1993), *Epic and Empire: Politics and Generic Form from Virgil to Milton.* Princeton, NJ: Princeton University Press.

Rae, Norman ([1957] 1997), 'Ione: Colourful but Academic', in Robert D. Hamner (ed.), *Critical Perspective on Derek Walcott*, 113–15. Boulder, CO, and London: Lynne Rienner.

Ramazani, Jahan (2001), *The Hybrid Muse: Postcolonial Poetry in English.* Chicago, IL, and London: University of Chicago Press.

Reed, Ethan (2018), '"I Heard That Voice at Troy": Resonance at The Other Place in Derek Walcott's *The Odyssey: A Stage Version*', *Cambridge Journal of Postcolonial Literary Inquiry*, 5 (2): 193–208.

Ricks, David (1989), *The Shade of Homer: A Study in Modern Greek Poetry.* Cambridge: Cambridge University Press.

Roberts, Neil (2002–3), 'Derek Walcott and English Metre', in Maria Cristina Fumagalli (ed.), *Agenda: Special Issue on Derek Walcott*, 39 (1–3): 267–74.

Roche, Helen (2018), '"Distant Models?" Italian Fascism, National Socialism, and the Lure of the Classics', in Helen Roche and Kyriakos N. Demetriou (eds), *Brill's Companion to the Classics, Fascist Italy and Nazi Germany.* Leiden and Boston, MA: Brill, 3–28.

Rodman, Selden (1974), *Tongues of Fallen Angels: Conversations with Jorge Luis Borges et al.* New York: New Directions.

Rohlehr, Gordon (1977/1978), '"This Past I Borrowed": Time, History, and Art in Brathwaite's *Masks*', *Caribbean Studies*, 17 (3–4): 5–82.

Rohlehr, Gordon (1985), 'The Problem of the Problem of Form: The Idea of an Aesthetic Continuum and Aesthetic Code-Switching in West Indian Literature', *Caribbean Quarterly*, 31 (1): 1–52.

Rohlehr, Gordon (2001), 'The Calypsonian as Artist: Freedom and Responsibility', *Small Axe*, 9 (5.1) (March): 1–26.
Rose, Margaret A. (1993), *Parody: Ancient, Modern, and Post-Modern*. Cambridge: Cambridge University Press.
Rose, Peter (1975), 'Class Ambivalence in the *Odyssey*', *Historia*, 24: 129–49.
Said, Edward W. ([1978] 1995), *Orientalism*, London: Penguin.
Said, Edward W. (1994), *Culture and Imperialism*. London: Vintage.
Sampietro, Luigi (n.d.), 'Derek Walcott on *Omeros*: An Interview'. Available online: https://www.modernamericanpoetry.org/content/derek-walcott-omeros-interview (accessed 7 October 2022).
Sauvy, Albert (1952), 'Trois Mondes, Une Planète', *L'Observateur*, 14 August, 5.
Savory Fido, Elaine (1986), 'Value Judgements on Art and the Question of Macho Attitudes: The Case of Derek Walcott', *Journal of Commonwealth Literature*, 21 (1): 109–19.
Scott, David (2004), *Conscripts of Modernity: The Tragedy of Colonial Enlightenment*. Durham, NC, and London: Duke University Press.
Scott, Dennis (1968), 'Walcott on Walcott', *Caribbean Quarterly*, 14 (1–2), 77–82.
Seeger, Sean (2018), *Nonlinear Temporality in Joyce and Walcott: History Repeating Itself with a Difference*. New York and London: Routledge.
Shakespeare, William (2017), *King Lear*, R. A. Foakes (ed.). London: Bloomsbury Arden Shakespeare.
Sharpe, Christina (2016), *In the Wake: On Blackness and Being*. Durham, NC, and London: Duke University Press.
Shaw, Rosalind, and Charles Stewart (1994), 'Introduction: Problematizing Syncretism', in Stewart and Shaw (eds), *Syncretism/Anti-Syncretism: The Politics of Religious Synthesis*, 1–26. London and New York: Routledge.
Shohat, Ella, and Robert Stam (2014), *Unthinking Eurocentrism: Multiculturalism and the Media*, 2nd edn. London and New York: Routledge.
Silk, Michael, Ingo Gildenhard and Rosemary Barrow (2014), *The Classical Tradition: Art, Literature, Thought*. Malden, MA, and Oxford: Wiley Blackwell.
Sophocles (1990), *Philoctetes*, R. G. Ussher (ed.). Warminster: Aris & Phillips.
Stanford, W. B., ed. (1987), *The Odyssey of Homer*, vol. 1. London: Macmillan.
Stewart, Charles (1999), 'Syncretism and Its Synonyms', *Diacritics*, 29 (3): 40–62.
Stone, Judy S. J. (1994), *Theatre*. London: Macmillan.
Taplin, Oliver (1991), 'Derek Walcott's *Omeros* and Derek Walcott's Homer', *Arion*, 3rd series, 1 (2): 213–26.
Taylor, Paul (1992), 'The Man Who Missed His Connection', *The Independent*, 4 July, 34.
Tempest, Kae (2013), *Brand New Ancients*. London: Picador.

Terada, Rei (1992), *Derek Walcott's Poetry: American Mimicry*. Boston, MA: Northeastern University Press.

Thelwell, Michael (1987), 'Modernist Fallacies and the Responsibility of the Black Writer', in *Duties, Pleasures, and Conflicts: Essays in Struggle*, introduction by James Baldwin, 218–32. Amherst, MA: University of Massachusetts Press.

Thieme, John (1999), *Derek Walcott*. Manchester and New York: Manchester University Press.

Thomas, Ned (1991), 'Obsession and Responsibility', in Stewart Brown (ed.), *The Art of Derek Walcott*, 83–98. Bridgend: Seren Books.

Thompson, Krista A. (2006), *An Eye for the Tropics: Tourism, Photography, and Framing the Caribbean Picturesque*. Durham, NC, and London: Duke University Press.

Tiffin, Helen (1987), 'Post-Colonial Literatures and Counter-Discourse', *Kunapipi*, 9 (3): 17–33.

Trouillot, Michel-Rolph ([1995] 2015), *Silencing the Past: Power and the Production of History*, with a foreword by Hazel V. Carby. Boston, MA: Beacon Press.

Tynan, Maeve (2011), *Postcolonial Odysseys: Derek Walcott's Voyages of Homecoming*. Newcastle upon Tyne: Cambridge Scholars Publishing.

Van Sickle, John B. (1999), 'The Design of Derek Walcott's *Omeros*', *Classical World*, 93 (1): 7–27.

Vásquez, Sam (2012), *Humor in the Caribbean Literary Canon*. New York: Palgrave Macmillan.

Vasunia, Phiroze (2005), 'Greek, Latin and the Indian Civil Service', *Cambridge Classical Journal*, 51: 35–71.

Vendler, Helen (1982), 'Poet of Two Worlds', *New York Review of Books*, 4 March, 23–7.

Virgil (1969), *Opera*, R. A. B. Mynors (ed.). Oxford: Clarendon Press.

Walcott, Derek (n.d.), *Ione*. Mona: University College of the West Indies Extra-Mural Department.

Walcott, Derek (1948), *25 Poems*. Port of Spain: Guardian.

Walcott, Derek ([1949] 2002–3), *Epitaph for the Young: XII Cantos*, reprinted in Maria Cristina Fumagalli (ed.), *Agenda: Special Issue on Derek Walcott*, 39 (1–3): 15–50.

Walcott, Derek (1956), 'Ruins of a Great House', in *New World Writing: Tenth Mentor Selection*, 159–60. New York: New American Library.

Walcott, Derek (1957), 'Modern Theatre', *Daily Gleaner*, 25 March.

Walcott, Derek ([1958] 1961), *Drums and Colours*, *Caribbean Quarterly*, 7 (1–2): 1–104.

Walcott, Derek (1962), *In a Green Night*. London: Jonathan Cape.

Walcott, Derek ([1964] 1997), 'The Necessity of Negritude', reprinted in Robert D. Hamner (ed.), *Critical Perspectives on Derek Walcott*. Boulder, CO, and London: Lynne Rienner, 20–3.

Walcott, Derek (1965a), *The Castaway and Other Poems*. London: Jonathan Cape.

Walcott, Derek ([1965b] 1997), 'The Figure of Crusoe', reprinted in Robert D. Hamner (ed.), *Critical Perspectives on Derek Walcott*. Boulder, CO, and London: Lynne Rienner, 33–40.

Walcott, Derek (1969), *The Gulf*. London: Jonathan Cape.

Walcott, Derek (1970a), 'Derek's "Most West Indian Play": *Ti-Jean and His Brothers*', *Sunday Guardian Magazine*, Trinidad (21 June): 7.

Walcott, Derek (1970b), *Dream on Monkey Mountain and Other Plays*. New York: Farrar, Straus and Giroux.

Walcott, Derek ([1970c] 1997), 'Meanings', reprinted in Robert D. Hamner (ed.), *Critical Perspectives on Derek Walcott*, 45–50. Boulder, CO, and London: Lynne Rienner.

Walcott, Derek (1974), 'The Caribbean: Culture or Mimicry?', *Journal of Interamerican Studies and World Affairs*, 16 (1): 3–13.

Walcott, Derek (1976), *Sea Grapes*. New York: Farrar, Straus and Giroux.

Walcott, Derek (1979), *The Star-Apple Kingdom*. New York: Farrar, Straus and Giroux.

Walcott, Derek (1980), *Two Plays: Remembrance & Pantomime*. New York: Farrar, Straus and Giroux.

Walcott, Derek (1981), *The Fortunate Traveller*. New York: Farrar, Straus and Giroux.

Walcott, Derek (1986), *Three Plays: The Last Carnival; Beef, No Chicken; A Branch of the Blue Nile*. New York: Farrar, Straus and Giroux.

Walcott, Derek (1988), *The Arkansas Testament*. London: Faber & Faber.

Walcott, Derek (1990), *Omeros*. New York: Farrar, Straus and Giroux.

Walcott, Derek (1993), *The Odyssey: A Stage Version*. London: Faber & Faber.

Walcott, Derek (1996a), 'Afterword: Animals, Elemental Tales, and the Theater', in A. James Arnold (ed.), *Monsters, Tricksters, and Sacred Cows: Animal Tales and American Identities*, 269–77. Charlottesville, NC, and London: University Press of Virginia.

Walcott, Derek (1996b), 'The Sea is History', in Frank Birbalsingh (ed.), *Frontiers of Caribbean Literature in English*, 22–8. London and Basingstoke: Macmillan.

Walcott, Derek (1997a), 'Reflections on *Omeros*', *South Atlantic Quarterly*, 96 (2): 229–46.

Walcott, Derek (1997b), 'A Letter to Chamoiseau', *New York Review of Books*, 14 August, reprinted in Robert D. Hamner (ed.), *Critical Perspectives on Derek Walcott*, 213–32. Boulder, CO, and London: Lynne Rienner.

Walcott, Derek (1998), *What the Twilight Says: Essays*. London: Faber & Faber.

Walcott, Derek (2002a), *The Haitian Trilogy: Henri Christophe; Drums and Colours; The Haitian Earth*. New York: Farrar, Straus and Giroux.

Walcott, Derek (2002b), *Walker and The Ghost Dance*. New York: Farrar, Straus and Giroux.
Walcott, Derek ([2004] 2005), *The Prodigal*. London: Faber & Faber.
Walcott, Derek (2009), *Another Life*, with a critical essay and comprehensive notes by Edward Baugh and Colbert Nepaulsingh. Boulder, CO, and London: Lynne Reiner.
Walcott, Derek (2010), *White Egrets*. London: Faber & Faber.
Walcott, Derek (2014), *O Starry Starry Night*. New York: Farrar, Straus and Giroux.
Webb, Barbara J. (1992), *Myth and History in Caribbean Fiction: Alejo Carpentier, Wilson Harris, and Edouard Glissant*. Amherst, MA: University of Massachusetts Press.
Wetmore, Jr., Kevin J. (2003), *Black Dionysus: Greek Tragedy and African American Theatre*. Jefferson, NC, and London: McFarland.
Whitaker, Richard (1996), 'Derek Walcott's *Omeros* and the Classics', *Akroterion*, 41 (1–2): 93–102.
White, J. P. (1996), 'An Interview with Derek Walcott', reprinted in William Baer (ed.), *Conversations with Derek Walcott*. Jackson, MS: University Press of Mississippi, 151–74.
Williamson, Margaret (2017), 'Africa or Old Rome? Jamaican Slave Naming Revisited', *Slavery & Abolition*, 38 (1): 117–34.
Williamson, Margaret (2020), '"Nero, the mustard!": The Ironies of Classical Slave Names in the British Caribbean', in Ian Moyer, Adam Lecznar and Heidi Morse (eds), *Classicisms in the Black Atlantic*. Oxford: Oxford University Press, 57–78.
Willis, Ika (2018), *Reception*. Abingdon: Routledge.
Wilson, Emily (2018), *The Odyssey*. New York and London: W. W. Norton.
Wynter, Sylvia (1989), 'Beyond the Word of Man: Glissant and the New Discourse of the Antilles', *World Literature Today*, 63 (4): 637–48.
Wynter, Sylvia (1997), '"A Different Kind of Creature": Caribbean Literature, The Cyclops Factor, and The Second Poetics of the Propter Nos', *Annals of Scholarship*, 12 (1–2): 153–72.

Index

Abrahams, Roger D. 100, 135 n.52, 159 n.179
Achille 8, 13, 16–17, 19–27, 29–30, 32–5, 81–2, 90, 108–9, 113, 125, 129, 138 n.117, 139 n.150, 139 n.158, 141 n.212, 155 n.91
see also Walcott, *Omeros*; and Walcott, *Ione*
Achilles 16, 19, 21–2, 35, 82
Adamic 3, 18–19, 29, 30, 34, 74, 103–5, 109, 115–16, 119, 122
adaptation 36, 38, 61, 75, 93, 98–101, 104–7, 110, 125–6, 136 n.74
Adorno, Theodor 23, 24, 66–8
Aegean 8, 18, 65, 94
Aeschylus 84–5, 141 n.228
  Agamemnon 80, 86
  Seven Against Thebes 80, 81
Aesop 65
Africa 6, 11, 17, 19–20, 24–6, 27, 29–30, 57, 72, 76–8, 93–5, 108–9, 125, 155 n.91, 161 n.33
Afrocentrism 27–8, 108–9, 139 n.158, 154 n.69
Ajax 57–8, 100
Alexander, Elizabeth 7, 31, 95
allochronism 38, 41–4, 51, 64
Amin, Samir 17
amnesia 3, 17, 22, 45, 65, 104, 110, 130
Anderson, Benedict 143 n.16
anthropology 38, 40–1, 64, 81, 137 n.107, 143 n.22
Antoine-Dunne, Jean 124–5
Antoni, Robert 165 n.126
Appadurai, Arjun 41
Aristophanes 9
  Frogs 9, 84–5
Aristotle 80–1, 114
Athene 126
Aulus Gellius 2
autobiographical 6, 8, 27, 57, 60, 85–7, 90

Balme, Christopher 72, 95–6, 151 n.1
baptism 89, 103–4, 113
Baudelaire, Charles 75, 130
Baugh, Edward 46, 55, 57, 59, 66, 134 n.26, 147 n.113, 147 n.120
Bearden, Romare 31, 95, 141 n.203
Benítez-Rojo, Antonio 3, 9, 25, 41, 71–2, 74
Benjamin, Walter 143 n.16
Bernabé, Jean 72, 152 n.12
  see also Creolists
Bernal, Martin 17, 94, 96, 142 n.9, 157 n.131
Bhabha, Homi 7, 11, 89, 96, 105–6, 110, 143 n.16, 158 n.153, 160 n.10
Black Power Revolution (Trinidad and Tobago) 38, 58–9, 142 n.7
Borges, Jorge Luis 64, 68, 150 n.175
Brand, Dionne 77, 153 n.53
Brathwaite, Kamau 3, 14, 33, 44, 74, 77, 87, 133 n.15, 136 n.77
  The Arrivants: A New World Trilogy 14, 19, 137 n.115
  History of the Voice 87, 136 n.77
  nation language 14, 87, 90, 136 n.77
Brecht, Bertolt 114
  Verfremdungseffekt 83, 100, 114, 159 n.182
Breiner, Laurence 32, 87–8, 109
Breslin, Paul 21, 45, 50, 76, 83, 85, 87, 106, 109, 113, 118, 142 n.7, 149 n.157, 156 n.107, 161 n.28
British Empire 36, 48, 52, 77, 78–9, 144 n.46
Brodsky, Joseph 152 n.26
Burnett, Paula 62, 94, 101

Caliban 115
  see also Césaire, *Une Tempête*; Shakespeare, *The Tempest*
Callimachus 13

calypso 9, 12–13, 98–9, 105–6, 110, 114, 116–18, 135 n.61
canonicity 2–3, 4, 5, 6, 10, 11, 12, 28, 33–4, 38, 44, 49, 59, 66, 73, 77, 78, 83, 85, 91, 104, 105, 110–11, 116, 117, 120, 121, 125–6, 127, 130, 132
Carnival 46, 49, 60, 83, 149 n.149, 154 n.69
carnivalesque (Bakhtin) 106, 160 n.10
Carpentier, Alejo 3, 45, 99, 135 n.56, 142 n.2
  Mediterráneo caribe 3, 99
  Los pasos perdidos 135 n.56
  El reino de este mundo 45
Cassandra 58, 82, 148 n.136
Césaire, Aimé 6, 23–4, 27, 57, 67, 97, 127, 165 n.126
  Cahier d'un retour au pays natal 6, 14, 23–4, 47, 56–7, 67, 86–7, 89, 139 n.145, 147 n.121, 150 n.192
  Discours sur le colonialisme 97, 133 n.18
  Une Tempête 115
Chakrabarty, Dipesh 6, 134 n.31, 144 n.38
Chamoiseau, Patrick 72, 82, 92
  Manman Dlo contre la fée Carabosse 82, 92
  Solibo Magnifique 98, 152 n.12
  see also Creolists
chorus 9, 49, 84–5, 109, 114
Christianity 29, 30, 92, 103–4
Christophe, Henri 45–50
chronology 18, 39, 41, 43, 62, 68
Circe 16, 52
Classics (discipline) 2–3, 5, 39, 60, 120, 130, 134 n.26, 163 n.98
Clifford, James 71, 139 n.154, 151 n.3
Clytemnestra 154 n.63
Cobham-Sander, Rhonda 3, 33, 133 n.3, 133 n.15, 136 n.77
code-switching 117
Coetzee J. M., 133 n.6
collage 30–1, 95
colonial gaze 18, 52, 63
colonialism 2, 4, 5, 14, 17, 18, 20, 24, 27–9, 34, 40, 41, 43–4, 52, 56, 59, 60, 62, 65, 67, 69, 71, 72, 76, 78, 79, 83, 87, 92, 96, 97–8, 100, 104, 107, 109, 110, 130–1, 134 n.21, 138 n.122, 145 n.55
coloniality 39, 51, 90, 131, 165 n.6
Columbus, Christopher 2, 42–3, 105, 145 n.55
comedy 85, 90–1
Confiant, Raphaël 72, 152 n.12
  see also Creolists
Creole (language) 2, 11, 13, 31–3, 82–3, 87–8, 90, 92, 108, 117–18, 121, 129, 130, 141 n.209, 154 n.64
Creolists (Jean Bernabé, Patrick Chamoiseau, Raphaël Confiant) 3, 72, 152 n.12
creolization 7, 25, 28, 29, 32, 71–2, 74, 88, 118–19, 143 n.15, 164 n.125
  see also syncretism
Cyclops 6, 23–4, 66–8, 100, 134 n.28, 159 n.180
  see also Polyphemus

Dacier, Anne 15
Dante Aligheri 11–13, 14, 20, 26, 34, 60, 75, 135 n.58
  La Commedia 12, 14, 20
Dash, J. Michael 43, 61, 71, 72–3, 116, 152 n.19, 164 n.125
Davis, Gregson 12, 13, 28, 86, 138 n.118, 147 n.121, 155 n.91
Defoe, Daniel 104–6, 111–12
  Robinson Crusoe 104–6, 111–12, 115
Demodocus 100, 159 n.181
'denial of coevalness' (Johannes Fabian) 6, 40–1, 137 n.107
Dessalines, Jean-Jacques 46, 47–9, 50
diaspora 11, 25, 27–8, 31, 57, 131, 152 n.15
Diop, Cheikh Anta 17, 94
double consciousness (W. E. B. Du Bois) 108
Duvalier, François 114

Eden, Garden of 19, 29, 34, 103–4, 109, 111
education 5–6, 21, 77, 83, 86–7, 121, 134 n.26
Egypt 16, 93–4, 96, 142 n.9
Eliot, T. S. 2–3, 4, 44, 61–2, 75–6, 130, 131
  'Tradition and the Individual Talent' 62, 131
  'What is a Classic?' 2–3, 75

Elizabethan drama 44, 49
Emerson, Ralph Waldo 147 n.113
Enheduanna 28
Enlightenment 45, 67
epic 1, 6, 8, 10–16, 18–19, 20, 26, 29, 30,
    33–6, 42, 55, 57, 60, 64, 67–8, 87,
    88, 93–100, 112, 135 n.43,
    142 n.229, 158 n.149
epistemology 4, 39–41, 42–3, 46, 52, 53, 66
Eumaeus 15, 75, 152 n.26
Euripides 16, 80, 85
    The Bacchae 47–8, 80–2, 154 n.62
    Medea 80–1
Eurocentrism 8–9, 10, 52, 53, 62, 72, 131
Eurycleia 15, 93–4, 101, 158 n.155

Fabian, Johannes 6, 38, 40–1, 51, 63, 64
    Time and the Other 40, 63, 137 n.107
Fanon, Frantz 6, 108, 109, 143 n.30
    The Wretched of the Earth 109
Figueroa, John 30, 117–19
Firmin, Joseph Auguste Anténor 157 n.131
folklore 80, 82–3, 84–5, 92, 100, 107,
    154 n.71, 155 n.83
fragmentation 7, 31, 40, 62, 71, 73–4, 78–9,
    80, 95, 108, 143 n.15
French (language) 2, 31–2, 108, 144 n.46
French Revolution 4–5, 145 n.51
Froude, James Anthony 23, 53, 56
    *The English in the West Indies: Or, The
    Bow of Ulysses* 23, 36, 56, 112

Garvey, Marcus 108–9
Gates, Jr., Henry Louis 7, 10–11, 15
    Signifying 7, 10–11, 13, 15, 34, 110, 112,
    135 n.52, 136 n.89, 164 n.107
Gauguin, Paul 4
Gikandi, Simon 69, 149 n.167
Gilgamesh 20
Gilroy, Paul 7
Glissant, Édouard 3, 7, 17, 37, 39, 41–3,
    59–61, 70, 71–2, 74, 99, 127,
    142 n.2, 143 n.30
    Le Discours antillais 39, 41, 71–2, 74,
    148 n.143
    Les Indes 42–3, 144 n.31
    Monsieur Toussaint 51
Goff, Barbara, 5, 25, 140 n.172
Goffe, Tao Leigh 39

Goodison, Lorna 5–6, 165 n.126
    I Am Becoming My Mother 6, 134 n.26
Goody, Jack 38
Greece, ancient 3, 5, 8, 10, 15, 17–18, 42,
    63–4, 65, 72, 84, 86, 92, 94, 96,
    99, 101, 103, 105, 111, 122,
    129–30, 132, 142 n.9
Greek, ancient (language) 6, 14, 29, 30–2,
    84, 99, 134 n.24
Greek, modern (language) 1, 31–2
Greenwood, Emily 4, 18, 42, 44, 66, 112,
    120, 131–2, 134 n.26, 147 n.114,
    150 n.182, 150 n.184, 163 n.98
    'omni-local' 4, 131–2
griot 13, 19, 28–9, 74

Haiti 29, 44–51, 114, 146 n.77, 164 n.107
Haitian Revolution 44–51, 142 n.2,
    145 n.51
Hall, Stuart 25, 26, 88, 152 n.15
hallucination 19, 21, 25, 29, 97–8, 108–9,
    129, 155 n.91, 158 n.159
Hardwick, Lorna 19, 58, 97, 98, 101,
    137 n.94
Harris, Wilson 3, 7, 17–18, 37, 39, 41, 43,
    127, 142 n.2, 143 n.27, 152 n.19
    The Mask of the Beggar 18
    'Quetzalcoatl and the Smoking Mirror'
    39, 143 n.27
Hawthorne, Nathaniel 57
Hearne, John 165 n.126
Hector 8, 16–17, 22, 28, 32–3, 82, 124–5,
    139 n.150
    see also Walcott, *Omeros*
Helen 8, 16–17, 19, 22, 24, 50, 58, 68, 81, 86,
    123, 144 n.46
    see also Walcott, *Omeros*
Henry, Paget 40
heroism 13, 15–16, 21–2, 23, 26, 36, 46–7,
    49, 61, 64, 75, 96, 98, 104, 114,
    162 n.61
Hesiod 29
Hesperides 52
Highet, Gilbert 130–1
Hill, Errol 77, 83–4, 148 n.136, 149 n.149,
    154 n.69, 154 n.71
    Man Better Man 148 n.136, 154 n.71
    *The Trinidad Carnival: Mandate for a
    National Theatre* 83–4

Holiday, Billie 82
homecoming 14, 25–6, 66, 85–7, 89–90, 120
  see also nostos
Homer 1, 3–4, 10–36, 50, 61, 62, 66–8, 74, 75, 81, 82, 89–90, 93–101, 112, 118, 135 n.56, 136 n.74, 137 n.104, 139 n.151, 140 n.191, 150 n.175, 158 n.155
  Iliad 15, 16, 31, 34–5, 66, 80–2, 100, 140 n.191, 142 n.229, 150 n.184
  Odyssey 6, 9–36, 61, 64, 65–8, 75, 86, 87, 90, 93–101, 134 n.26, 135 n.56, 138 n.138, 150 n.184, 158 n.155
Horace 77, 79, 100
Horkheimer, Max 23–4, 66–8
Hutcheon, Linda 125, 135 n.64, 164 n.114
hybridity 7, 151 n.2
  see also creolization; syncretism

Iliad, see Homer, *Iliad*
imitation 6, 8–9, 55, 60, 64, 75–6, 92, 110–11, 116, 118
  see also mimicry
imperialism 1, 4–5, 10, 13, 16, 24, 33–4, 40–1, 43–4, 49, 55, 62–3, 65, 67, 73, 77, 79, 80, 85, 92, 105–7, 109, 113, 120, 133 n.6, 134 n.24
Indigenous 4, 6, 9, 24–5, 28, 50, 67, 72, 92
infantilization 4, 134 n.21
Iser, Wolfgang 7
Ismond, Patricia 74, 79, 105, 136 n.77, 153 n.40

Jacobean drama 49, 90, 146 n.74
James, C. L. R. 45, 49, 142 n.2
  The Black Jacobins 47–9, 142 n.2, 162 n.61
James, George G. M. 17, 94
JanMohamed, Abdul 72
Jauss, Hans Robert 7, 75
Johnson, Samuel 118
Joyce, James 11, 18, 57–8, 59, 61, 62, 69, 130, 149 n.158, 149 n.161
  Ulysses 15, 57–8, 61, 69
Julien, Isaac 164 n.106
Juvenal 118

katabasis 19–27, 29, 86–7, 139 n.158, 140 n.172
Kenya 76–8
King, Bruce 114, 139 n.145, 163 n.104
Kingsley, Charles 57
kleos 23, 35, 138 n.140
Kristeva, Julia 110

Lamming, George 74–5
Latin 5, 6, 14, 31–2, 77, 120–2, 134 n.24
Leclerc, Charles 48
Lévi-Strauss, Claude 28, 84, 101, 139 n.154
Little Carib Theatre (Port of Spain) 84
Lovelace, Earl 119
Lucian 67

Malcolm X 115
Marlowe, Christopher 77
Martial 118
Martindale, Charles, 75
Mau Mau uprising 76–8
McClintock, Anne 4, 6
Mediterranean 3, 93–5, 99, 129, 130, 157 n.135
Medusa 58–9, 63
Meeropol, Abel 82
Melantho 100–1
messenger speech 47–9
metre 12–15, 33, 78, 117–18, 153 n.46
Midas 58
Middle Passage 20, 24, 25–6, 30, 31, 44, 45, 54–6, 90, 95, 129, 143 n.15
mimicry 9–11, 31, 38, 45, 60, 64, 96, 105–7, 110–11, 116–20, 126, 150 n.176, 158 n.153, 158 n.154
  see also imitation
Modernism 4, 44, 60–2, 149 n.157
monuments 3, 53, 56, 62, 63–4, 69–70, 78, 151 n.205
Mudimbe, Valentin 134 n.42
Mukherjee, Ankhi 133 n.6
Murray, Albert 4
Muses 34–5, 37, 63

Naipaul, V. S. 3, 8, 23, 46, 53, 54, 62–3, 133 n.15
  The Middle Passage 23, 46, 56
naming 6, 9, 19, 20–4, 30–1, 34, 43, 49–50, 54–5, 67, 81–2, 88–9, 104–5,

107–9, 114, 115–16, 120–2, 126, 138 n.128
narrator 8, 12–15, 19, 22, 26–7, 31, 44, 66, 76, 87, 89, 98–9, 121, 122–4, 137 n.94, 138 n.123, 140 n.172, 140 n.173
nature 3, 20, 24, 32, 56, 78, 85, 92, 113, 138 n.123, 147 n.120, 150 n.190
Nausicaa 66, 100
négritude 24, 26, 57, 134 n.42, 139 n.146
Ngũgĩ wa Thiong'o 107
Nobel Prize 2, 73, 91, 127
nostos (homecoming) 25–6, 86–7, 89–90, 120
'nothingness' 21, 23–4, 46, 53–7, 62–3, 122, 147 n.106

Odysseus 22–4, 35, 52, 57, 61, 65–8, 75, 88, 90, 93–101, 112, 113, 120, 139 n.151, 140 n.173, 158 n.152
Odyssey, see Homer, *Odyssey*
Okpewho, Isidore 56, 141 n.209
Omotoso, Kole 71, 72, 84, 107, 112
orality 9, 12–13, 82–3, 92, 98–9, 100, 107–8, 130, 135 n.52
originality 6, 37–8, 39, 60, 62, 68, 101, 104, 110–11, 116–19, 125–6, 132
Ortiz, Fernando 3, 71–3, 95
Ovid 53–6, 88, 119–20, 126–7, 162 n.57
    Metamorphoses 53–6, 63, 88, 120
    Tristia 120

Pan 92
pantomime 105–7, 160 n.11
    see also Walcott, *Pantomime*
Papa Bois 85, 92
Parks, Suzan-Lori 135 n.46
parody 7, 13, 61–2, 136 n.89
pastiche 7, 136 n.89
Patterson, Orlando 21
    'natal alienation' 21
    'social death' 21–2
Penelope 96–8, 101, 134 n.26, 158 n.155
Philip, Theophilus (Mighty Spoiler) 116–19
Philoctete 8, 16, 19, 20, 25, 27–30, 33, 103–4, 109, 141 n.228
    see also Walcott, *Omeros*
Philoctetes 104, 112–15

Piñera, Virgilio 114
Plutarch 90
Polyphemus 6, 23–4, 66–8, 100, 134 n.28, 159 n.180
    see also Cyclops
polyphony 117, 156 n.120
Pompeii 53
Pompey 21–2, 49–50
Pope, Alexander 118
Pound, Ezra 60, 75, 148 n.146
postcolonialism 1, 2–10, 26–8, 38, 40, 44, 125–6, 130–1, 165 n.4
'primitivism' 4, 7
Prospero 115
    see also Shakespeare, *The Tempest*

Rae, Norman 80–3
Ramazani, Jahan 27, 31, 156 n.111
re-creation 6, 8, 9, 18–19, 30–6, 103–27, 130, 132
'reverse simile' (Helene Foley) 97
rhapsode 30–1
Rome, ancient 2–3, 5, 8, 10, 42, 63–4, 92, 99, 103, 105, 111, 129–32
Royal Shakespeare Company 93
ruins 3, 53, 63–4, 70, 75, 78–9, 122
Rushdie, Salman 10

Said, Edward 40, 96–7, 134 n.21, 163 n.78
St Lucia 1, 2, 8, 15, 20, 25, 26, 30, 33, 36, 57, 79, 80–1, 83, 86–7, 93, 96, 112–14, 121, 144 n.46, 161 n.54
    Castries 2, 57–8, 75
    Gros Islet 8, 16, 32, 112–14, 126, 161 n.54
    Soufrière 26
St Omer, Dunstan 140 n.188
St Omer, Garth 86
Sainte-Beuve, Charles Augustin 2–3
Sartre, Jean-Paul 109, 134 n.42
satire 76, 106, 108, 110, 116–19
Saturnalia 160 n.11
Scott, David 47, 114, 142 n.2, 162 n.61
Scott, Dennis 82, 154 n.63
    The Crime of Anabel Campbell 154 n.63
Senghor, Léopold Sédar 134 n.42
Servius Tullius 2
Shakespeare, William 49, 54, 77, 90–1, 93, 106, 115, 130

Antony and Cleopatra 90–1, 156 n.115
Hamlet 49
King Lear 54, 101, 155 n.83
Richard III 49
The Tempest 115
Troilus and Cressida 100
simultaneity 4, 8, 17–20, 28, 37–44, 52–6,
    57–8, 59, 62–70, 101, 104, 125,
    129–32, 143 n.16
slave trade 11, 13, 25, 30, 54–5, 70, 104,
    115, 129
    see also Middle Passage
Sophocles 85, 112–13, 136 n.74, 141 n.228
    Philoctetes 112–13
space 4, 11, 17, 23, 28, 41, 44, 51–2,
    65, 115
Spartacus 50
Spiralism 122, 164 n.107
Stesichorus 16
suitors 96–8, 112, 158 n.155
syncretism 2, 3, 6–9, 14, 16, 19, 24–33, 49,
    54, 68–70, 71–101, 103, 107–9,
    111–12, 115, 116–19, 122,
    129–32, 140 n.191, 151 n.1,
    151 n.2, 152 n.13, 153 n.45,
    157 n.140, 159 n.173, 164 n.125
    see also creolization

Taplin, Oliver 15, 16–17, 135 n.43
Tate, Nahum 101
Teiresias 35, 82, 141 n.228
Telemachus 75, 93
Tempest, Kae 15
Tennyson, Alfred 90
Terada, Rei 110, 118, 119, 150 n.176,
    161 n.33
terza rima 12–14, 136 n.74
Thieme, John 55, 68, 88, 146 n.74,
    156 n.120
'Third World' (Albert Sauvy) 4–5
time 3–4, 6, 8–9, 13, 17–20, 22, 27–8,
    37–70, 79, 99, 100, 104, 111, 125,
    129–32, 134 n.31, 143 n.16,
    144 n.35, 149 n.161
    see also simultaneity
tourism 20, 86, 113, 125, 138 n.122,
    161 n.54, 164 n.112
Toussaint L'Ouverture 45, 47–51, 145 n.55,
    162 n.61

tragedy 47–51, 54, 80–2, 98, 113–14,
    155 n.83, 162 n.61
transculturation 71–3, 95, 152 n.10
Treaty of Paris 144 n.46
Trinidad 9, 13, 38, 58–9, 73, 83, 88–90, 114,
    116–18, 129
    Port of Spain 84, 90–1, 119
    Rampalangas 55, 129
Trouillot, Michel-Rolph 39–40, 45–6, 51,
    145 n.51, 146 n.77
Trojan War 16–17, 34–5, 58, 68, 82,
    112–13, 124–5
Troy 16, 58, 68, 75, 112, 119, 124–5

underworld 14, 19–27, 35, 85–7
    see also katabasis

Van Gogh, Vincent 4
Vendler, Helen 117–18, 163 n.78
vernacular 7, 11–13, 14, 87–8, 94
violence 9, 27–8, 31, 40, 45, 47–50, 65, 69,
    71, 76–8, 98, 104, 114, 161 n.38
Virgil 11, 13, 20, 22, 25, 34, 77, 119
    Aeneid 20, 22, 25, 87, 119, 148 n.136
    Eclogues 13
Voice of St Lucia, The 1

Walcott, Derek
    Essays
        'The Antilles: Fragments of Epic
            Memory' 73–4, 91
        'The Caribbean: Culture or
            Mimicry?' 11, 38, 45, 60, 110–11,
            126, 142 n.7
        'The Figure of Crusoe' 55, 105,
            111–12
        'Meanings' 77–8
        'The Muse of History' 8, 13, 17, 19,
            33–4, 37–8, 58–65, 111, 119, 132,
            142 n.7 159 n.186
        'Necessity of Negritude' 24,
            139 n.146
        'Reflections on *Omeros*' 8, 18, 20, 31,
            62, 94–5
        'What the Twilight Says' 31, 47,
            55, 84–5, 107–8, 115–16,
            155 n.83
    Film script
        Omeros, 9, 122–5

Plays
   Batai 148 n.136
   A Branch of the Blue Nile 76, 90–1
   Dream on Monkey Mountain 107–9
   Drums and Colours 46, 49, 51
   The Haitian Earth 46, 49–50
   Henri Christophe: A Chronicle in Seven Scenes 37, 44–51, 146 n.74
   The Ghost Dance 140 n.183
   Ione 48, 79–84, 113–14, 153 n.58
   The Isle is Full of Noises 111–16
   O Starry Starry Night 4
   The Odyssey: A Stage Version 9, 58, 84, 93–101, 125
   Pantomime 105–7, 111, 156 n.117
   Remembrance 156 n.117
   Steel 156 n.117
   Ti-Jean and His Brothers 9, 80, 83–5, 90, 92
Poetry
   'The Acacia Trees' 164 n.112
   'Air' 23, 56–7, 112
   'The Almond Trees' 53–6, 57
   Another Life 27, 46, 57–8, 74, 103, 129, 146 n.106
   The Arkansas Testament 92, 121
   'Blues' 136 n.77
   The Castaway 104–5
   'Crusoe's Island' 104, 111
   'Crusoe's Journal' 104–5, 111
   'Egypt, Tobago' 156 n.115
   Epitaph for the Young: XII Cantos 60, 74–6
   'A Far Cry from Africa' 76–8, 79, 85, 87, 108, 153 n.46
   The Fortunate Traveller 68, 116–17, 119
   The Gulf 23, 87, 147 n.106
   'Homecoming: Anse La Raye' 85–7, 90, 120, 138 n.118
   'The Hotel Normandie Pool' 119–20, 126, 162 n.57
   In a Green Night 51, 76, 78, 147 n.106
   'A Latin Primer' 119, 120–2
   'A Map of the Antilles' 51–2, 68, 144 n.31
   'Map of the New World' 68–9
   'Names' 151 n.205
   Omeros 1, 8, 10–36, 44, 49, 50, 52, 58, 60–1, 64, 66, 68, 70, 74, 76, 80–1, 84, 89–90, 93, 103–4, 108, 109, 113, 122–5, 126, 133 n.3, 136 n.77, 137 n.114, 140 n.183, 141 n.209, 149 n.161, 150 n.182, 155 n.91
   The Prodigal 125–6
   'Roots' 3–4
   'Ruins of a Great House' 78–9, 122, 153 n.53
   'Sainte Lucie' 2, 133 n.3, 136 n.37, 140 n.191
   'The Schooner *Flight*' 5, 70, 83, 87–90, 136 n.77
   'Sea Grapes' 51, 65–8
   'The Sea is History' 69–70
   'The Spoiler's Return' 116–19
   The Star-Apple Kingdom 69, 87
   Tiepolo's Hound 149 n.161
   25 Poems 74
   White Egrets 126, 141 n.203, 152 n.26
   'White Magic' 9, 91–3
Ward Theatre (Kingston) 83
Watt, Ian 38
ways of knowing 4, 10, 39–41, 56–7, 129, 132
   see also epistemology
West Indies Federation 51–2, 112
Wilson, August 141 n.203, 165 n.126
Wynter, Sylvia 6, 143 n.30

xenia (guest-friendship) 6, 101

Yoruba 29

www.ingramcontent.com/pod-product-compliance
Lightning Source LLC
Chambersburg PA
CBHW052120300426
44116CB00010B/1735